THE Principal's Companion

THIRD EDITION

Dedicated to David J. Robbins, a lifelong leader who believed that, in the end, "it's all about relationships"; Rebecca Pearl Alvy, a champion of all children; and Pat and Loyd Wolfe.

THE Principal's Companion

THIRD EDITION

Strategies *for* Making *the* Job Easier

Pam Robbins | **Harvey B. Alvy**
Foreword by Kent D. Peterson

CORWIN
A SAGE Company

For information:

Corwin
A SAGE Company
2455 Teller Road
Thousand Oaks, California 91320
(800) 233-9936
Fax: (800) 417-2466
www.corwinpress.com

SAGE Ltd.
1 Oliver's Yard
55 City Road
London, EC1Y 1SP
United Kingdom

SAGE India Pvt. Ltd.
B 1/I 1 Mohan Cooperative
    Industrial Area
Mathura Road, New Delhi
India 110 044

SAGE Asia-Pacific Pte. Ltd.
33 Pekin Street #02-01
Far East Square
Singapore 048763

Printed in the United States of America.

Library of Congress Cataloging-in-Publication Data

Robbins, Pamela.
The principal's companion: strategies for making the job easier / Pam Robbins and Harvey B. Alvy.—3rd ed.
        p. cm.
Includes bibliographical references and index.
ISBN 978-1-4129-6549-1 (cloth)
ISBN 978-1-4129-6550-7 (pbk.)
    1. School principals—United States—Handbooks, manuals, etc. 2. Educational leadership—United States—Handbooks, manuals, etc. 3. School management and organization—United States—Handbooks, manuals, etc. I. Alvy, Harvey B. II. Title.

LB2831.92.R63 2009
371.2'012—dc22   2008056035

This book is printed on acid-free paper.

09   10   11   12   13   10   9   8   7   6   5   4   3   2   1

Acquisitions Editor:	Debra Stollenwerk
Associate Editor:	Julie McNall
Production Editor:	Cassandra Margaret Seibel
Typesetter:	C&M Digitals (P) Ltd.
Proofreader:	Anne Rogers
Indexer:	Jean Casalegno
Cover Designer:	Rose Storey
Graphic Designer:	Scott Van Atta

Contents

Foreword

Kent D. Peterson

University of Wisconsin–Madison

Many authors come out with new editions with no newness. This is not the case with the third edition of *The Principal's Companion* by Robbins and Alvy. This edition is even better than the second, and the second was very good. Several outstanding sections have been added that provide new knowledge and concrete strategies for principals facing new staff, standards, and stakeholders. The third edition adds sections that address issues related to data, brain research, social justice, and ethical leadership. New material on technology makes this book current with the variety of new sources and types of communication facing principals.

These and other new topics enhance an already rich book for principals—and probably expand the audience to policymakers, staff developers, and parents who are concerned about supporting and building successful, high-quality schools. This book continues to be one of the most important contributions to the literature designed to help principals enhance their leadership and management skills with the most current research-based practice.

The Principal's Companion focuses on the critical work of school principals, with practical wisdom, conceptual ideas, and useful examples from many different settings. It helps answer the questions, "What skills and knowledge will help principals lead and manage better schools?" and "How can principals become successful leaders?" This book adds extremely relevant knowledge and skills for preservice courses, new principals, and experienced leaders.

Let me make a few observations about the importance of school leaders, especially principals. To begin with, the daily work of school principals is extremely complex, demanding, intense, and, at times, surprising. Daily, principals must solve complex problems of practice, deal with demands and conflicts from parents and students, and maintain an intense work schedule filled with drama (will the new content standards fly with parents?), tragedy (a student is killed in a car accident), and, thankfully, comedy (a class accurately copies the principal's mannerisms for a school play). The days of principals are full of surprises, and most days have a mix of totally unexpected happenings, from the birth of gerbils to the wonderful successes of students. It is within the flow of these days that leadership, decision making, school improvement, and change occur. This book will help those filling this important role.

The second key feature of principals and their complex work is the paradox that although they must gain certification through university training, much, if not most, of their learning occurs later, on the job. In the best cases, preservice training affords aspiring administrators concepts and models as well as a modicum of practical knowledge that will get them started. But once on the job, these concepts and models get forged in the press of daily work. This book contributes significantly to both preservice and inservice realms, increasing the cache of available and easily readable information for this difficult but important role. This book provides a detailed, useful, and rigorous set of absorbing and shrewd suggestions for making the most of the panoply of these days—approaches that can be used immediately by practicing principals. It also presses school leaders to consider new techniques such as walk-through supervision, teacher leadership, and storytelling to shape culture.

This third edition is the product of two educators who have worked with hundreds of educators, schools, and other organizations around the world. Their wide experience and insights permeate this book. The 22 chapters supply an excellent mix of the conceptual and the practical, the concrete and the abstract, the most current and classic concepts. *The Principal's Companion* should bridge the needs of preservice programs and inservice professional development as well as be useful to the individuals who can learn on their own. Teacher leaders would also benefit from reading this book.

Books for principals should foster careful thinking and relevant new skills in an easily accessible format. *The Principal's Companion* accomplishes these things. The richness of ideas, breadth of examples, and thoughtful questioning make this book a unique tool for the development of more successful leaders. Effective principals should not be a luxury that schools only occasionally enjoy. Rather, effective leadership is needed and required in all schools. This third edition provides an enhanced array of ideas and suggestions for achieving this important end.

Preface

A principal interacts with hundreds of individuals on a daily basis, but the work life is ironically often one characterized by isolation, for there is no colleague on site with the same role. Although constantly engaging in social interaction, the principal often recalls feeling isolated when reflecting on the merit of key decisions. Alone, the principal often wonders, "Am I doing the right thing? Is this the best and most ethical way to approach the task?" For example, alone in her office a high school principal wonders about the subtle and not-so-subtle remarks students are making about ethnicity. Having 54 nationalities represented in the school could make it a potential tinderbox or an incredible context for teaching tolerance, valuing diversity, and building understanding. Her leadership actions will have a profound affect in determining which of these situations becomes reality.

Many principals reflect on the nature of their work and describe it as characterized by paradox. For instance, some say that they feel like they are alone and in the spotlight at the same time. Alone, in the privacy of his office, a middle school principal, having heard from teachers about students suffering from respiratory symptoms, contacts the central office about the need to have the air conditioning filters replaced and the roof checked for mold. As the principal gets off the phone, the secretary lets him know that three reporters from local papers are waiting to interview him about environmental health hazards in the school. Now in the spotlight, the principal must quickly prepare to speak with reporters who were alerted to the potential environmental problem by a parent who had been volunteering in the school.

Principals feel alone when asked to lead an effort in an area in which they have no formal training. One district sent out a memo to all principals indicating that their evaluation will be based in part on their ability to lead efforts to improve test scores in their schools. Upon reading this message, an elementary principal reflects, "I value the notion of using student data to drive instructional decisions, but how do I get the training to do this? How do principals get data from various sources, interpret it, and make decisions for instruction? It is a big part of my job, yet I have never really had any help on how to do this."

Creating a learning environment that capitalizes on diversity to promote lessons on tolerance as well as academics, ensuring school safety, adhering to environmental guidelines that protect the health and general welfare of staff and students, raising student test scores, promoting social and emotional learning . . . never before has the principal's role as a public figure been so demanding. What's more, there is pressure to perform in a context where others frequently offer "expert" advice. After all, everyone's been to school! But, what is the best decision? How can the principal ensure what is in the best interest of students and staff? Because of questions like these, we wrote *The Principal's Companion*.

■ WHY A THIRD EDITION?

Although some educational issues remain constant, practitioners, researchers, and the daily news remind us that much of the educational landscape has changed since the 2003 second edition of

The Principal's Companion. In response to these changes, the third edition examines the principal's role in relation to various topics, including the following:

- federal legislation that affects practice
- shifts in curriculum, instruction, and assessment
- data-driven decision making and high-stakes accountability
- teacher leadership
- a prescription for student learning (a new graphic, Figure 9.3, The Student Learning Nexus Model, has been added to assist supervisors and teacher leaders)
- teacher supervision and evaluation that focuses on enhancing the quality of student work, including walk-through supervision approaches
- forms of professional development that build individual and schoolwide capacity to address differentiated student needs in ways that leave their mark on policy and practice
- shaping school cultures to promote professional learning communities
- instructional implications of brain research
- social justice
- storytelling as a powerful culture-shaping leadership tool
- social and emotional learning
- the high school dropout crisis
- the Individuals with Disabilities Education Act of 2004
- ethical leadership
- technology
- opening a new school
- addressing cyberbullying and social responsibility

Some of these issues have historically been part of the administrator's work life, but many are new or are being spotlighted more emphatically now than in the past. As authors, we continue to feel compelled to explore both research and practice to support principals in their quest to effectively address important issues. However, we are quite cautious about taking on topics simply because they are in vogue. Our focus in *The Principal's Companion* is steered by a continuing commitment to promoting those actions that best serve all students and a belief that relationship building and communication skills represent critical leadership abilities. For example, high test scores on challenging state and national performance measures are certainly important. But equally important is developing within students a reverence for learning and those social and emotional skills that enable them to become contributing citizens in a democratic society. Although these attitudes and skills often are not measured formally, research shows that they are essential to leading a satisfying life and fostering a healthy society.

ENDURING FEATURES OF THE BOOK ■

The Principal's Companion seeks to explore both classical issues of leadership and current issues that are likely to impact student learning for many years to come. The primary purposes of this book remain the same—to provide ideas, approaches, strategies, resources, tools, techniques, and reflective opportunities for practicing and aspiring principals and to facilitate educational improvement when and where it counts, in every classroom and school, each and every day.

There are countless theories and ideas about leadership, but there is no one secret formula for success. Effective leaders invent creative solutions as they face challenges associated with new demands on their role or new situations. As one principal put it, "I try to make thoughtful decisions. Operating by the seat of one's pants is not the best way 'to do' the principalship. Yet the work demands that one address issues as they emerge. The bottom line is you try to do what is best for students and staff." Although principals cannot succeed without a fundamental understanding of theory, because of the immediacy of workplace demands, they often hunger for tried-and-true practices. Both theory and practice are essential for effective leadership.

Experience tells us that many principals have discovered strategies to tackle problems similar to those faced by their colleagues. However, because of the isolation that characterizes the principalship, there are seldom avenues to tap this tremendous potential treasure. *The Principal's Companion* mines multiple sources to provide practical strategies for principals who often operate alone. School principals need to know that they are part of a learning community of educational companions working together to help colleagues be the best they can be. This combined collegial effort will help principals create the kind of teaching and learning environment that supports teachers' efforts to bring about successful student performance. The interactive nature of the book, with reflective questions at the end of each chapter, is intended to help principals feel as if there is a colleague out there with whom to interact. The reader also will "hear" the voices of many practitioners who are quoted throughout the text. This will give aspiring principals a perspective of what it is like in the field and help them connect with others. Ultimately, these newcomers will learn that all of us make mistakes, meet challenges, and succeed.

Although this book is written primarily for current and aspiring principals, it will also be of interest to staff developers, university professors, school board members, directors of national and international principals' centers and associations, and leadership consultants. To assist programs using *The Principal's Companion* and the *Educational Leadership Policy Standards* (2008), a matrix aligning the book's chapters with the standards can be found on the inside cover.

Recognizing that principals are quite busy and have little time to waste, the chapters in this book have been kept short and to the point. Each one reflects a topic that principals have indicated is important. The ideas, experiences, strategies, and techniques described in each chapter are grounded in research and practice. Each chapter concludes with a set of questions, and there is space between the questions for the reader to write reflections inspired by the chapter or note strategies that he or she wants to try. This is an invitation to write between the lines, to add to one's collective knowledge base, thus enhancing the value of the book for the reader. Each chapter is designed to stand on its own and can be read in one sitting. Because of this feature, some ideas will appear in several chapters but may be addressed with a different perspective.

Success in the principalship depends on many factors. This book addresses these factors in seven parts, with chapters included under umbrella themes:

Part I: The Principal's Many Roles describes the roles of learner, manager, communicator and leader during a crisis, co-creator of the learning organization, and shaper of school culture. This section makes a strong case for recognizing that effective principals play a variety of roles—all of which are necessary for success. Fulfilling the roles that create a climate for growth, making sure schedules work, and setting a personal example of learning from successes and mistakes are some of the issues we address in this section.

Part II: Critical Skills for Effective Leadership examines and makes many suggestions regarding effective human relations strategies characterized by Emotional Intelligence and the vitally important function of time management and working effectively with the central office. We emphasize that these are critical areas because one cannot get the job done without succeeding in cultivating, practicing, and maintaining collegial relationships at the school site and central office and without taking control of one's time.

Part III: Honoring the School's Mission concentrates on the importance and process of mission building as a guiding force in the organization. We examine how to implement change in a way that provides meaning and constant renewal of the school's mission and generates commitment to the change among organizational members.

Part IV: Working Together to Build a Learning Organization links a variety of components that must interact synergistically if a school is to truly be a learning community. These components include building a collaborative environment; addressing critical issues in instruction, curriculum, and assessment that relate to classroom decisions that enhance student work; effectively using faculty meetings as a tool for capacity building; and meeting a variety of professional growth needs focused on building teachers' collective capacity to promote student learning. Additional components include supervision and evaluation of teachers to promote quality teacher decision making based on student learning and strategies to maximize feedback to teachers regarding their performance in meeting professional goals and student needs.

Part V: Starting Effectively and Staying the Course looks at the importance of providing meaning to traditional events such as the first days of school or the opening of a new school. Often principals miss opportunities to see how these events can serve as key tools for shaping the school's culture and providing a foundation for continuous growth. We also include an expanded section on tips to enhance a principal's effectiveness. Here, the reader will find ideas about organizing time, using technology efficiently, and incorporating helpful strategies to stay on task.

Part VI: Understanding Your Constituencies provides strategies to enhance one's interactions with students, parents, and the greater community, including businesses, emergency service personnel, social services, senior citizens, politicians, and the media. This section takes a holistic approach, viewing parents and the greater community as an integral part of the school, and examines social justice and the high school dropout crisis.

Part VII: The Principals' Professional and Personal Worlds looks at the individual principal. The focus here is to examine ways for the principal to grow, personally and professionally, and to remain vibrant, healthy, and continuously engaged in the pursuit of best practice regarding teaching, learning, and ethical school leadership.

The individual chapters serve as a menu of options from which the reader can select to meet pressing needs, assist in planning, or use as a resource. Many readers of the first and second editions commented that *The Principal's Companion* validated their existing practices, foreshadowed situations that needed to be addressed, and raised the bar for professional practice. In lonely moments of reflection, it also served as a companion. Collectively, the chapters offer a concise library of both research-based and tried-and-true practices. As professional colleagues, we welcome you in joining a continuous conversation about the principalship and wish you much success in what we believe is one of the most sacred professions.

PAM ROBBINS
Napa, CA, and Mt. Crawford, VA
HARVEY B. ALVY
Cheney, WA

Acknowledgments

We are indebted to many professional educators and family members who by their example have helped to steer the direction of this book. First and foremost, we would like to acknowledge Pat Wolfe, who brought us together to write this book and greatly influenced our thinking.

Harvey Alvy's first principal while teaching in the Harlem section of New York City, Lionel McMurren, will always remain as an example of an ethical leader whose support for new teachers inspired them to reach great heights in the classroom. Harvey is especially indebted to other administrators, teachers, school secretaries, and friends who have shared ideas, provided constructive criticism, and supported him while he served as an elementary, middle, and high school teacher, as an elementary and secondary principal, and currently as the William C. Shreeve Endowed Professor of Educational Administration at Eastern Washington University. These include Bob Gibson, Richard Shustrin, Alan Siegel, David Chojnacki, Steve Kapner, Forrest Broman, Elaine Levy, Jane Liu, Don Bergman, Roger and Betty Bicksler, Rob Beck, Joan Dickerson, Mike Dunn, Nelson and Lisa File, Bob Connor, Drew Alexander, Bob Stockton, Paul Schmidt, Ted Coladarci, Sandy Bensky, Les Portner, Billie Gehres, Sharon Jayne, Sharon Mowry, Jim Howard, Boni, and Leonie Brickman, and the late Phil Snowdon and William C. Shreeve. In addition, I would like to acknowledge the wonderful administrators, teachers, and support staff of the American Embassy School in New Delhi, India, the American International School in Israel, the Singapore American School, and Eastern Washington University. To Norman Alvy and Vicki Alvy, "you're the best." Harvey's wife, Bonnie, and daughter Rebecca, as always, deserve a degree of recognition that cannot be measured.

Pam Robbins would like to acknowledge Percy Haugen and Ernie Moretti, educators who provided inspiring induction experiences for her and created a strong sense of meaning and enthusiasm for her work. Special thanks are due to Margaret Arbuckle, Terry Deal, Karen Dyer, Linda Gaidimas, Carl Glickman, Tony Gregorc, Roland Barth, Lynn Seay, Allen Haymon, Kent Peterson, Jane Scott, Dennis Sparks, Karen Steinbrink Koch, Leslie and Mike Rowland, Jeff White, Patrice Newnam, DeWitt House, Pat Montgomery, Helene Paroff, Kathleen McElroy, Lou Martin, Ann Cunningham-Morris, Gayle Gregory, Stephanie Hirsh, Tom Guskey, Jay McTighe, Jane Bailey, Betsy Dunnenberger, Doug Guynn, Judith Warren Little, Debbie Brown, Scott Willis, Maurice Elias, and the late Susan Loucks-Horsley for their professional colleagueship, insights, wisdom, thoughtful feedback, and willingness to collaborate. The late Judy Arin Krupp deserves special mention for her expertise regarding adult learning and for the inspiration she provided as a friend and professional colleague.

Heartfelt thanks are due to Ray Cubbage for his sage advice, companionship, love, patience, support, and inspiration. D. D. Dawson deserves special acknowledgment for her support, wisdom, good humor, reflections, insights, and friendship.

Gracia Alkema, founding president of Corwin, deserves sincere thanks for her friendship and recommendations regarding the book's content and organization, as well as that little "push" she provided *when* we needed it! We thank Leigh Peake, president of Corwin, for her earnest support. Cassandra Seibel, production editor, deserves special acknowledgment for her expertise and editorial assistance. Debbie Stollenwerk, senior acquisitions editor, is to be thanked for her assistance throughout the project.

Finally, to our parents David and Muriel Robbins and Daniel and Rebecca Pearl Alvy, thanks for the good humor, wisdom, encouragement, support, modeling of perseverance, and lifelong learning.

About the Authors

Pam Robbins earned her doctorate in educational administration from the University of California, Berkeley. Her professional interests include leadership development, supervision, developing learning communities, brain research and brain-compatible instruction, teaching in the block schedule, peer coaching, mentoring, promoting quality teaching, and presentation skills.

Her teaching career began in 1971 in special education. She later taught intermediate grades, and coached high school basketball. As an administrator, she served as Director of Special Projects and Research for the Napa County (CA) Office of Education and Director of Training for the North Bay California Leadership Academy. She has lectured at several universities, authored and co-authored books, developed videotapes, and consulted with principals' academies in Alaska, California, Kentucky, Tennessee, Massachusetts, Utah, Pennsylvania, Europe, Great Britain, the Far East, and South America.

In addition, she has provided national and international training sessions for the Department of Defense Education Equity Division, the Ford Motor Company, the Association for Supervision and Curriculum Development (ASCD), the American Society for Training and Development (ASTD), the Wisconsin Academy Staff Development Initiative (WASDI), the National Staff Development Council (NSDC), Phi Delta Kappa (PDK), the National Association of Elementary School Principals (NAESP), and the National Association of Secondary School Principals (NASSP).

Currently, she is consulting with school districts, state departments of education, educational service centers, and corporations throughout the United States, Canada, Europe, Great Britain, and the Far East. She may be contacted at 1251 Windsor Lane, Mt. Crawford, VA 22841, or by e-mail: probbins@shentel.net. For additional information, visit Pam's Web page at user.shentel.net/probbins.

Harvey B. Alvy served as a practicing principal for 14 years and had the opportunity to gain both elementary and secondary administrative experience. His teaching career began as an inner-city elementary school teacher in the Harlem section of New York City. He later taught in middle and high schools in the United States and abroad. His experience in multicultural, international schools is extensive. His international experiences have taken him from the American School in Kinshasa, Zaire, to the American International School in Israel, the American Embassy School in New Delhi, India, and the Singapore American School. Harvey is a founding board member of the Principals' Training Center for International Schools. In 1991, the National Association of Elementary School Principals selected him as a National Distinguished Principal for

American Overseas Schools. In 2004 he received the Eastern Washington University (EWU) CenturyTel Faculty Achievement Award for Teaching Excellence.

In 1983, Harvey earned his doctorate in educational administration from the University of Montana, focusing on the problems of new principals. He has conducted seminars, workshops, and presentations both nationally and internationally on the newcomer to the principalship, moral leadership, instructional leadership, effective supervision of teachers, characteristics of great teachers, shaping collaborative school cultures, educational change, and the leadership of Abraham Lincoln.

Presently, Harvey holds the William C. Shreeve Endowed Professorship in Educational Administration at EWU, where he specializes in educational leadership and foundations. He can be reached at: 312 Williamson Hall, Department of Education, Eastern Washington University, Cheney, WA 99004, phone: (509) 359-6093, email: harvey.alvy@mail.ewu.edu. His Web site is http://www.ewu.edu/x21525.xml.

PART I

The Principal's Many Roles

1

Leader as Learner

Just when I'm ready to retire, I'm beginning to learn what this job is all about.

—A principal's voice[1] (after 33 years of service)

■ PRINCIPAL AS LIFELONG LEARNER

There is no setting in which the concept of the lifelong learner is more important than a school. In fact, many professionals now conceptualize the school as a Professional Learning Community (DuFour & Eaker, 1998) not only for students but also for administrators, teachers, support staff, and parents. This is a powerful notion that can impact student success. As Barth (2001b) notes, "more than anything else, it is the culture of the school that determines the achievement of teacher and student alike" (p. 33).

Bennis and Nanus (1985) remind us that successful leaders take responsibility for their own development and are *perpetual learners.* Schlechty (2001) stresses that "if the principal is to help teachers improve what they do, the principal must continuously be learning to improve what he or she is doing" (p. 145). Senge (1990) suggests that a characteristic of the successful leader is the ability to instill in others the desire to learn what is necessary to help the organization reach its mission. And George (2007) reflects that "authentic leadership is empowering others on their journeys. This shift is the transformation from 'I' to 'We.' It is the most important process learners go through in becoming authentic" (p. 44). Applying this notion to the principal of a school, the leader can model for everyone in the workplace what lifelong learning means. For modeling to be effective, though, it should be sincere, consistent, purposeful, and empowering. There are several ways to do this.

■ LEARNING IN MANY CONTEXTS

One way the principal can model lifelong learning is by continuing to participate in the development and demonstration of effective teaching practices. For example, a principal collaborating with teacher leaders can help create faculty meetings in which conversations about teaching, learning, and assessment become institutionalized through various activities. During these conversations, principals should purposefully support the remarks of both new and veteran teachers to model a high regard for the contributions of all faculty. Another context in which the principal can function as learner is during the supervision process. The following scenario demonstrates how the leader-as-learner theme is played out in two ways: learning about not only behaviors and activities that facilitate student and teacher learning but also behaviors and strategies that enhance the principal's effectiveness in the supervisory process.

An effective and common supervisory technique includes a preobservation conference in which the principal and a teacher, through a questioning process, work together to "unpack" the teacher's thinking about the lesson to be taught. Together they discuss planned teaching behaviors and expected student outcomes. They solve potential problems and fine-tune the lesson plan. The teacher identifies the focus for the observation, and collaboratively the teacher and the principal decide on the best method for data collection. During the observation, the principal, steered primarily by the teacher's request for information, collects data. Collectively, teacher and principal learn about curricular, instructional, and assessment practices that produce desired student outcomes. In addition, both professionals identify the types of data collection that capture the essence of the desired supervisory focus.

In the postobservation conference, the principal and the teacher often examine student work and ask questions that foster reflection on and analysis of the lesson. Together they discuss what worked to facilitate student learning. At the conclusion of these reflections, they analyze what would be done the same and what would be done differently if the lesson were to be taught again.

Additionally, the principal asks, "Thinking about this conferencing process, what strategies and techniques did I use that facilitated your thinking as a teacher?" The principal might also ask, "What might I have done differently?" Thus the principal and the teacher collaboratively analyze the conferencing practices that enhance or hinder teacher thinking and learning about curriculum and instruction. Together they find ways to make the conferencing experience worthwhile for both.

Principal-as-student experiences can be an innovative way to provide a new perspective and important insights about a school. The principal can spend time in classrooms taking on the student role as a participant in a discussion, a team member in a cooperative group, or a reader or teacher. A particularly successful principal-as-student strategy is "Principal for the Day." One high school principal that we know of holds an essay contest each year that results in a student exchanging roles with the principal for one day. The principal takes on the class schedule of the student selected as principal and completes the student's homework assignments, attends classes, and takes examinations. This is a wonderful way to celebrate learning, remain visible, attend classes, and build relationships with students. It also increases the principal's awareness of the quality of classroom learning. These experiences can be shared on a schoolwide basis, in faculty meetings, or with the school's parent teacher organization. Students and teachers appreciate the interest in them and enjoy the novelty of the situation. If a principal has not functioned in these roles before, it is critical to let teachers know ahead of time "what you're up to."

The principal can teach demonstration lessons, possibly on technology, and digitally record the lessons to use at a faculty meeting. This provides an opportunity to apply new ideas and practices. Then the principal can talk with staff about experiences in teaching and learning associated with presenting lessons. If the principal's lesson is only fair, and the "rough edges are showing," this can be comforting to staff. It is nice to know that leaders are not flawless. This builds trust because teachers realize that the principal has walked in their shoes, is willing to accept feedback from the faculty, and has an understanding of classroom conditions.

The principal can also function as a learner by reading and sharing research with teachers and parents. By writing or speaking about new learnings, the principal can pass on knowledge of recent research while modeling a love of learning.

Still another way that the principal functions in the learner role is by participating in professional development sessions. Too often principals introduce speakers and run off to another meeting.

Principal participation emphasizes the importance of these professional development opportunities and validates the teachers' time spent in these sessions.

When the principal attends a conference, there are frequently opportunities to purchase CDs, DVDs, or podcasts of sessions. Teachers should be encouraged to do the same. Try picking out the best sessions, purchasing recordings of them, and starting a collection in the staff room, teachers' center, or library. These resources can be borrowed by staff or parents. The principal can also send a follow-up report on the conference via e-mail or hard copy or sponsor a volunteer brown-bag lunch on key conference ideas to the staff. If there is sufficient interest in a topic, blogs can be initiated to engage in a discussion forum on a school district Web site.

Principals can help encourage Action Research projects by individuals or groups of teachers on educational ideas of interest to the staff. To illustrate, in one school district several elementary and high school teachers engaged in an Action Research project exploring the use of student portfolios. The teachers met periodically to discuss their experiences and student reactions, and the principal facilitated the process by helping to gather articles on portfolios, keeping a record of the project, and helping to develop an Action Research report with the staff. Staff who were planning to pursue the project during the following school year used several recommendations from this report:

- continuing the project on a voluntary basis
- developing portfolio partners among the faculty to compare notes every couple of weeks during the year
- having students in one class share portfolios with other classes
- collecting more nuts-and-bolts ideas on portfolios
- finding a quiet area to digitally record student work
- refining ways to help students reflect on and evaluate their progress through self-assessment and use of rubrics
- helping teachers fine-tune their conferencing skills with students
- providing strategies to help teachers structure classes to engage in frequent conversations with individual students
- considering strategies to present portfolios to parents during an evening or afternoon of student-led conferences

These suggestions by teachers assisted both the principal and the teachers in their quest to continually learn. By allowing teachers to use the resources of a principal's office, including secretarial services, and maintaining a database on portfolio progress, principals send a clear message of support for professional development and can be a great help to teachers engaged in learning activities designed to enhance students' classroom experiences.

Another strategy to support learning includes organizing book study groups or clubs among teachers and parents. (See Chapter 17 for a detailed explanation of such a group.) When principals are involved in these groups as facilitators or participants, the leader-as-learner role is strengthened and modeled. In one high school a successful book study group read *A Tribe Apart,* by Patricia Hersch (1998), and *Reviving Ophelia,* by Mary Pipher (1994).

Principals who solicit comments about their job performance from staff members at the end of the year send a strong message that they seek and appreciate staff input as another resource to promote learning. Furthermore, asking for staff feedback models a stance of openness and a commitment to ongoing learning. The following form has been used for several years by one of the authors to gain faculty input on a principal's performance:

Dear Faculty,

Over the years I have asked each faculty member with whom I have worked to give me helpful hints to improve my job performance. I know that you are all very busy, but I would appreciate it if you could take a few minutes to answer the questions below and help me evaluate my performance so I can do a better job next year. Obviously, your comments will remain confidential. If you would like to remain anonymous, please word process your comments. Please put your comments in the "Harvey" envelope on Prema's desk. I would appreciate your comments by the last faculty day, May 27.

Thanks, Harvey

1. What are some of the things that I am currently doing that you would like to see me continue?

2. What am I currently doing that you would like to see me discontinue next year?

3. What suggestions do you have to help me improve my job performance (e.g., Is there a particular area that I should pursue for additional training? Is there a book or article that you suggest I read?)?

4. Do you have any additional comments?

This procedure is simple to execute and often yields constructive feedback and helpful ideas. It also provides an opportunity for the principal to assess the perceptions of staff in relation to his or her self-perception. Feedback can be enhanced when the perspectives of students, classified staff, parents, assistant principals, and community members are solicited. This type of feedback, often referred to as *360-degree feedback,* can offer multiple perspectives for consideration.

Principals who keep reflective journals often share insights derived from this activity with staff, which sometimes encourages staff members to become reflective about their own craft experiences and practices. Supporting the notion of leader as learner, Barth (1990) emphasizes principals' tremendous capacity to release energy in a school by becoming sustained, visible learners. Barth also describes the phenomenon of an "at-risk" principal as any educator who leaves school at the end of the day with little possibility of continuing learning about the work that he or she does (cited in Sparks, 1993, p. 19). Rolf P. Lynton of the World Health Organization has also offered some powerful insights about reflection by noting that we all go through events on a daily basis. What distinguishes an *event* from an *experience* is that an event only becomes an experience after you have time to reflect.[2] Each experience offers an opportunity to learn. When teachers, students, and parents see a principal's desire to learn and share ideas, norms and expectations that celebrate learning can develop within a school. Moreover, the leader-as-learner model transfers to the classroom, where teachers demonstrate for students that they, too, are both leaders and learners.

THE SCHOOL AS A POWERFUL ■ CONTEXT FOR LEARNING

Finding time for such reflective endeavors is a challenge, yet doing so is critical. "We must also find imaginative ways of separating adults from youngsters at times during the school day for conversation, brainstorming, reflection and replenishment" (Sparks, 1993, p. 20) so that the learning and the growth process continue. Barth (1990) believes that "the schoolhouse itself is the most powerful context for the continuing education of educators" (p. 20). Creating a learning community in some cultures is so valued that a considerable amount of time within the work day is allocated to this endeavor. For instance, in some Japanese schools, 40 percent of the work day is devoted to teacher planning, often in a collaborative context. Reflecting on the conceptualization of leader as learner, one can see that there are numerous ways to learn while on the job. Once time is identified, learning experiences can come from workshops, class visitations, demonstration lessons, Action Research projects, analyses of student data, reflective journal writing, books, educational journals, conferences, and discussions with and visits to other principals.

■ A GLOBAL PERSPECTIVE

A leader's commitment to promoting lifetime learning throughout an organization is simply a smart strategy and an ethically wise decision when contemplating the world from a global perspective. In his influential book *The World Is Flat,* Thomas Friedman (2005) discusses the fact that successful corporations are cross-training their workers to develop multiple skills because future employment will depend on a worker's ability to be flexible and mobile: "The whole mindset of a flat world is one in which the individual worker is going to become more and more responsible for managing his or her own career, risks, and economic security" (p. 284). Based on his observations of India and China as well as the instrumental role that technology and initiative play, Friedman stresses that, in recent years, "the global competitive playing field was being leveled. The world was being flattened" (p. 8). Not surprisingly, he says that schools need to support math and science education as well as technology and critical thinking for both women and men.

School leaders who seek to understand the demographic changes in their own schools gain a greater perspective on the changes, and engage in lifetime learning, by recognizing the world as a dynamic, interdependent global community in which the "distance'" between cultures and world issues is shrinking. In the United States today, there are more and more students who are nonnative English speakers from multicultural, immigrant, or migrant backgrounds. These students and their families have left their native countries to be a part of the U.S. historical narrative, the story of a nation of immigrants that has succeeded because of the ingenuity and hard work of its people.

School principals, as active and influential citizens, have a moral obligation to promote the success of each child in the school, regardless of race, class, ethnicity, gender, or country of origin. At the local school level, this commitment to the success of each child can be realized through the promotion of heterogeneous classes from prekindergarten through Grade 12. That local act sends a powerful message with global implications.

■ WHEN OLD AND NEW IDEAS CONVERGE

The Value of Repertoire

As principals' knowledge and experience increase, they are often faced with new ideas that appear to conflict with previous learning. Educators are expected to make either/or decisions regarding innovations that affect instructional practices and, consequently, students. To illustrate, suppose a district commits to a professional development focus on brain-based learning. Does this mean that the previous insights and learning from Madeline Hunter's direct instruction model are no longer valid? Certainly not. Rather, the strengths from both instructional approaches should be celebrated. Too often we are encouraged to discard one idea for another. However, leaders as learners should develop the ability to take the best from each new idea and synthesize information into an eclectic model. Doing so enables principals to diagnose a situation and draw from a repertoire of strategies to meet particular needs.

A critical learning for leadership is acknowledging that there will always be a need to learn more. Some of the most essential behaviors a principal can model is a devotion to lifelong learning and a willingness to dialogue with members of the learning organization about how new learning can reshape existing knowledge. To demonstrate this ongoing pursuit of knowledge, one principal we know regularly hangs a sign on the doorknob of her office that reads "Out Learning." This reminds all members of the learning organization about the importance and power of learning about learning.

From ESEA to NCLB: Implications for the Future

When studying the history of education in the United States, it is clear that the federal government initially had little intent of playing a major role in statewide education decisions. Remember, education is not mentioned in the U.S. Constitution. However, by the middle of the 20th century the federal position had permanently changed because of three major acts. First, President Eisenhower decided to use National Guard troops in Little Rock, Arkansas, to enforce the Supreme Court's decision in *Brown v. Board of Education*. Second, in response to the Russian launch of Sputnik in 1957, U.S. leaders decided that this country was falling behind in math and science education, so in 1958 they passed the National Defense Education Act to upgrade schooling in the scientific fields. Third, passage of the Elementary and Secondary Education Act (ESEA) in 1965, as part of President Johnson's War on Poverty, directly involved the federal government in compensatory programs, from Title I to Head Start, to lift up the poor and help them succeed in schools. It is helpful to conceive of the No Child Left Behind Act (NCLB), signed into law in January 2002 by President Bush, as part of the federal government's continued intervention in schools.

Although there are as many critics as supporters of NCLB, important components of the NCLB movement have impacted schools significantly and will likely remain important educational objectives and trends regardless of which party controls the White House or Congress. School principals will need to address the following components to meet legislative and public expectations (Alvy & Robbins, 2008; Armstrong, Henson, & Savage, 2009; Koch, 2009):

- Each student, regardless of race, ethnicity, socioeconomic status, gender, or exceptionality, is entitled to a high-quality education.
- Schools and teachers must be accountable for student learning.
- The achievement gap among different groups must be closed.
- High averages on statewide tests will no longer be acceptable if students from minority, impoverished, or other selected groups perform below standard. Disaggregating test scores will remain critical to ensure that the needs of each group are addressed.
- High-stakes statewide tests will remain an important measure of state, district, school, and individual student success. However, school leaders will continue to fight for multiple measures of student progress (e.g., both traditional and alternative assessments, including portfolios, culminating projects, and interim formative testing) to gain a more accurate portrait of student success. Value-added data will likely be a component of the testing equation to assess student progress over time.
- School leaders will continue to struggle with not only the pressure to provide one-size-fits-all testing results to meet the public's desire for accountability and transparency but also educators' desire to address individual student needs based on teacher voice and authentic assessments.

- Because the federal government has mandated that standards and assessments should be developed by individual states, there will continue to be a controversy concerning the variety of content and testing expectations demanded across the nation. Inconsistency in standards and testing expectations will likely contribute to confusion about whether all students in the country are meeting equally high expectations.
- High-quality curriculum standards, guided primarily by the national professional associations (e.g., National Council of Teachers of Mathematics, National Council of Teachers of English), will continue to be developed and used in each state. Teachers and administrators will work to ensure that tests are aligned with these curriculum standards and do not simply assess minimum competencies, but rather critical thinking skills as well.
- The alignment of statewide tests with curriculum standards will remain a topic of controversy as teachers and other school leaders struggle with issues such as "teaching to the test"; "covering the curriculum"; determining whether a test actually is aligned with standards; and dealing with a possible reduction of problem solving, higher-level thinking, and project-based work.
- Decisions related to curriculum, instruction, assessment, and classroom management primarily should be made based on Best Practice research.
- Hiring highly qualified teachers in each core subject area regardless of the economic base of the local school district will remain an important social justice objective. Statistically, less qualified teachers, based on certification status and college majors, have been hired disproportionally in schools with greater poverty (Peske & Haycock, 2006, cited in Morrison, 2009).
- States, districts, and individual schools must provide data to parents and the community, a report card that indicates how schools are doing in several categories, including test scores. Schools that do not achieve Adequate Yearly Progress will be expected to take corrective action. Parents will play a greater role in determining their children's educational setting within the realm of school choice.
- Districts and schools will continue to struggle with determining the best ways to assess exceptional students, including English Language Learners, students with disabilities, and all students with special talents. This has become an important ethical issue for schools. As one elementary school principal responding to the consequences of poor test scores under NCLB stated, "I think it is immoral in fact to require students who are disabled to take a test that is way beyond their ability" (quoted in Smith, 2005).
- The alarming number of high school dropouts and underprepared graduates, especially in urban areas, must remain a focus of states. The movement toward smaller schools that press for academic rigor and high expectations, supported by major educational organizations (e.g., National Association of Secondary School Principals) and public and private funding (e.g., Bill and Melinda Gates Foundation), will continue to address the dropout issue by promoting meaningful school options that personalize learning.
- Although the standards and assessment movement has emphasized success in core academic subject areas, the neglect of the visual and performing arts, social and emotional learning, physical education, and health-related schooling responsibilities must be addressed.

A final but important note: Learning leaders armed with essential understanding of how the old and new converge will find themselves equipped with the wisdom to effectively and confidently guide the school into the future.

NOTES

1. Authentic principal voices from interviews, workshops, writings, and informal conversations will be heard throughout the book.

2. We thank Dr. Steve Atwood of UNICEF for introducing us to Dr. Lynton's ideas.

REFLECTIONS

This space provides a place for you to write down ideas that have been generated by this chapter, things you want to try, or adaptations of ideas presented here.

1. What are some things you might do to model leader as learner?

2. What might be some observable indicators or artifacts of a school that is functioning as a Professional Learning Community?

3. How can principals facilitate a learning environment for adults within a school?

4. What questions should principals or assistant principals ask to gain helpful feedback on their performance?

5. In what ways do federal legislation and state mandates impact the role of the principal?

6. Why did you become a school principal, or why would you like to become a principal?

7. What insights or new questions do you have as a result of reflecting on the ideas presented in this chapter?

2

Leader as Manager

To facilitate learning, the instructional leader also makes sure that the classroom lights are working.

—A principal's voice

As practitioners, we need to ensure that schedules work, whiteboard markers are in classrooms, and transition times run smoothly. Instructional leadership behaviors will have a greater impact on student success and often reflect effective long-range leadership planning, but teachers, students, parents, and the community are more likely to notice immediate problems due to management glitches (R. Grant, personal communication, October 2007). These problems include the less-than-glamorous flooding toilet, school bus breakdown, schoolwide computer server or Internet problem, scheduling error, and leaking ceiling. The long-range vision may make you a great leader tomorrow, but today the public notices the poorly lit hallway (which is interpreted by some as displaying minimal regard for safety and security). However, we should not be fooled into thinking that success as an educational leader ends with neat bookshelves, quiet hallways, or the latest software for student records. We must not forget that students should be the ultimate beneficiaries of all management actions. Yet much of the leadership literature contains a subtle disdain for management.

Although the concept of the principal has shifted from gatekeeper (Deal & Peterson, 1994; Goldring & Rallis, 1993) to instructional leader, collaborative decision maker, leader of leaders, and results-oriented instructional leader, any discussion of leadership can become a romantic concept if leadership is not discussed hand in hand with management. One has to manage leadership. Part of management is paying attention to a school's physical environment; it is difficult to focus on learning if the physical environment does not promote it. For example, simply changing the contents of a display case outside of a high school office each month can send a strong message about student learning. If the display case includes work from various subjects and extracurricular activities, the school is honoring each discipline.

GOOD LEADERSHIP REQUIRES ■ EFFECTIVE MANAGEMENT

Effective principals are effective managers. They must communicate and develop relationships with teachers, assistant principals, custodians, secretaries, counselors, librarians, students, cafeteria workers, parents, transportation workers, and central office and security personnel. As managers, it is critical to display respect for every individual who serves the school. When considering the primary purpose of schooling, principals should always remember that, although some employees may appear to be on the periphery, everyone contributes in his or her own way to a school's success. Principals must model in all their relationships the behavior that they expect throughout the school and the community. To illustrate, principals or assistant principals should work closely with classified staff, such as bus drivers, who appear on the fringe of the classroom experience because they can offer a valuable perspective. Principals, assistant principals, or district personnel should share with classified staff the school goals and advocate important programs (e.g., decreasing harassment). Because of their unusual schedule, bus drivers are in the community, the diners, the barbershops, and other public places during part of the school day. What individuals say about the school in these venues can go a long way toward influencing how the school is perceived in the community.

Honoring these workers can have a very positive affect on them. To illustrate, Johnston (2001) relates the story of Ramon Curiel, who recruits and hires the 6,000 bus drivers, teacher aides, custodians, and other classified staff in Long Beach, California. Curiel gave credit to and celebrated their contribution to the overall improved grades of the students in the district because of the role they played in developing school climate. To the classified staff he said, "Look, you had something to do with this" (p. 18). As a bus driver in Harrisonburg, Virginia, reflected, "I am the first point of contact kids have with the school. A friendly greeting from me when they step on the bus brings a smile to their faces. My positive attitude influences what teachers experience on a daily basis."

A principal's work produces many additional management challenges involving policies, resources, behaviors, procedures, and data. These challenges can be classified into four categories that reflect the various arenas in which the leader must function as manager: classroom, school site, community, and support services. (An additional category, working with the central office, is discussed in Chapter 6.)

MANAGEMENT RESPONSIBILITIES ■ AND STRATEGIES

Classroom

Principals must help to maximize the availability of sufficient and high-quality classroom supplies and instructional resources to enable teachers to focus on student learning. Principals need to be on top of the classroom supply inventory so that key items are available during the year for teachers and students. Some principals delegate this job to a responsible supply clerk or secretary. In small schools, principals retain this function for themselves. Although it is important to know how to delegate, one can never give up the responsibility for the task. When you delegate, you need to check for clear understanding, provide support, and follow up regularly. If the person to whom you have delegated comes up with an innovation, assure the person that you have confidence in him or her and encourage the resourcefulness, but make sure you are not the last one to find out about the innovation.

The availability of classroom supplies and instructional resources for staff is heavily reliant on data relating to curricular needs and the quality of the material. One must ask teachers whether the resources are serving their purposes. Does a particular instructional resource improve the quality of the educational program? Are the resources helpful for gathering assessment data to measure student progress? Is there enough money in the budget for a year's supply of computer paper? What classroom supplies were consumed completely last year? What instructional resources are in great demand at the start of the school year? What are some of the new resources available to make life easier for the staff (e.g., flash drives)? How can the resources be distributed more efficiently? Is waste taking place, and if so, why? The answers to these questions can be provided by a variety of people as well as through observations. System checks are crucial and should include input from the staff regarding the adequacy and appropriateness of supplies.

Staff members' perceptions of resource availability are another important consideration. The policies for allocating classroom supplies and instructional resources reveal much about the values and beliefs of the organization. For example, is the supply room locked and materials strictly allocated, or is it open with a sign-out sheet? Are the veteran teachers in possession of the best resources? With your own school in mind, reflect on how "the system" works. Does it match the mission of the school? If your school promotes enrichment for all students, then you must have enrichment material and classroom options available for various instructional disciplines (e.g., novels, technology resources, independent science projects, challenging math manipulatives) that can be used by all classroom teachers. A teachers' resource center in a school or district office can serve as a central area in which to keep instructional material to be used by all teachers, which may diminish greatly the desire to hoard the best instructional material.

With regard to the environment, is your school ecologically conscientious? Do the school office and each classroom collect paper to be reused or sent to a recycling plant? Are plastic containers, cans, and bottles collected for recycling? Helpful ideas about being more environmentally conscious can come from a variety of sources. One high school ecology club convinced the superintendent to purchase copier paper for the district that was ecologically superior to paper purchased previously.

Some principals encourage staff input on the creation of policies and procedures related to resource requisition and allocation, which expands the leadership function of many staff members. These new roles build ownership of school-level practices and policies. Some principals also provide site-based teams and individual teachers with school and classroom budgets to be used according to their discretion. If greater teacher involvement in resource allocation follows expanded teacher involvement in curricular and instructional decisions, then the resources will surely be used more efficiently and with greater meaning.

Another managerial responsibility is record keeping for a variety of purposes, including attendance and tardiness, lunch count federal aid to dependent children, and cumulative records. In general, teachers disdain these responsibilities (as they should!) because they subtract from teaching. The principal must carefully review these chores to see what can be removed from the teacher's task list. How can the secretary assist? How can technology be used to free up teachers? What responsibilities can be picked up by students, teacher aides, or parent volunteers? For example, students can help with lunch count chores. Each school has a unique set of routines and chores. Important questions to ask are: How do the current routines and tasks support the educational program? Which routines and tasks can be eliminated or trimmed to increase instructional time?

School Site

A safe environment contributes to an effective school. Furthermore, the physical appearance of a school can contribute to and reflect positive or negative school climate or morale. For example, graffiti and vandalism negatively affect the school and its administration, teachers, students, and community. Thus principals should inform school custodians to remove graffiti immediately and quickly repair broken lights and windows, loose banisters, or damaged lockers to ensure safety and maintain pride in the appearance of the school.

There are many ways to positively influence the physical environment of the school. For example, one school staff collectively designed a hallway mural that depicted key standards addressed in K–5 classrooms; images of the Nile River, pyramids, and Egyptian mummies underscored essential social studies learnings. Classes at some schools have donated benches, trees, and flower gardens as an indication of their commitment to the school. This has significantly decreased vandalism and enhanced social and emotional competence.

Principals and teachers need to recognize that a school's physical environment or air quality may be a contributing factor if students appear to be lethargic or are experiencing frequent nasal, throat, eye, skin, or lung problems. U.S. Environmental Protection Agency (EPA) officials have noted that "the air quality in many schools could be improved dramatically simply by replacing filters on heating and air conditioning units on a regular basis" (Sack, 2002, p. 12). According to Michelle Guarneiri, an EPA official, "the worst problem is mold, and most schools have mold, everywhere from Alaska to Florida" (quoted in Sack, 2002, p. 12).

Working with health department officials, school principals can identify issues relating to the air quality and environment by developing a questionnaire for teachers and students that addresses topics relating to noise, ventilation, lighting, wall or ceiling leakage, and various odors such as gas, propane, sewage, mold, glue, smoke, dust, and ammonia. The EPA has published on its Web site guidelines and resources to help schools with environmental concerns (www.epa .gov/iaq/schools).

A related responsibility is maintaining a litter-free environment. Principals have organized "trash patrols" and other activities to assure an attractive campus. One principal developed a program called The Eagle's Eyes. The eagle is the school's mascot, and anytime someone was observed doing something to enhance the campus—from picking up litter to planting a tree—that person would be acknowledged with a note written on stationery headed with "The eagle's eyes saw. . . ." These individuals could also be celebrated during assemblies.

Another area of management responsibility is transportation. To address teacher and office confusion about which bus a new student should ride, transportation supervisors work with principals to keep an alphabetical listing of all streets, subdivisions, and day care centers with the appropriate bus number listed by each entry. The route times might also be listed. This document enables teachers to look up a student's address by street name and assign the student to the proper bus quickly and accurately.

Often overlooked as a management responsibility is the need to keep support personnel informed about student behavior and expectations. Principals find student behavior to be an essential topic, not only for teachers but for parent volunteers, paraprofessionals, and support personnel such as school bus drivers, cafeteria workers, classroom aides, and library personnel. To address this topic, seminars can be planned to discuss issues related to student behavior as well as motivation and reinforcement theory. When the emphasis is on organizing, teaching, and reinforcing students during the first 3 weeks of school, the staff and support personnel generally report fewer discipline referrals. Thereafter, attention to behavior should continue with a focus on "catching students being good." These strategies will contribute to a safe, vibrant learning environment.

Leading and Learning By Wandering Around

In addition to physical appearance and air-quality issues, plant maintenance and safety are also critical management dimensions. One way to ensure safety is through Leading and Learning by Wandering Around (LLBWA), which involves the principal purposefully getting out from behind the desk and walking around the school (Robbins & Alvy, 2004). Research by Marzano, Waters, and McNulty (2005) reveals that a key principalship responsibility correlated with student achievement is "Situational Awareness . . . leaders' awareness of the details and the undercurrents regarding the functioning of the school and their use of this information to address current and potential problems" (p. 61). It is our belief that LLBWA is a technique that uniquely enables a leader to monitor the pulse of a school by keeping abreast of the undercurrents and potential problems. Marzano et al. suggest that one should not be surprised that situational awareness is an important principalship responsibility because "it makes intuitive sense that a school leader must understand the innermost workings of the school at the nuts-and-bolts level to be effective. The more one knows about the inner workings of an organization, the more one is able to lead and manage that organization" (pp. 64–65).

In this chapter, the strategy of LLBWA refers primarily to maintenance concerns. However, LLBWA has an additional, powerful application: promoting instructional excellence (discussed in Chapter 9). A key attribute of this technique is that the principal must have a clear plan for where the "wandering" will occur. Some principals create a checklist of key areas, from classrooms to storage sheds. The goal is to visit these areas frequently, with classrooms being the top priority. Many principals keep a clipboard by their desk and post this checklist on it. Figure 2.1 provides an elementary school example.

Others keep the checklist on a personal digital assistant (PDA) or an index card. Then, whenever they have a few minutes here or there, they look down the checklist, determine where they have not visited during the month, and purposefully wander to one of those locations. In doing this, one principal discovered that an electrical outlet was located next to a sink in the boys' restroom. A call to the maintenance department quickly corrected this hazardous condition. A great way to visit classrooms and the rest of the school is to do so with the school custodian. A principal might meet with the custodian once a month, and they walk around the school (the custodian with a notepad or PDA in hand). This enables them to see maintenance needs and communicate about school programs and activities as well as get input from teachers. On these walking tours the building "talks." A strong message is conveyed to students, teachers, parents, and visitors by what is on the hallway walls, on the walls of the cafeteria, in the display cases, or on the floor. A walk in one school revealed that the lawn was being watered five minutes before physical education classes were going to play on the field.

Usually, there are 5–10 maintenance requests that result from these walks. The walks provide maintenance personnel with undivided attention from an administrator and opportunities to receive treasured feedback. Also, these walks let the staff know that the principal is interested in the day-to-day running of the school.

Spending time in corridors, classrooms, stairwells, and other areas throughout the building gives the principal a chance to oversee plant safety and spread good news and caring words to staff, students, community members, and parents. Using this approach, the principal is able to communicate, plan proactively, and minimize interruptions.

Another proactive management technique is to visit classrooms before or after school to see bulletin boards, special displays, learning centers, and student work. A principal can note, for example, whether a computer lab or journalism classroom is used actively during these times. When staff members receive a complimentary note from the principal about their rooms, it is a great way to start the day and reinforces the notion that the classroom is the center of the school.

Figure 2.1 Example of a Leading and Learning by Wandering Around Record

	September	October	November
Kitchen Cafeteria Custodian's office Girls' restroom Boys' restroom Library Storage shed Bike rack Kindergarten playground Regular playground Baseball diamond			
Classrooms—Wing A			
Room 1 Room 2 Room 3 Room 4 Room 5 Room 6			
Classrooms—Wing B			
Room 7 Room 8 Room 9 Room 10 Room 11 Room 12 Kindergarten room Computer lab			

These visits also increase a principal's awareness of each classroom's current activities, which allows for channeling of resources in particular areas. When fliers, pictures, or book samples come across the principal's desk, they can be forwarded to the appropriate classrooms.

LLBWA is also an excellent time management technique. The principal uses precious minutes in an efficient way to manage what is important. One principal talked of conducting "one-legged conferences" during her walks about campus. As an example, she cited talking with a custodian about his excellent care of the front lawn and simultaneously requesting that he mow the lawn by the primary wing at a time other than 12:45, when students were doing sustained silent reading. She invited him to participate in the reading program at that time so that students could see him modeling reading as a lifelong skill. Another idea might be to invite the custodian into the classroom to talk about how he uses math in his daily work. Cafeteria staff, the nurse, librarians, teachers, parents, and community members could be asked to share how they have applied learnings from school.

One of the most troubling and sensitive problems facing principles is managing individuals who are not succeeding, whether they are teachers or other school personnel. LLBWA increases the principal's awareness of these situations. Unless there is an immediate act that necessitates dismissal, long-term documentation is usually necessary. The principal should take detailed notes during LLBWA visits, following both legal standards and collective bargaining agreements. It is essential to keep careful documentation of incidents that could be admissible in court hearings.

Additionally, LLBWA can help principals determine whether an employee's poor performance is due to systemic failure or professional inadequacy. Consider the view of W. Edwards Deming, the management expert, who maintained that systemic failure accounts for up to 85 percent of employee problems, whereas workers are responsible for only 15 percent of the problems (Walton, 1986).

Community

Principals manage the image of the school in the community and the communication flow between school and community by adopting a proactive stance. This can greatly affect the community perception of the school and support for school activities and funding, as well as students' perceptions of parental support for the school. Several examples that follow were shared at a job-alike session (in which individuals with "like" job titles meet) sponsored by the NAESP and held in Washington, DC, for Nationally Distinguished Principals.

Principals can conduct a regular "Neighborhood Walk and Watch" designed to take the principal into the neighborhood that surrounds the school to talk with community members, spread good news about the school and students, find out about community developments, and lend an interested ear.

One principal organizes a late spring "Dinner on the Grounds." Each class prepares for this event by writing letters of invitation and sending them to family members and key civic leaders, all of whom must make reservations to attend this function. At a special assembly held during the evening, the school takes the opportunity to highlight its mission and important values by conducting a ceremony in which awards are given for the most improved student, student leadership, good citizenship, and academic excellence. Following the assembly, quilts and blankets are spread out, sack dinners are handed out, and the school band plays.

Many principals enhance the image of the school in the community by joining civic service clubs and regularly reporting on school affairs. In addition, they meet with education reporters and editors from the local newspaper and cultivate positive relationships with them.

One principal challenged the president of a large international seed company to trade places with him for a day. This joint get-acquainted venture resulted in a delightful school–business partnership. Scientists and other personnel from the company worked with the teachers to develop a project in which students formed greenhouse companies in their classrooms and produced plants for a Mother's Day plant sale.

Another principal initiated an e-mail pen-pal program between students and a local navy submarine unit. In one high school, students corresponded with scientists at the South Pole.

Recognizing the rising costs of feeding families, one school extended a hand to community members by organizing a bulk food purchase. This involved placing large orders for frozen foods to secure a substantial discount for community members. In a Bronx, New York, school, selected students were discreetly given backpacks of food to provide some nourishment during the weekend.

Still another example of managing the school in the community occurred when the principal and staff of a school in Hawaii realized that many parents of preschoolers had negative school experiences themselves and were therefore reluctant to come to school. So the principal and staff decided to go to the community. They set up blankets and provided refreshments in a local park and invited the parents to visit. On each blanket was a learning station for parents. This activity demonstrated to the community that the school was approachable and had much to offer.

In Rockingham County, Virginia, a school's staff volunteered to conduct parent conferences at a local chicken-processing plant where a large number of immigrant parents worked. The school administration provided Spanish and Russian interpreters to communicate with parents who didn't speak English. This increased parents' understanding of student learning and access to the school, and greatly enhanced school-community relationships.

Support Services

Societal conditions and increased social service agency cooperation have made support services in the community still another facet of principals' management responsibilities. That is, to serve students, staff, and parents, principals need to know about the community resources available to support the local school. Many principals, especially in full-service schools, work with agencies that provide support, including Big Brothers and Big Sisters organizations, the community clothes closet, the county health department, mental health service agencies, child protective services, crisis lines, the community library, and services for the homeless. Some schools establish resource files in the school office with the name, address, and phone number of each agency. The files might also contain literature collected during get-acquainted visits to these organizations. Having well-organized files enables easy access to this information for parents and students in need. During Open House or Back to School Night, a directory of information regarding support services can be distributed to parents. This same information can also be provided to students. (For further discussion of community-based organizations that assist schools, see Chapter 17).

CRISIS MANAGEMENT PLANNING   ■

The American Academy of Experts in Traumatic Stress defines a crisis as "a traumatic event that seriously disrupts our coping and problem-solving abilities. It is typically unpredicted, volatile in nature and may even threaten our survival. A crisis can present a drastic and tragic change in our environment. This change is generally unwanted and frightening, and may leave us with a sense of vulnerability and helplessness" (Lerner, Volpe, & Lindell, 2003, p. 11). Each school faces the possibility of an emergency at any time. Weather emergencies may include excessive rain, windstorms, floods, earthquakes, tornadoes, or hurricanes. School, medical, or drug emergencies may include kidnappings, shootings, cyberbullying, a drug overdose, a severe allergic reaction, fires, traffic accidents, a sudden death of a classmate or teacher, or a tragedy in the community.

Tragic preK–12 school shootings in the United States and abroad, and the horrific events of September 11, 2001, have been wake-up calls for everyone associated with schools to proactively develop crisis management plans. More recent incidents at Virginia Tech and Northern Illinois University have taught us that even universities are vulnerable to terrible shooting tragedies. An effective plan is the best opportunity to reduce the chance of a tragedy and to minimize injuries and save lives when a tragedy does occur.

Shortly after the tragedy of September 11, some of the nation's chief executives were asked to "offer a vision for tackling an overwhelming disaster. Their wisdom, distilled, came down to four basic truisms: be calm, tell the truth, put people before business, then get back to business as soon as possible" (Wayne & Kaufman, 2001, p. 1). Following this wisdom entails being prepared. If crisis management tactics and practices are well planned and in place, they provide the scaffolding for leadership action when an unexpected crisis occurs. Bill George (2007) reminds us that an important precursor to developing an effective crisis management plan is to be aware of one's values and their impact on action:

> It is under pressure—when your success, your career, or your life hangs in the balance—that you must decide what your values are. When you are forced to make trade-offs between your values under difficult circumstances, you learn what is most important in your life and what you are prepared to sacrifice for. Those who develop a clear sense of their values *before* they get into a crisis are better prepared to keep their bearings and navigate through difficult decisions and dilemmas when the pressure mounts. (p. 87)

Of course, when acts against students or staff occur, it is essential that the missing social and emotional ingredients that may have contributed to the alarming events are not lost, given the immediate need to respond to the crisis.

Every school must have a crisis management planning manual that includes appropriate steps for each type of emergency. Procedures should be developed through collaboration with teachers, students, administration, and classified and support staff as well as local safety officers. Such collaboration increases the knowledge base and the number of personnel able to cope with emergencies. Developmental work of this type also increases ownership for the manual and its contents.

Developing a Crisis Management Planning Manual

The following guidelines for a crisis management planning manual were adapted from several excellent sources (Bagin & Gallagher, 2001; Dwyer, Osher, & Warger, 1998; Lawton, 2002; Lerner et al., 2003; National Mental Health Association, 2006; National School Public Relations Association, 1996; Warner, 2000). An effective plan should include the following parts:

- the rationale for the plan (e.g., zero tolerance for bullying, monitoring of hallways), noting that prevention is the first step to avoiding a crisis
- a list of crisis team members; although the school will have a core team on campus for the initial crisis period, an expanded team should be included in all planning and used during the crisis (e.g., principal; assistant principals/deans; counselors; school psychologists; classified representatives such as secretaries, teacher aides, and custodians; central office personnel; school nurse; school security officers; appropriate safe and drug-free program coordinators; law enforcement, fire, and emergency service personnel; community social service and health service agency representatives; clergy; media representatives; parent and student representatives)
- a generic form to define and assess a crisis situation
- generic procedures that go into effect for all crises
- a regularly updated emergency phone tree with chain-of-command information
- an updated list of faculty with current Red Cross Training Certification
- a description of types of crises covered and procedures for each crisis, with clearly coded or separate colored pages for each type of crisis
- a list of crisis code signals for faculty; students; and fire, police, and emergency service personnel
- maps of facilities with areas for a crisis control center, distributed to faculty and fire and police personnel
- maps clearly delineating evacuation procedures, distributed to faculty and fire and police personnel
- a designated crisis spokesperson for faculty, media, and parent communication
- a description of communication procedures with emergency service personnel for immediate contact
- information on faculty and community training procedures and school drill schedules (e.g., lockdown, earthquake, fire drill)
- a plan to ensure that all critical parties have received the crisis management planning manual
- copies of brochures that have been distributed to parents relating to school crisis planning
- templates of "backpack" letters that address specific crises
- procedures to ensure that students, staff, parents, and community members are kept informed and comforted during the aftermath of the crisis
- an evaluation process to update plans each year or following a crisis

Developing a Plan for the
Prevention of Serious Violence

To be truly proactive, preventive measures relating to the possibility of serious violence should also be part of crisis management planning. The U.S. Department of Education report *Early Warning, Timely Response: A Guide to Safe Schools* (Dwyer et al., 1998) includes many excellent strategies to help schools prevent and deal with violent incidents. The difference that one individual can make in connecting with a potentially violent student is a primary theme of the report. All members of the community, administrators, teachers, families, fellow students, classified staff, and community members must collaborate to develop positive relations with students. As former Secretary of Education Richard Riley notes in the report's introduction, "every school in the nation [should have] a comprehensive violence prevention plan in place" (p. 2). The authors of this report make the following essential points:

- Safe and responsive schools are characterized by a focus on academic achievement; welcoming and involving families in the school; links to important community agencies, including the police, emergency and health services, and the faith-based community; an emphasis on positive relations among students and staff; an open school discussion concerning safety issues; fair and equal treatment by faculty, staff, and students in terms of racial groups, ethnic background, religious preference, and sexual orientations; eliminating targeting or bullying of students; creating safe and nonintimidating ways for students to share concerns with administration, faculty, counselors, or parents about potential violent acts; and disciplinary policies that include a code of conduct with specific consequences and clear policies concerning antiharassment, antiviolence, and due process rights.

- Early warning signs of possible violence include feelings of rejection, persecution, or social withdrawal and isolation; having been a victim of violence at home or in school; low interest in school and academics; expressions of violence in drawing, writings, or speech; impulsive, threatening, and bullying behavior; disciplinary and violent history; intolerance and prejudicial attitudes; drug or alcohol abuse; gang affiliation; and access to firearms.

- Imminent warning signs of serious violence include severe physical fighting at home or school, vandalism of property, rage for minor reasons, detailed threats and plans to harm or kill others, possession and use of firearms, and self-injurious behaviors or threats of suicide.

- Intervention practices, depending on severity of threat, include contacting the principal, guidance counselor, school psychologist, family, health service, or law enforcement agency; persistent efforts to help a student and cut through the bureaucracy even when the threat is diminished; avoiding inappropriate labeling of a student because of profiling; and enforcement of the Gun Free School Act, requiring expulsion of students for a minimum of one year for bringing a firearm to school.

- Intervention practices to improve the behavior of violent students include access to a team of education specialists to assist students; parents and teachers sharing responsibility with child and family service agencies, law enforcement, the juvenile justice system, and other agencies; working closely with parents of troubled children; maintaining confidentiality when appropriate; developing the capacity of staff, students, and families to help; simplifying staff requests for assistance; implementing early intervention procedures; developing social skills programs; and referring children for special education evaluation.

- Action steps for students to create safe schools include participating in peer mediation and conflict resolution programs, listening to friends and encouraging them to seek out a trusted adult, joining organizations that oppose violence in schools, joining community youth-oriented activities, working with teachers and the administration to create a safe and nonbureaucratic process for reporting violence-related activities, knowing the school's code of conduct, working with law enforcement officials in the school on safety audits and safety tips, role modeling appropriate behavior when intensive feelings of anger arise, and seeking help from a trusted adult.

- Suggestions by experts to maintain a safe physical environment include maintaining supervised access to buildings and grounds; reducing class and school size; adjusting schedules to minimize time in hallways or other potentially dangerous locations; modifying traffic flow patterns to limit conflicts; conducting a safety audit; closing campuses during lunch; supervising key areas at critical times; prohibiting congregating students in at-risk areas; having adults, including parents, visible in the school; staggering dismissal and lunch periods; monitoring areas around the school; and coordinating safe routes to and from school with law enforcement officials.

- Critical and immediate intervention procedures during a violent crisis include using well-planned lockdown or evacuation procedures to protect students and staff, immediately identifying safe areas during the crisis, having a fool-proof communication system with designated roles for members of the crisis management team, and creating a process for securing immediate support from law enforcement officers and appropriate medical and emergency service personnel (Dwyer et al., 1998).

After a series of school shootings in September and October of 2006, safety experts stressed three key points related especially to the tragedy of shootings by students or outsiders. First, it is critical that all students are "visible to others in meaningful, responsible ways" (Chaltain, 2006, p. 48) and that they are valued by adults in the school. The movement toward smaller middle and high schools in which each student has a mentor or advisor can be viewed as one way to help students feel like their lives are meaningful. Second, Gregory Thomas, New York City's former security chief of schools, states that "creating real and imagined barriers around schools is another way to deter intruders who are looking for a vulnerable target. 'Imagined' barriers are signs that tell visitors to report to the front office for a pass, or reminders that the school is in a 'gun-free, drug-free zone that tells people there will be more dramatic consequences for certain behaviors'" (quoted in Maxwell, 2006, p. 17). Third, Thomas emphasizes that adults and students must be sensitive to the environment, with students helping adults identify intruders who are strangers inside or outside of the immediate school area. Adults need to respond and challenge intruders if necessary, either personally or with the assistance of security personnel.

Excellent sources to enrich your school crisis plan can be found on the Internet. Examples include the National School Public Relations Association's (1996) guidelines for the first 30 minutes of a crisis and the U.S. Department of Education's (2007) *Practical Information on Crisis Planning Brochure.*

Final Thoughts on Crisis Management

Douglas Huston, a nuclear safety specialist, noted during a crisis communication conference that "you have a moral and ethical obligation to be truthful. People are more afraid of what they don't understand than what they do understand. [Providing accurate information during a crisis] is about reducing uncertainty" (quoted in Lawton, 2002, p. C5). Providing honest information during a crisis helps individuals gain a sense of control. They also feel control when they contribute to minimizing the effect of a tragedy. For example, promoting and participating in a blood drive can help citizens cope with a disaster.

If a school leader is asked for information during a crisis, a "no comment" remark will likely lead to speculation about what is being concealed. Rudolph Giuliani's honesty during the moments

LEADER AS MANAGER **21**

and days following the September 11 attacks helped New Yorkers and the nation gain strength to deal with the aftermath of the horrific tragedy.

Once developed, procedures should be taught, modeled, and practiced. Although drills interrupt instructional time, if the school principal is serious about the importance of these drills with staff and students, then these emergency preparation procedures can be a useful educational experience. In some schools, teachers integrate teaching about AIDS and disaster or emergency preparedness into reading, writing, science, and history classes. Some schools have students write letters home explaining the disaster preparedness procedures to their parents. Crisis planning teaches a great deal about decision making as well.

Bringing in key community members involved in emergency work (e.g., firefighters, protective service workers, trauma unit personnel) to speak with students helps develop a respect for and awareness of emergency procedures. Furthermore, having a strong public relations program with the local police department, including officers speaking at the school about proactive crime prevention or automobile safety, could later prove very valuable if the police need to be called into the school's vicinity because of an emergency.

It is helpful to provide time for school student service teams (e.g., nurses, school counselors, social workers) to have regular contact with related community health professionals. Communication between school personnel and community professional groups can increase knowledge and significantly inform actions. In the most serious cases, this can lead to valuable coordination regarding potential teenage suicides or gang violence. The contact also keeps school personnel informed about current research to help students who are bulimic or anorexic. Child protective service personnel can offer useful information about child abuse—how to recognize it, how to raise teacher and student awareness, and how to work with abused students. Administrators and teachers are required by federal law to report suspected cases of child abuse. Indicators related to physical abuse, physical neglect, sexual abuse, and emotional abuse must be followed up on by school personnel (Morrison, 2009).

Although very rare, students have died from eating foods with ingredients to which they are extremely allergic. The ultimate tragedy for a family, school, and community is, of course, a child's death. Schools must ensure that they have updated information regarding students' health, medication, and psychological needs. Those who need to know should be informed. Health and emergency procedure cards should be updated regularly. Computer files that include student emergency information and yearbook photos are vital during a crisis. Key facts such as food allergies or medical/health problems, custody issues, and other important information should be highlighted and communicated to appropriate personnel, including the school secretary, the nurse, cafeteria workers, counselors, social workers, and teachers.

Many schools offer workshops for teachers, support staff, and administrators to prepare for emergencies. Medical preparedness can include training to cope with shock victims, people who are choking or having epileptic seizures, people who are bleeding severely, and those who need CPR. Areas where accidents might occur should be identified and procedures developed to address each possible accident. Obvious locations are playgrounds, hallways, locker rooms, cafeterias, and bus stops. An emergency crisis kit might include a flash drive with current student data, a crisis management manual, a bullhorn, a phone tree, permanent markers, wristbands, legal pads, pens, a fully charged cell phone, and a current yearbook, in addition to typical first-aid resources.

Also, to be sure that all possibilities have been considered, the staff might brainstorm potential emergency situations and design related precautions to be included in the crisis management manual. An example might look like this:

Possible Situation	Plan
Evacuation of building	Evacuation plans taught and practiced as well as posted on each classroom, library, office, and gym door Busing plans posted
Shooting on the playground or in the classroom	Locations of phones to dial 911 specified Contact school nurse Lockdown plan implemented Provide counseling for those impacted by the event

Planning ahead can pay off dramatically in speeding up effective response and reaction time. When every second counts, it may spell the difference between life and death. Finally, the authors strongly recommend that each state, district, and school review the guidelines suggested by the American Academy of Experts in Traumatic Stress in *A Practical Guide for Crisis Response in Our Schools* (Lerner et al., 2003; www.schoolcrisisresponse.com).

■ A FINAL OBSERVATION REGARDING SCHOOL MANAGEMENT

When considering the classroom, school site, community, and support service management responsibilities of the principal, it is interesting to note that the responsibilities seem to move from the inside of the school (the classroom) to the outside world (support services). Clearly, the classroom, school site, community, and support services are linked, and the principal's ability to successfully take advantage of this linkage will rest to some extent on his or her ability to see the linkage as based on relationships among people, not simply as structural entities that need to remain in communication with one another. Certainly, leadership and management go hand in hand.

REFLECTIONS

This space provides a place for you to write down ideas that have been generated by this chapter, things you want to try, or adaptations of ideas presented here.

1. Separately, consider several characteristics of effective leaders and of effective managers. What conclusions can you draw about management or leadership from your selected characteristics?
2. Develop a key area checklist for LLBWA at your school.
3. Make a list of various types of crises that should be addressed in your school's crisis management plan. Are there some generic planning elements that would apply to most crises on your list? If so, what are these elements?
4. Explore and select Internet resources that would complement or enhance your crisis management plan.
5. What insights or new questions do you have as a result of reflecting on the ideas presented in this chapter?

3

Leader as Shaper of School Culture

There is a subtle spirit that can be sensed the moment one walks into a school. . . . That subtle spirit is the school culture.

—California School Leadership Academy

Within any organization, there is an *inner reality* (Deal & Peterson, 1993) or culture that influences the way people interact, what they will and will not do, and what they value as "right and rude" (Little, 1982). This inner reality reflects what organizational members care about, what they are willing to spend time doing, what and how they celebrate, and what they talk about. It is evident in daily routines. The inner reality or culture of a school influences its productivity, professional development, leadership practices, and traditions. The same stable culture that brings meaning to a school can also frustrate efforts to implement new, innovative ideas, especially if they are contradictory to the existing culture. Consider, if you will, the open classroom of the 1960s. It soon became walled up because the culture of the one-room schoolhouse was so strong.

Despite its pervasive nature, culture or inner reality is often overlooked as a critical force. Instruction, curriculum, quality assessment, staff, and leadership surely all contribute to a quality school. But "the inner, unspoken set of values and purposes that weave quality into the daily routine and motivate everyone to do his or her best" (Deal & Peterson, 1993) is equally if not more powerful in moving a school toward achieving a vision of quality. A school's culture is reflective of its organizational members. The culture is the meaning that individuals create in their world of work. Bennis (1991) has written "Each employee is, to a remarkable extent, the organization in miniature" (p. 156). This explains both why culture is such a critical force and how individual interactions influence culture. Because the way people interact daily or "do business" at a site dramatically influences its ultimate productivity for all members, culture is a powerful school improvement tool. As Goleman, Boyatzis, and McKee (2002) explain, "when people feel good, they work at their best" (p. 14). It is not surprising that if a culture is a negative one, it can serve as a hindering force to school improvement efforts. In such cases, the culture must first be studied and then transformed if school improvement efforts are to thrive.

Figure 3.1 illustrates the interactive elements of school culture. Each element is dynamic in nature; that is, it influences the current culture and is sensitive to competing elements that may threaten its existence and reshape the culture. If the culture is cohesive, all of the elements should reflect the core values and beliefs. In the stories from a variety of schools that follow, you will see how these elements function. These accounts, which combine practices used successfully in several schools, demonstrate some of the ways that principals and staff can use culture as a quality tool for school improvement.

■ CORE BELIEFS AND VALUES ARE THE HEART OF CULTURE

The principal at Lincoln School endeavors to facilitate a learning culture. He believes the leader's role is to provide an environment that contributes to teacher empowerment. In a recent interview, the principal explained that to construct a context within which this can occur, principals should help create a culture that celebrates growth, teacher leadership, and shared decision making. Teachers need to feel confident and safe. It is very important that, regardless of what takes place outside of the school, the school culture must remain positive and clearly aimed at making the school a better place for students. The culture should emphasize that the school is a community of learners and that all can learn from one another. As one teacher stated, "The belief in teaching [as] a learning experience has enabled me to deal with problems as opportunities for problem solving."

In this setting, risk taking and experimentation—if they are directed toward goals of enhanced learning—are recognized and rewarded. According to Barth (quoted in Sparks, 1993), "to unlock energy and inventiveness, people have to take risks" (p. 18). Teachers, students, and parents are far more likely to take risks when principals frequently and visibly take risks themselves. The willingness of people who inhabit a school to take risks directly influences their capacity to learn. Learning from one's "mistakes"—risk taking—and exploring heretofore undiscovered dimensions of one's competencies can contribute to an environment characterized by teaching and staff collaboration committed to continuous improvement. Moreover, every aspect of the program should emphasize quality, and all personnel should feel professional and personal pride as individuals and as part of the group, from teachers, principals, and aides to lunchroom personnel, custodians, and school security officers. Quality should be emphasized in interpersonal relationships, resources, teacher meetings, playground equipment, and the physical condition of the school.

■ THE PHYSICAL ENVIRONMENT REFLECTS CORE VALUES

In a culture that values learning, collaboration, and quality, there are visible places where this occurs. The teachers' center is one such example. A key aspect of this center at Lincoln School is a professional library that includes current journals and professional development DVDs. It is a setting where ideas are exchanged and books, articles, lessons, and podcasts are discussed. Teachers find resources there to develop curriculum materials, plan instruction, or assess the impact of curriculum and instruction on students.

Activities are also in place to remind organizational members of the importance of learning, collaboration, and quality and to provide avenues for such ends. Examples of this include a schedule for peer coaching or a time when, on a schoolwide basis, everyone reflects through journal writing.

Figure 3.1   Interactive Elements of School Culture

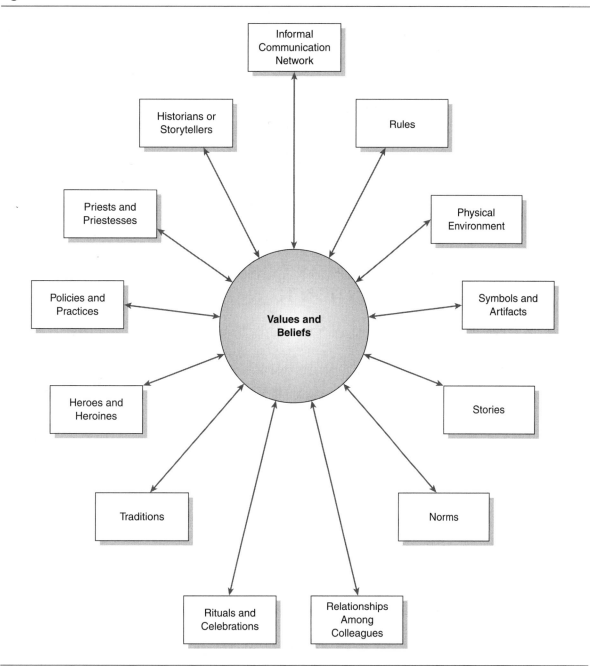

A celebration of student work also reflects core values. This can occur with an "On Showcase" bulletin board that highlights the work of different classes every two weeks. It is generally in a prominent area of the school, such as on the wall outside of the main office. Items for display may include work from a recent unit, a special project emphasizing the value of diversity, or an idea such as respect being promoted on a schoolwide basis as a result of an emphasis on social and emotional learning. What is most important is that the display calls attention to student work and core values of the school culture.

One school in Israel displayed a bulletin board depicting a vineyard in the entry hall. Interspersed with the vines was every student's name. This symbolically communicated the importance of each student as well as their connection to each other and the learning community. On a similar note, a principal commented, "You can tell what's important in a school by what you see when you walk in the front door. What's on the walls, what's in the trophy case, sends a strong message to all who enter the building."

■ RITUALS DISPLAY CORE VALUES AND CALL ATTENTION TO WHAT IS IMPORTANT

There are many rituals in a school. A familiar one is the faculty meeting. In a culture that values learning from one another, a faculty meeting can become a forum for learning. Meetings can be organized to have teachers share ideas that are working in their classrooms. For example, teachers who are experiencing success with differentiating instruction or publishing student work can show samples and lead a discussion on their experiences. If an atmosphere of trust exists, ideas that were not successful can also be shared. The principal can share successes and failures. This promotes the idea of leader as learner. How can one learn without making mistakes and taking risks? A CEO of a large corporation once stated, "Failure is the opportunity to begin again more intelligently." To promote this idea, the principal encourages teachers to try lessons that are experimental and demonstrates his or her support.

Another activity that can be used to foster learning and model a classroom instructional strategy is the jigsaw. For example, in reviewing schoolwide test data, a leadership team analyzed that an achievement gap existed for several groups of students. The team planned a faculty meeting that would promote staff understanding of what an achievement gap is and provide practical strategies to close the gap. The meeting opened with school-level data that revealed an achievement gap. The leadership team explained that in today's meeting a powerful cooperative learning strategy called a jigsaw would be used to convey the content of four articles on closing the achievement gap. Staff members formed "home groups." In each group, individuals counted off from one through four. "Ones" would read the first article, "twos" the second article, and so on (see Figure 3.2a). Following this, staff members who shared the same number met to become "expert" in the content of the article they read. This involved discussing key points, identifying helpful examples, and deciding how they would teach others what they read (see Figure 3.2b). Finally, home groups reconvened, and each member explained to the others what he or she had read (see Figure 3.2c) and the implications for their own teaching practices.

At the conclusion of the teaching episodes groups synthesized their collective learnings and reported out to the total group. The principal functioned as a group member during the entire jigsaw process.

Many principals use the jigsaw technique with different types of content. For instance, at the beginning of the year, some use it to review information contained in the faculty or school handbook. Others use it to share articles about working with special education students and at-risk students,

Figure 3.2 Jigsaw Activity

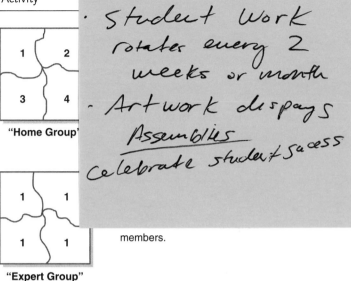

"Home Group"

"Expert Group"

"Home Gr

members.

effective teaching practices, or ... tegy celebrates individual accountability and ... culty members. These attributes reflect the val ... ure.

Another technique that ... ts" activity. The faculty meeting facilitator as ... ussion, such as differentiated instruction, w ... g rubrics, and homework. Topics for discus ... om. Individuals gather around topics of interest and ... roup's ideas are recorded on butcher paper posted around the room. These ideas are often word processed and later distributed to the faculty. Following the discussion, each group prepares a 2-minute summary of its conversation and reports out. Many times the "reporting out" phase plants seeds of interest among other faculty members. A variation of this activity is the use of classrooms instead of areas of the room as listening posts. This has the added value of getting faculty members into classrooms other than their own.

Another learning ritual is the brown-bag lunch. One staff member at Lincoln School who attended several cooperative learning workshops shared her experiences with interested staff during lunch. Teachers followed up these sessions by experimenting with cooperative learning techniques in their classrooms. At the final session, teachers decided they wanted to support one another in their cooperative learning activities. As a consequence, they continued meeting once a month at lunch to exchange ideas. The principal supported this activity by publicizing the meetings and providing logistical support and refreshments.

■ CELEBRATIONS CALL ATTENTION TO WHAT IS IMPORTANT

In a Professional Learning Community, learning is valued and celebrated publicly. Student recognition assemblies are held every six to eight weeks to celebrate student successes. Students are cited for helping out a new classmate, citizenship, improving attendance, making significant academic improvement, or teaching another student. Groups of students are complimented for excellent behavior in the cafeteria or keeping the campus clean. Whatever is celebrated reflects what is being emphasized in the culture. Following a recognition assembly, the principal sends notes home to parents, informing them of their child's accomplishments. It is important that the celebrations and recognition program reflect the culture's values. For example, if the school culture places value on teamwork, it is important to recognize teams or groups of students rather than a "student of the month."

Celebrations put the school's values on display. At one school, Martin Luther King Day was celebrated by faculty, parents, and students. First, the principal gave a presentation about what Martin Luther King Jr. stood for, emphasizing values such as the love of fellow human beings, nonviolence, and equal opportunity. Next, he pointed out how these same values were shared by the school and cited specific examples that students could relate to. As an example, the principal asked the students how they would feel if, because of their hair color, they had to use separate drinking fountains, restrooms, and cafeterias. Finally, students and faculty sang songs such as "Lift Every Voice and Sing" and "We Shall Overcome" and then viewed a YouTube video of Martin Luther King Jr.'s "I Have a Dream" speech. The assembly provided some insight into what it was like to live through the 1960s. When the ceremony was over, many participants had tears in their eyes. One teacher remarked, "As a school, we're closer now, and have a feeling of what we're all about."

In the wake of September 11, one high school had an assembly around the themes of developing tolerance and acceptance, and valuing diversity. It is important to make sure that all programs—even holiday programs—have meaning and reflect the core values of the school.

■ HOW PEOPLE SPEND TIME REFLECTS CORE VALUES

A middle school's staff saw the value of providing an integrated course of study for its students. As a result, the schedule was reorganized so that teachers had 74 minutes of common planning time to develop rich learning experiences for students. Other ideas include organizing charity drives in schools or sending middle or high school students out to volunteer in the community for service credit; this sends a clear message that the school is concerned about others. Such activities also teach about empathy and community service. The December holiday season is an excellent time to have a food, clothing, or toy drive for those in need. The student government can help organize these events, assisted by faculty advisors so that it becomes a collaborative enterprise.

History reminds people about what an organization has stood for over time. On the 40th anniversary of the American Embassy School in New Delhi, India, a teacher received a stipend to write a history of the school. This went a long way toward building the idea of tradition. The middle school buried a time capsule with a video of the school and samples of schoolwork. The elementary school student council took the lead in renaming two school buildings after famous people who exemplified the values for which the school stood. In addition, the following school song was written by one of the teachers to reflect the core values, and there was a student contest to select the title:

The World of AES

To the city of New Delhi
We come from far and wide
Boys and girls of every nation
Standing side by side
In the beauty of the gardens
We learn to take good care
Of ourselves and of each other
And this world that we all share
At AES, AES the finest school we know
Where the boys and girls and grown-ups
All really like to show
That we're smart and clean and friendly
And we lend a helping hand
In this very special school
In a very special land
Each day we try our very best
In everything we do
The school is like a sailing ship
And we are all the crew
We work and play together
As we sail upon the sea
There's no other place in India
That we would rather be than . . .
AES, AES the finest school we know
Where the boys and girls and grown-ups
All really like to show
That we're smart and clean and friendly
And we lend a helping hand
In this very special school
In a very special land

—Marilyn Ferguson

NORMS ARE THE UNWRITTEN ■ RULES OF CULTURE

Generally, individuals within an organization behave toward one another according to the expectations they perceive to exist within the culture. These group expectations are usually a function of an unwritten code for behavior called *norms*—or, as Terry Deal said, "the way we do things around here" (personal communication, 1989).

In some schools, for example, there are norms that encourage people to voice their opinions, even if those opinions go against the grain of the majority voice. As a teacher from Maine explained, "At our school, everyone has a right to disagree. No one must voice his or her opinion. But, if you don't take responsibility for voicing your opinion and a decision is made by the rest of the staff, you must agree not to stand in the way of the wheels of progress." In schools where this type of norm is strong, individuals who risk offering an opposing viewpoint have often become celebrated as heroes because they make others think about their attitudes and actions. One teacher noted, "At our school, we can always count on Andy. He has his feet planted firmly in concrete . . . but he reminds us, who often have our heads in the clouds, of brass tacks reality!"

When norms at a school encourage prospecting for internal resources, the activities reflect that stance. Peer-coaching programs are an example. At one school, a peer-coaching program has been operating successfully for three years. To keep the project going, teachers formed mixed new-comer and veteran groups. There are strong norms within this culture that emphasize the impor-

> *During orientation*
> *share stories*
> *about how teachers*
> *have shaped the*
> *school.*

When practices such as peer coaching support [...] me embedded in the fabric of school life.

[...] nities are needed in collaborative cultures, the [...] rich reservoir of talent to see what we might [...] ttee surveyed the teachers about what they were [...] ng questioning techniques was a major area of [...] egrown talent to put on a staff workshop. Topics [...] d on Bloom's taxonomy, Socratic seminars, and [...] a result of the workshop.

[...] toxic ones. At one school, at the beginning of the [...] ve referrals, six inches high, on the desk of his pre- [...] sitive as opposed to negative behavior. The assis- [...] ey referred a student to the office for misbehavior [...] ffice for positive behavior within six weeks. Within [...] climate and culture of the school.

In schools that oper[...] rning Communities, there is a shared norm: each staff member will do whatever it takes to help every student in the school thrive.

■ POWERFUL STORIES COMMUNICATE AND REINFORCE CULTURAL VALUES

The use of story is one way to inform and remind new and existing members of a culture about its values. Every school has stories that, as a matter of tradition, are passed on to new staff members. Generally, these stories signal important values or beliefs. For example, at one school, new teachers are told about a former teacher who always had special techniques for helping at-risk youth. Through the story, they learn that because the school did not at that time have a forum for staff sharing, when that teacher retired, a library of knowledge "burned." Hence that teacher left her mark on students, but not on the teaching profession. Because of this great loss, teachers at the school now take special care to make sure that quality time is set aside for professional dialogue and the sharing of ideas and practices. A ritual called "See Them Teach Before They Leave" is instituted each spring; returning faculty members are encouraged to visit classrooms of departing teachers. Following this ritual, an assembly is held at which the bronzed classroom doorknob of each departing teacher, affixed to a wooden plaque and inscribed, is presented to that teacher. The plaque inscription reads, "Thank you for opening your door and sharing your classroom secrets. You kept a library of knowledge from burning."

In addition to reminding organizational members about important values, stories can also provide a way of talking about sensitive issues with a more comfortable distance. One principal used the following story during the first faculty meeting to remind teachers of the tremendous influence they have on students' lives beyond the academic arena. The story is taken from a speech by Sir Winston Churchill before the British House of Commons on June 4, 1940.[1]

The Honorable Profession of Teaching

Teddy Stallard certainly qualified as "one of the least." Disinterested in school, he wore musty, wrinkled clothes, and his hair was never combed. He was one of those kids in school with a dead-pan face, expressionless—sort of a glassy, unfocused stare. When Miss Thompson spoke to Teddy, he would always answer with a "yes" or a "no." Unattractive, unmotivated, and distant, he was just plain hard to like. Even though Miss Thompson said she loved all of the students in her class the same, deep down inside she wasn't being completely truthful.

Whenever she marked Teddy's papers, she got a certain perverse pleasure out of putting Xs next to the wrong answers, and when she put Fs at the top of the papers, she always did it with flair. She should have known better; she had Teddy's records and she knew more about him than she wanted to admit. The records read:

First grade: Teddy shows promise with his work and attitude but has a poor home situation.

Second grade: Teddy could do better. His mother is seriously ill. He receives little help at home.

Third grade: Teddy is a good boy, but much too serious. His mother died this year.

Fourth grade: Teddy is very slow, but well behaved. His father shows no interest.

Christmas came, and the boys and girls in Miss Thompson's class brought her Christmas presents. They piled their presents on her desk and crowded around to watch her open them. Among the presents was one from Teddy Stallard. She was surprised that he had brought her one, but he had. Teddy's gift was wrapped in brown paper and held together with Scotch tape. On the paper were written the simple words, "For Miss Thompson, from Teddy." When she opened Teddy's present, out fell a gaudy rhinestone bracelet, with half of the stones missing, and a bottle of cheap perfume.

The other boys and girls began to giggle and smirk at Teddy's gifts, but Miss Thompson at least had enough sense to silence them by immediately putting on the bracelet and putting some of the perfume on her wrist. Holding her wrist up for the other boys and girls to sniff, she said, "Doesn't it smell lovely?" And the children, taking their cue from their teacher, readily agreed.

At the end of the day, when school was over and the other students had left, Teddy lingered behind. He slowly came over to her desk and said softly, "Miss Thompson . . . Miss Thompson, you smell just like my mother . . . and her bracelet looks real pretty on you, too. I'm glad you liked my presents." When Teddy left, Miss Thompson sobbed.

The next day when the children came to school, they were welcomed by a new Miss Thompson. She had become a different person, a person committed to loving all of her students, especially the slow ones. Especially Teddy Stallard. By the end of that school year, Teddy showed dramatic progress. He had caught up with most of the students and was even ahead of some.

The school year quickly came to an end, and Teddy went on to another school. Miss Thompson didn't hear from Teddy for a long time. Then one day, she received a note that read:

> Dear Miss Thompson,
> I wanted you to be the first to know. I will be graduating second in my class.
> Love, Teddy Stallard

Four years later, another note came:

> Dear Miss Thompson,
> They just told me I will be graduating first in my class. I wanted you to be the first to know. The university has not been easy, but I liked it.
> Love, Teddy Stallard

And four years later:

> Dear Miss Thompson,
> As of today, I am Theodore Stallard, MD. How about that? I wanted you to be the first to know. I am getting married, the 27th to be exact. I want you to come and sit where my mother would sit if she were alive. You are the only family I have now; Dad died last year.
> Love, Teddy Stallard

Miss Thompson went to the wedding and sat where Teddy's mother would have sat. She deserved to sit there; she had done something for Teddy that he could never forget.

After telling this story, the principal conducted an activity in which staff members reflected on the legacy that they would like to leave with their students.

The staff members frequently referenced this story when speaking with one another. It became a part of the culture. It served as a constant reminder about how fragile students are and how, in small ways, teachers can make big differences in students' lives.

At report card time, the principal reminded the teachers about the Teddy Stallard story. The point was to emphasize how a comment that may at first glance appear to be insignificant may, in fact, have an enduring positive or negative effect on students and parents. A report card manual, prepared for the teachers, was distributed as a guideline to assist in the development of report card comments. The significance of the manual has heightened meaning because so many contemporary report card software programs have canned response options. Yet these programs do not preclude adding more personalized comments that pertain to student performance. The manual began with the following words:

> This manual is made up of report card comments written by you and your colleagues. Different types of comments have been selected to provide you with a variety of ideas and styles for you to review. Overall, the quality of the comments is very impressive. It is easy to take pride in the sensitivity, care, and thoughtfulness that went into the report cards written by our staff.
>
> The comments are divided into primary and intermediate sections and subdivided by subject area and general comments. I've culled through all the report cards so that each comment has a little different angle to offer. Interestingly, as I read through the comments, I recognized that some of the comments from the primary grade teachers have a lot to offer as suggestions to the intermediate grade teachers and vice versa. I would suggest taking an hour to read through the manual, marking comments that you find of interest— that address your class—before beginning report cards this quarter. Of course, thanks to everyone for writing comments that contributed to this project.

After reading hundreds of comments on previous report cards, I would like to make a few nuts-and-bolts suggestions relevant to our specific report cards and concerning report card comments in general.

1. Consider relating comments in curriculum areas to specific curriculum issues as related to the student. Mention areas of strength and weakness that identify for the parents what is being studied in class. This should be considered also when discussing behavior.

2. If you want to make a general point, use the "additional comments" section on the back of the report card instead of the designated subject area section. Mentioning that "Beverly is a pleasure to have in class" or "Steven is often late to school" should not be the primary point under the math section of the report card. Furthermore, summary comments about the student's overall performance belong in the additional comments section.

3. When discussing a problem, be specific and try to provide recommendations. For example, "Appu is not doing well in social studies and needs to try harder" gives very little guidance. Consider: "Appu's oral presentations in social studies should be organized more carefully. Please consider 'rehearsing' the presentations at home before the classroom presentation. I am sure her work will improve with this effort!"

4. Remember that the report card is a permanent record. Thus every comment should be meaningful. "Juan forgets to date his papers" can be mentioned at a parent conference instead of as part of the language arts comment section.

5. To preserve overall class confidentiality, it is not recommended to state, "Willie has the top math grades in the class." Furthermore, this tends to overemphasize competition.

6. Make sure your report card comment matches the grade. A glowing comment next to a "needs improvement" grade does not really make sense.

7. Avoid insensitive comments such as "Jacob is slow."

As you read through the manual, note which comments or ideas strike you and/or could be helpful in developing appropriate comments about students in your class. Consider e-mailing me additional ideas for comments. I will update the manual with your new ideas, which can be added to or drawn from by colleagues.

Thanks, Steve

Report card comments by grade level and subject area were included in the manual following the guidelines. The members of the school culture were, in this way, celebrated for their efforts and reminded of core values. Schools that share strong beliefs and values related to student outcomes can increase the attention, time, feedback mechanisms, and resources directed toward helping students learn. This occurs because the focus on the student and the quality of student–teacher relationships become part of the school's operating procedures, actions, rules, and reward systems.

Thus far, through anecdotal examples, we have discussed a framework of interactive elements for thinking about school culture. In the pages that follow, we consider how a culture might be transformed if it is not a positive one, or if it is not in keeping with a school's vision.

READING, TRANSFORMING, ■
OR SHAPING A CULTURE

Effective leadership must be both administrative and cultural in scope (Schein, 1985). Deal and Peterson (1993) suggest that the principal shapes a culture through a variety of means. They believe that it begins with "reading" the existing culture and then progressively moving to actions or behaviors that "mold or reinforce desirable core values and norms." Reading a culture involves "reconstructing a school's history by listening to the stories of past events, examining artifacts, such as faculty meeting agendas and minutes, reviewing newsletter stories and school goals" (Deal & Peterson, 1993).

Prior efforts at school improvement, crises faced by the staff, traditions, and information about the former principal's leadership style also yield valuable data for constructing a profile of the existing culture. Once this information is garnered, the principal, in concert with the staff, identifies specifics related to the vision of a school as a learning community. In keeping with this vision, detailed plans are made to gradually transform the culture so that the rituals, rewards, routine activities, stories, and norms call attention to the values embedded in the new vision. Deal and Peterson (1990), in a series of case studies, noted that principals shape culture in both formal and informal ways. They identified six major culture-shaping strategies:

1. Developing a sense of what the school should and could be

2. Recruiting and selecting staff whose values fit with the school's

3. Resolving conflicts, disputes, and problems directly as a way of shaping values

4. Communicating values and beliefs in daily routines and behaviors

5. Identifying and articulating stories that communicate shared values

6. Nurturing the traditions, ceremonies, rituals, and symbols that communicate and reinforce the school culture

What one principal does will differ dramatically from another. One cultural transformation may take a year, whereas another may take five. What is essential is that the principal holds the values and beliefs in focus as he or she conducts daily tasks and that these values and beliefs are articulated widely. Continuous growth and improvement must be emphasized.

The following are some questions to ask yourself regarding leadership and culture building (Deal & Kennedy, 1982; Schein, 1985):

- What do you pay attention to?
- What do you react strongly to?
- What do you model, teach, and coach?
- How do you allocate rewards?
- What criteria do you use to recruit, select, and excommunicate teachers?
- What ceremonies, rituals, and traditions reinforce your vision?
- Who are the heroes and heroines of your school?
- What stories do you tell about the successes and accomplishments of the faculty and students?
- What school symbols communicate your vision?

You might also ask: When do I have meetings? What items have priority placement on the agenda? How is time spent? Where are the meetings held? Are humor and smiling rituals of daily life? Each answer provides valuable data about the culture.

For change to be effective, the change masters—whether they be the principal, teachers, students, or parents—must first sincerely examine the ceremonies, rituals, norms, values, stories, and traditions of the culture. Then culture-shaping techniques should be used to help the organizational culture reflect desired core values.

Consider the following story. The faculty at one school reflected that it was often the high achievers or the students who got in trouble who received the most attention. Wanting to change this trend, they asked one another: "Who are the students who get ignored? Who are the students who are likely to slip through the cracks?" They decided on a plan of action. Each faculty member collected pictures of the students who often slipped through the cracks or were ignored. They published a compilation of each faculty member's students. The document was called "The Vanilla Kids." The name comes from the notion that vanilla is not as memorable a flavor as blueberry, cherry, or butter pecan. Each faculty member was to reach out and communicate every time he or she saw a vanilla kid. "You could see a difference in the students and in the culture of the school within three weeks," one staff member reflected.

Shaping the Culture Through Storytelling

As a reader, perhaps you were moved by the "vanilla kids" or Teddy Stallard story in this chapter. Certainly you have been moved by compelling stories told within your own culture. Hoar (quoted in Kouzes & Posner, 2006) asserts that "in the end it's all about the story that gives people meaning to not only what we're doing but to what we're aspiring to achieve" (p. 63). This explains why stories are powerful tools for transforming cultures and changing behavior in organizations.

Research documents the tremendous capacity of storytelling. Consider the following account from Kouzes and Posner (2006):

> Stanford University organizational sociologists Joanne Martin and Melanie Powers studied the impact of stories on MBA students, an often numbers-driven, highly competitive, skeptical audience. Martin and Powers compared the persuasiveness of four methods of convincing the students that a particular company truly practiced a policy of avoiding layoffs. In one situation they used only a story to persuade people. In the second, they presented statistical data that showed that the company had significantly less involuntary turnover than its competitors. In the third, they used the statistics *and* the story, and in the fourth, they used a straightforward policy statement made by an executive of the company. . . . As you probably anticipated, the most believable was number 1, the story only. The students who were given only the story believed the claim about the policy more than any of the other groups and remembered it better several months later. The executive delivering the policy statement was the least convincing. (pp. 63–64)

Kouzes and Posner's (2002) landmark book *The Leadership Challenge,* underscores the use of storytelling as a leadership tool. The authors make the following insightful points:

- It is important to "lead by storytelling" and "put storytelling on your meeting agenda" (pp. 98–100).
- "Telling great stories is one of the most effective ways leaders can model the values and beliefs essential to organizational success" (p. 381).
- "Stories aren't meant to be kept private; they're meant to be told. And because they're public, they're tailor-made for celebrations. In fact, stories are celebrations and celebrations are stories" (p. 359).
- "Well-told stories reach inside us and pull us along" (p. 383).

How can the power of storytelling shape the culture of the schoolhouse (Alvy & Robbins, 2008)? Consider the following scenario: In one school the principal became aware that the sixth-grade team was dysfunctional. Backbiting, bullying, and self-serving battles replaced the resource sharing, problem solving, and collaboration that benefited students whose teachers were on other teams. The principal was distressed that the human toll, in terms of student learning, would be great if the sixth-grade team members were unable to resolve their differences. In an effort to ameliorate the toxic energy that was rampant in this underperforming team, the principal shared the following story about President Abraham Lincoln:

Building a Team for the Nation's Greater Good

In 1855, Abraham Lincoln expected to be co-counsel with the well-known and respected Pennsylvania lawyer Edwin M. Stanton on the celebrated McCormick Reaper patent case in Cincinnati, Ohio. Lincoln, with a passion for inventions and new mechanical gadgets, prepared extensively for the case and looked forward to working with Stanton. Stanton, however, viewed Lincoln "as a Western hick and snubbed him throughout the trial . . . [and] supposedly referred to him as 'that giraffe' and that 'creature from Illinois'" (Oates, 1994, p. 103). Lincoln, always the lifetime learner, remained in the courtroom and learned much from Stanton's performance. Seven years later, on January 13, 1862, Lincoln appointed Stanton to the Secretary of War cabinet position. Stanton was

> astonished that Lincoln had appointed him Secretary of War. After all, Stanton had humiliated Lincoln back in the McCormick Reaper case. And in Washington this past year, Stanton had vilified this "imbecilic" President, this "original gorilla." . . . But Lincoln made it clear that he bore Stanton no ill will. If the McCormick Reaper episode had been one of the most humiliating episodes of his life, Lincoln had put that aside now. He never carried a grudge, he said later, because it didn't pay. (p. 278)

Stanton's appointment was but another example of Lincoln's greatness; he did not let petty differences serve as obstacles to the greater good. As the nation's leader, Lincoln's objective was to fill the cabinet with those most able to carry out the national purpose: to serve as a democracy of, by, and for the people. In *Team of Rivals,* Doris Kearns Goodwin (2005) observes that "Lincoln's choice of Stanton would reveal . . . a singular ability to transcend personal vendetta, humiliation, or bitterness. As for Stanton . . . he would . . . come to respect and love Lincoln more than any person outside of his immediate family" (p. 175). When Lincoln died on April 15, 1865, at 7:22 a.m., it was Stanton who stated the immortal words, "Now he belongs to the ages" (p. 743).

In this example, the principal drew on a period of national crisis as a tool to resolve petty differences for the greater good: student learning.

■   FINAL THOUGHTS ON CULTURE

One principal noted, "Culture is really the stage on which leadership gets played out. If, for example, the shared vision for a school is to be a 'home' for the heart and mind, one has to ask, 'To bring this to reality, what will it take? What will be in the halls, on the walls, in the trophy case? What will the stories be like that are told to newcomers? What will be the traditions, celebrations?' And, what's more, as a principal I always have to be aware of how my behavior—what I attend to, put last on my priority list; what I participate in, what I don't—shapes the culture of the school." As Kent Peterson once reflected, "Probably one of the most important things a leader does is to create, shape, and manage culture."

NOTE

1. The authors thank Tim Hansen, former director of the American School in Abu Dhabi, for sharing this story.

REFLECTIONS

This space provides a place for you to write down ideas that have been generated by this chapter, things you want to try, or adaptations of ideas presented here.

1. Reflect on the school culture in your organization. What are the core values and beliefs? How are they depicted in traditional ceremonies, rituals, reward structures, artifacts, and stories? Are they consistent with the vision of the school? Why or why not?

2. Are there traditions or rituals in your school that are contrary to the values of the school? If so, why do you think this is the case? How might you transform them if need be?

3. Identify key behind-the-scenes staff members who play a major part in the school culture. What parts do they play?

4. What are the stories that are told in your school's culture? How do they shape the behavior of organizational members?

5. What insights or new questions do you have as a result of reflecting on the ideas presented in this chapter?

PART II

Critical Skills for Effective Leadership

4

The Art of Human Relations

Getting the Job Done

You must be able to deal with people and communicate with them, or just bag it. . . .
That's the crux of the whole thing.

—A principal's voice

Displaying effective and ethical human relations is a key to leadership on every level. It is a thread that runs throughout the organization and affects the culture, climate, personnel practices, and every individual who has contact with the school. It impacts the relationship between the school and the larger community.

Human relations skills include working with people, building trust, creating a climate for teachers to comfortably discuss their own classroom practice, and helping individuals reach their potential. When positive human relations skills are manifested, people feel comfortable taking risks, experimenting, collaborating, and communicating ideas and feelings. These behaviors enable students and staff to perform at high levels.

■ TASK AND RELATIONSHIP BEHAVIORS

One of the difficult aspects of the principal's human relations role is that task and relationship behaviors must be addressed simultaneously. If too much weight is placed on task behaviors as a measure of success, organizational members may feel stressed or pressured. If too much emphasis is placed on relationship behaviors, people may feel as if it's all fluff, and no progress is being made. The dialogue regarding the tension between task and relationship responsibilities has been with us since the emergence of management literature. Frederic Taylor's industrial model stressed individual and bureaucratic efficiency, whereas Mary Parker Follett and Elton Mayo emphasized interpersonal dynamics and "change-oriented and informal structures" (Stewart, 2006, pp. 4–5). In fact, Stewart creatively (and humorously) reduces the history of task and relationship literature: "Between them, Taylor and Mayo carved up the world of management theory. According to my scientific sampling, you can save yourself from reading about 99 percent of all the management literature once you master this dialectic between rationalists and humanists. The Taylorite rationalist says: Be efficient! The Mayo-ist humanist replies: Hey, these are people we're talking about! And the debate goes on. Ultimately, it's just another installment in the ongoing saga of reason and passion" (p. 5).

It can be helpful to reflect on key routine events—faculty meetings, newsletters, daily bulletins and announcements, meetings with the staff—and consider in planning for these how you might balance task and relationship behaviors. For example, one principal plans faculty meetings with a principal's advisory committee made up of teachers. This allows him to sense the staff's attitudes toward key issues on the agenda. The agenda is constructed with time allocations for each item. Then it is distributed to the staff ahead of time so that items may be added prior to the meeting. During the meeting, in between every few agenda items, drawings are held or jokes are swapped for a brief period of time. On items that require staff input, table group discussions occur and collective group summaries are shared. At the end of the meeting, feedback is requested. In these ways, attention to both task and relationship behaviors is modeled.

One principal brainstormed a list of things she could do to balance attention to task (getting the job done) with relationship-oriented behavior (taking care of people). Elements of this list follow:

Task Orientation	Relationship Orientation
Begin and end meetings on time.	Allocate time for collaborative activities.
When you ask for behavior change or products, give concrete examples of what you expect.	Plan interactive activities during faculty meetings.
Request feedback on agenda construction and coverage at the end of meetings.	Protect faculty members from verbal attack when ideas are discussed.
Take written notes on requests, and follow up.	Ask for input regarding decisions to be made; allocate time for discussion.
Assign time limitations to agenda items. If additional discussion time is needed, ask the faculty for more time or for permission to continue the discussion at the next meeting.	Schedule time for faculty members to work together (sharing ideas, trading lessons, integrating curriculum, reviewing state curriculum standards, teaching one another instructional approaches, developing rubrics of student work).
	Follow up on staff development experiences with opportunities for staff members to share how they have applied recent learnings.

DIFFERENTIATED SUPPORT ■

Another effective human relations skill is being sensitive to the individual needs of personnel. For example, teachers new to the profession may need very directive support as they struggle and triumph in the early stages of their careers. This assistance may begin with a tour of the school and a review of basic policies and procedures, with time to ask questions. Additional support can be provided by a variety of people: the principal; a group of teachers; a mentor, coach, or lead teacher; or a combination of these. Support might include consultation, modeling, feedback, and opportunities to visit other teachers or to talk with trusted colleagues.

Successful experienced teachers, on the other hand, may prefer reflective listening and coaching as opposed to directive support. Opportunities to work with colleagues on professional growth topics may be a stimulating aspect of the support provided to experienced teachers (see Chapter 10).

■ PERSONALITY STYLES

A principal's human relations skills may be enhanced by considering the impact of a staff member's *mind style* (Gregorc, 1985). School leaders would benefit from examining the literature on style and applying the lessons appropriately. For example, Gregorc identifies four basic mind or learning styles that affect how individuals think, what they value, and how they behave. These styles reveal preferences for ordering and perceiving information. Ordering preferences range from sequential to random. Perception preferences range from concrete to abstract. Thus a principal who, because of style, relates and perceives in an organized, concrete manner may have difficulty communicating with a staff member who operates through a more abstract, random approach. (Providing a workshop on style can be a lively, informative, and enjoyable professional development activity.)

Style represents one tool to enhance relationships among staff members. Focusing on style as a staff will also impact classroom practices as teachers become more aware of how their styles influence the lessons they design and, consequently, student learning. In addition, success in human relations may result as a consequence of interpreting how individuals are affected by the context of a particular situation and acting appropriately.

■ RECOMMENDATIONS FOR SKILLFUL HUMAN RELATIONS

Following are some commonsense suggestions for a principal to consider in working to help staff and students reach their highest levels of performance. These recommendations emerged as a result of observing and talking with many principals.

1. *Project yourself as a person first, and as a principal second.* Show your human side. Let the staff know that you are approachable and genuine. This helps colleagues feel that they, too, can be themselves. When you show your "rough edges" it gives people permission to show theirs, and authentic relationships have a chance to flourish. Although the leader strives to do the right thing, mistakes happen. In a sense, the leader is saying, "We are all humans, we make mistakes, and through our humanness, we learn."

2. *Be consistent about what matters.* As a leader, consistency is a great asset if words and actions are communicating the important values of the school. Furthermore, matching actions with words helps create credibility and provides the staff with a sense of security about what can be expected of the leader. Also, trust develops when the staff knows what to expect—what can be predicted—in the leader's actions.

3. *Never lose sight of the vision and your role in fostering the vision.* Maintaining a focus on the vision while working with teachers, students, and parents in the workplace allows one to stay on course and create positive attitudes and perceptions among others in the workplace. Focus on the people side while working on the vision.

4. *Take time to look at people; smile, respond, and laugh.* Taking time to interact sincerely, with a smile or a meaningful "hello," shows others that you care. Moreover, the nonverbal gestures

that you make, and respond to, really count. Your ability to read nonverbals can make the difference in communicating effectively with a staff member. The message may not always be obvious, but it is still there to be received.

5. *Use active listening so people sense that you are really listening and that you care.* Active listening demonstrates that you are hearing what is being communicated. People are more likely to be motivated when they feel heard and understood. Active listening tells the speaker that his or her time is important and that a full explanation is welcome and can benefit the listener's understanding. Active listening usually includes asking clarifying questions to enhance understanding as well as paraphrasing. Unfortunately, we often listen only to respond. This communicates a message that what we have to say is more important than the contribution of another.

6. *Dignify people, and take the high road.* When you look for the best in people and communicate by dignifying them, you can expect that the best will come back to you. Dignifying people includes taking the high road in all relationships. If you embarrass or insult someone, it is difficult to build bridges, and you will likely regret your actions later. Dignifying people shows respect, which can foster trust, and trust is the most critical attribute in building a learning organization.

7. *Walk a mile in your colleague's moccasins.* Taking another person's perspective often reveals insights that we would not otherwise be privy to. This provides a greater appreciation of the other's needs, viewpoints, and, possibly, an inside view of what that person considers when making important decisions. Considering another's perspective can provide a measure of empathy as well. The ability to empathize is one of our most sophisticated and valuable human gifts. Also, appreciating another's point of view enhances our capacity to fine-tune communication as a result of greater understanding. As the world and the school become smaller and more global in their constituency bases, taking time for individuals to share the unique perspectives afforded by their cultures or experiences enriches understanding and adds a valuable asset to the organization.

8. *Respect, nurture, and celebrate diversity of ideas and people.* Diversity brings richness to a school. Encouraging and nurturing the diverse ideas of individuals can tap a new level of creativity that enables the staff to collectively face challenges. Diversity reflected in different ideas and cultural perspectives can enable the leader to see with many different eyes. This enhances one's overall perspective. Moreover, the person who might not share the leader's viewpoint, or the viewpoint of the majority, may be offering an important idea or thought that has been overlooked.

9. *Seek feedback from multiple constituencies—take the 360-degree option.* One practice that capitalizes on the value of diverse perspectives is called *full-circle evaluation* or *360-degree feedback* (Dyer, 2001). This process involves soliciting feedback from multiple and diverse sources so that leaders can gather data about their performance from those who interact with them. Examples of data sources include teachers, parents, students, classified staff, central office personnel, and community members. Several organizations have excellent instruments that can be used to gather 360-degree data. For example, a first-rate instrument is the National Association of Secondary School Principals' (NASSP; 2008) Leadership Skills Assessment, which provides data on 4 skill areas that are divided into 10 skill dimensions. The instructional leadership area includes setting instructional direction; the resolving conflict area includes judgment, results orientation, and organizational ability; the communication area includes oral communication and written communication; and the developing self and others skill area includes understanding one's own strengths and weaknesses and developing the strengths of others. After one completes the self-assessment, NASSP encourages the principal to get feedback from up to 15 colleagues in order to compare perceptions (NASSP, 2008; www.principals.org).

Recently, Vanderbilt University and the University of Pennsylvania teamed up to develop and field-test a 360-degree instrument that measures behaviors associated with student achievement and is aligned with the Educational Leadership Policy Standards (Olson, 2008). Vanderbilt Assessment of Leadership in Education (VAL-ED) measures six components of student achievement: high standards for student learning, rigorous curriculum, quality instruction, culture of learning and professional behavior, connections to external communities, and performance accountability.

10. *Be accessible, open, and supportive.* People have a need to connect with one another, especially during the change process when many people feel lost, needy, incompetent, vulnerable, and out of control. Be there for them. Support can help individuals make the transition from old to new practices. Support entails listening, problem solving, reflecting, clarifying, and helping people develop workable solutions. Support may also mean spending time with people when tragedy or medical emergencies occur. One's physical presence at difficult times is deeply valued. Research in intensive care units has shown that the comforting presence of another person not only lowers the patient's blood pressure but also slows secretion of fatty acids that block arteries (Goleman, Boyatzis, & McKee, 2002). Thus, one's presence not only provides emotional comfort but also has the impact of changing a physiological state!

11. *Know your authentic self.* Experts on ethical leadership stress that knowing one's authentic self is a first step to understanding others and displaying positive human relations skills (Starratt, 2004). Harvard Business Professor Bill George (2007) reflects, "First, you have to understand yourself, because *the hardest person you will ever have to lead is yourself.* . . . Second, to be an effective leader, *you must take responsibility for your own development*" (p. xxxiii, italics in original).

12. *Take time to smell—and water—the roses.* One superintendent took five minutes to play catch with a lonely boy, and two months later learned that it had meant a great deal to the student. A principal walked into a small class of students receiving special assistance and asked a boy, "Jonathan, how are you doing?" Later, the principal was told that after he left, the child smiled at the teacher and said, "Wow, the principal knows my name!" Remember that in small ways we can make a big difference in people's lives. Portraying interest in a student's or staff member's work, for example, can be invigorating to the principal as well as the recipient. It communicates care.

The Chinese characters for *ear, eyes, you, undivided attention,* and *heart,* when combined, make up the verb *to listen* and remind us of the critical components necessary for effective human relations. (See Figure 4.1.) Consider posting this symbol near your desk or near a table at which you frequently hold conferences.

■ THE ROLE OF EMOTIONS IN THE ORGANIZATION: REMEMBERING THE HEART

Experience tells us that when organizational members perceive that they are genuinely valued as people, feel recognized for their efforts, and are seen as important because of the contribution they are making, climate is enhanced and productivity soars. Indeed, leaders have a profound role in affecting the emotions of individuals within the workplace; their commitment to work, school, and climate; and, ultimately, productivity!

All of us, at one time or another in our lives, have been inspired by a great leader who brought out the best in us. Daniel Goleman and his colleagues Richard Boyatzis and Annie McKee (2002) explain in *Primal Leadership* that "great leadership works through the emotions" and that "the best

Figure 4.1

leaders have found effective ways to understand and improve the way they handle their own and other people's emotions. Understanding the powerful role of emotions in the workplace sets the best leaders apart from the rest—not just in tangibles such as better business results and the retention of talent, but also in the all-important intangibles, such as higher morale, motivation and commitment" (pp. 3–5).

The leader who is skillful in human relations has the power to influence organizational members' emotions in a variety of ways. Goleman et al. (2002) suggest that the leader acts as a group's emotional guide. The leader's behavior literally influences whether staff members' emotions will be driven in a positive or negative direction. Staff will look to the leader for guidance, especially during times of crisis. In times of tragedy, they will look to the leader for emotional support. Goleman et al. explain that "we rely on connections with other people for our own emotional stability" and "other people can change our very physiology" (pp. 6–7). They support this statement by citing Lewis, Amini, and Lannon's (2000) research that "one person transmits signals that can alter hormone levels, cardiovascular function, sleep rhythms and even immune function inside the body of another" (p. 7). Reflecting on this research, a principal noted, "So that's why when negative information is churned out through the rumor mill people often complain of losing sleep and feeling grumpy! And, conversely, that's why when I give positive feedback to staff about their efforts with students they seem to get all pumped up." Indeed, researchers have found that human beings tend to mirror the emotional states of one another—positive or negative—when they are together. For example, people who are in rapport during a conversation often even mirror one another's body language.

Using Emotions Intelligently

How skillfully and successfully a leader models human relations skills largely depends on his or her *Emotional Intelligence.* Goleman (1995) defines Emotional Intelligence as "a basic flair for living—being able to rein in emotional impulse; to read another's innermost feelings; to handle relationships smoothly." Goleman et al. (2002) identify four dimensions of Emotional Intelligence and divide these into two areas. The first area has to do with personal competence, how we manage ourselves; the second area has to do with social competence, managing relationships with others.

The **Personal Competence** component includes *Self-Awareness* and involves knowing one's own emotions and understanding their impact on others. It also means knowing one's strengths and limitations and having a sense of one's self worth. *Self-Management* involves emotional self-control, being trustworthy, and having the capacity to be flexible when the need presents itself. Having an internal performance drive, the capacity to take the initiative, and a spirit of optimism are also competencies related to self-management.

Social Competence involves *Social Awareness* and *Relationship Management*. *Social Awareness* areas include empathy for individuals and the organization, organizational awareness, and a service commitment to recognizing and meeting client needs. *Relationship Management* includes inspirational leadership, the kind that involves guiding and motivating others with a compelling vision. It also refers to the ability to influence others, which usually means possessing a wide range of strategies for persuasion. Another key area of relationship management is the capacity to develop others through feedback and guidance. The person who manages relationships well often functions as a change catalyst and is skilled in conflict management, building bonds with individuals and fostering teamwork and collaboration.

Being aware of the dimensions of Emotional Intelligence and striving to model them as well as reflect on them during and after daily interactions will enhance relationships with staff members, central office personnel, other professional colleagues, parents, community members, students, and one's own family. These competencies also will inform actions that will contribute to the well-being and productivity of the organization. When people feel good about their working relationships with others, they will be able to focus on the centerpiece of school activity: making a difference for students.

REFLECTIONS

This space provides for you a place to write in ideas that have been generated by this chapter, things you want to try, or adaptations of ideas presented herein.

1. Make a list of things you do that have a task focus. Then make a list of things you do that have a relationship focus. Examine the lists to determine which one is longer. Why do you think this is the case? State what you do to simultaneously "get the job done" and "take care of people."

2. After reviewing the Recommendations for Skillful Human Relations, consider these questions: Are there particular recommendations that you should work on? What other recommendations would you add to the list?

3. Reflecting on the four dimensions of Emotional Intelligence, what are your areas of personal strength? What are areas that you would like to strengthen?

4. What insights or new questions do you have as a result of reflecting on the ideas presented in this chapter?

5

Managing Time

What you pay attention to, and spend time on, communicates what you value.

—Kent Peterson

Time is the one resource we all share. However, what we choose to do with the time we have, how we actually spend our time, differs widely across individuals. No one actually "manages time." However, we can manage our use of time by clearly identifying our personal and professional goals and scheduling our time to reflect those goals. Easier said than done! In a study of time use among new principals, a major discrepancy was apparent between the time that principals wanted to spend and the time that they actually spent in the areas of curriculum and instruction. These principals were very dissatisfied with the amount of time they were able to spend on curriculum and instruction versus such items as pupil problems and facility management (Alvy, 1983).

■ BREVITY, FRAGMENTATION, AND VARIETY

Part of the difficulty associated with principals' efficient use of time lies in the characteristics of their work lives. In a study of principals' work, Peterson (1982) notes three attributes of their work lives: brevity, fragmentation, and variety. Peterson found that 85 percent of the principals' tasks lasted nine minutes or less. Often there was a sense of fragmentation related to the work because frequently principals were interrupted by forces over which they had no control, and in many cases these interruptions were unexpected. Furthermore, there was tremendous variety in the nature of their tasks. This variety demanded a wide range of emotions and technical skills, some for which the administrator had no previous experience or preparation. With federal mandates, a constant demand for data, and the variety of state and local curricular and instructional initiatives, the demands on principals' time are greater than ever before. The reality of brevity, fragmentation, and variety accentuates the need for systematically and thoughtfully addressing the multitude of tasks that beg for the principal's attention.

Although brevity, variety, and fragmentation make planned work very difficult to get done, paradoxically these attributes present an opportunity to work more effectively. For example, when taking a morning walk through classrooms (an important professional goal), a principal may be interrupted by a parent who is picking up make-up work for a sick child. This brief encounter presents the principal with an opportunity to express concern for the child and share the purpose of the morning walk through classrooms. This simultaneously communicates an interest in students and the school's commitment to instructional excellence. As the principal continues walking, he or she collects information about individual classrooms' culture and climate. So, in a sense, the brevity, fragmentation, and variety often give the principal an opportunity to do two or more things at once, an authentic example of Leading and Learning by Wandering Around.

Time-Study Strategy

Due to these attributes of _____ ____'s work life, principals must work hard to take control of their use of time. Otherwi__ _____ ___ ill control them. The first step to effectively managing the use of time is to _____ _____ ___ __ssionally and personally through a time study. (Additional time m_____ _____ _____ ____ in Chapter 16.) For example, professional items of impor_____ _____ _____ ____ns, halls, and playgrounds; giving feedback; devel___ _____ _____ ____ professional reading. Personal items of _____ _____ _____us, jogging, golf, or basketball; and tim__ _____ _____ _____hings are developed, think about other _____ _____ _____ven your role. Make a list of these, too__ _____ _____ _____lead to potential problems. For insta__ _____ _____ _____cords or fire-drill procedures, or wor__ ____

Then cr__ _____ _____ _____oals. Think about the activities associa__ _____ _____ _____goal of spending quality time with your family m___ _____ _____ _____going to dinner, having discussions, reading together, or ____

After your goals are develope__, _ _____ ____nd conduct a study of your use of time. Do this for two weeks. You may choos__ _____ __ely, at the end of each day, or as you move from task to task. Some principals use a di___ ___ ___r or personal digital assistant (PDA) because they find it easier than writing down each task. Another option is to look back at your calendar for the previous month, noting how you spent time.

When your time study is complete, review your use of time against your goals. Use a marker to highlight those events, tasks, or activities that relate to your goals. Looking for a match in this way will help you determine whether you are spending time in accordance with your priorities. Now take out your list of mundane tasks. How much time are you spending on these tasks? Carefully analyzing your use of time in this way will help you determine what you want to do more of and what you want to do less of.

■ TECHNIQUES FOR TIME MANAGEMENT

One principal remarked, "It is important to take control of one's schedule. That means long-range scheduling. If you think something is important—like visiting classrooms—build it into your schedule. That's the only way it will happen. Take care of yourself, and don't shortchange yourself on personal goals. I know that may seem selfish, but if your personal life is 'together,' it will help your professional life." Another principal reflected, "If you don't build what's important to you into the schedule, it will never get done . . . because unimportant events always are there to fill the void. Everyone wants a piece of the principal's time, but if the slices are too small, then you can't taste the accomplishments!"

Many time management consultants have developed models to help principals reflect on which responsibilities and tasks are essential and nonessential and to determine which tasks should receive immediate attention but often remain on the back burner (e.g., Covey, 1989). Unfortunately, important activities such as long-range planning, building relationships, reflection, and self-renewal often receive little or no attention because of responsibilities that press one's time. To illustrate, daily interruptions that are difficult to avoid (e.g., telephone calls, drop-in sales visits, some administrative meetings) frequently overshadow essential responsibilities to the organization and to oneself (e.g., visiting students on the field or in the classroom, talking with teachers, reading a professional journal).

MANAGING BIFOCALLY ■

One way to use interruptions as leverage points to get more done is to manage bifocally. Kent Peterson, noted researcher on principals' work lives, suggests that bifocal leadership and management actions can actually help a principal accomplish two things at once. Here is how it works. Suppose you are working with a school improvement team on a budget committee. At the same time that you are working on the budget, you may seize the moment to educate the committee about the school's reading program—one of the budget line items. Or suppose you receive a phone call from an angry parent. Use the call as an opportunity to build positive bridges between the school and this parent, collaboratively problem solve, and gather data about how this segment of the parent population views the school. This approach uses the call as a leverage point for changing the perception of the principal and the school from negative to positive. Another way to manage time with insight involves the use of a pocket planner. The box that follows outlines how this process works.

Managing Time With Insight: The Pocket Planner

The "pocket planner" can be used so that the barrage of demands become leverage points for accomplishing tasks. One may use 3″ × 5″ index cards or a PDA as a pocket planner. Here's how they work:

1. To track progress toward realizing the vision:
   - Post the school's vision.
   - Identify key goals.
   - Anytime you are out and about, receive a phone call; interview a student, parent, teacher, or community member; observe student work; and so on. For anything that relates to the vision, jot down the date, the event, and your perceptions regarding how it relates to accomplishing the vision.
   - When it comes time for report writing, take out the data you've recorded and examine it.

2. As a management tool:
   - Anytime you see something that needs to be done, jot it down on a 3″ × 5″ card or PDA.
   - Decide whether you need to delegate the task to someone or do the task yourself.
   - For those cards with tasks not delegated, carry them with you. When you have a few extra minutes, take out the cards and select one that is doable, given your time. You'll be surprised how you can use fragmentation to your advantage.

3. For keeping track of supervisory visits, with a goal of distributing one's proximity across staff members, gaining a sense of classroom work, increasing storytelling capacity, and building schoolwide norms of practice:
   - List staff members' names down the left side of an index card or PDA screen.
   - Write the months across the top—three or four to a card or screen.
   - Every time you visit a staff member, jot down the date, time, and what you did during your visit (e.g., IS—interviewed a student, ESW—examined student work, LN—left a note, TOT—conducted a time-off-task scan, WT—walk-through visit).
   - When you have a few minutes—perhaps due to a canceled appointment—take out your pocket planner and visit someone you have not seen in action this month.

■ MULTITASKING: A MODERN-DAY SOLUTION OR HAZARD?

Our modern, fast-paced society applauds the benefits of multitasking. We take pride in telling our colleagues that we can complete six tasks at the same time. However, many experts warn us to embrace multitasking with caution. Consider Walter Kirn's (2007) observation:

> This is the great irony of multitasking—that its overall goal, getting more done in less time, turns out to be chimerical. In reality, multitasking slows our thinking. It forces us to chop competing tasks into pieces, set them in different piles, then hunt for the pile we're interested in, pick up its pieces, review the rules for putting the pieces back together, and then attempt to do so, often quite awkwardly. (. . . A brain attempting to perform two tasks simultaneously will, because of all the back-and-forth stress, exhibit a substantial lag in information processing.) (p. 72)

Kirn also warns us of the extreme hazard of multitasking: "For every driver who's ever died while talking on a cell phone (researchers at the Harvard Center for Risk Analysis estimate that some 2,600 deaths and 330,000 injuries may be caused by drivers on cell phones each year), there was someone on the other end who, chances are, was too distracted to notice" (p. 76).

Communicating effectively is a critical competence for principals. Giving a colleague undivided attention during a conversation communicates interest and respect. Word processing or text messaging during this encounter can diminish understanding of the communication and impair one's ability to respond meaningfully. Further, multitasking in this situation conveys a lack of genuine interest in the speaker and what he or she is saying.

The need to multitask will not fade away. The nature of the principalship makes multitasking very seductive. Embrace this temptation with caution. It may be the simplest but not the best solution for every circumstance a principal may encounter. Heed H. L. Mencken's sage advice: "There is always a well-known solution to every human problem—neat, plausible, and wrong."

FINAL THOUGHTS ON USING TIME ■

Many principals have pointed to the importance of reflecting on the effectiveness of daily work routines to determine whether they actually help get things done in a time-efficient way or their use tends to inhibit creative abilities. By abandoning or altering a routine, a principal will have the opportunity to approach a familiar task in a new way and, in doing so, possibly become more productive.

All of us probably have recognized that our performance tends to peak at certain times during the day. Some refer to themselves as morning people. Others jokingly remark, "Don't even ask me to think before 10 a.m." There is a note of seriousness in all this talk. Sensitivity to one's most creative or best "thinking" time can help you schedule those tasks that require the greatest concentration at times when your performance is optimal. Of course, this will not always be possible. To support your plan for the effective use of time, communicate your priorities and philosophy to the secretary and the staff. This can enable them to assist and support you in sheltering peak performance time as well as provide a model for them. It might be appropriate to provide examples of how you would like the secretary to respond (e.g., "Mr. Smith is visiting classrooms now, may I schedule an appointment or have him call you back?").

Furthermore, principals must be sensitive to the demands of the day, week, or year that constrain the time of others in the organization. When scheduling personal appointments and all-school activities, principals need to consider how time can be most effectively used to acknowledge the important role that others play in the organization and to send the message that time does not revolve around the principal. For example, personally asking a teacher about the best time to schedule a professional appointment, or directing the secretary to do the same, can go a long way in setting the proper tone for the appointment. In one school, no faculty meetings are held on Friday, at the request of teachers, so they can take care of pressing professional needs before the weekend. Another example of respecting teachers' daily work lives is providing monthly and yearly calendars that identify important deadlines and events (e.g., report card due dates, Martin Luther King Jr. assembly, statewide testing dates). It is imperative to adhere to these deadlines, whenever possible, out of respect for teachers.

One final thought: When your behavior aligns with your values and beliefs, you will feel comfortable with yourself, your colleagues, and your environment. Professionally, you will feel better about your day because you will know that you have made every minute count.

REFLECTIONS

This space provides a place for you to write down ideas that have been generated by this chapter, things you want to try, or adaptations of ideas presented here.

1. Think about your goals. Conduct a time study.

2. Is your use of time aligned with your goals? Are any changes necessary?

3. When are your peak performance times? What do you usually do during these times?

4. What are some effective use-of-time strategies that you can implement on the job?

5. How have federal and state mandates impacted your use of time? What strategies have you used to effectively address these mandates?

6. Who needs to be aware of your goals in relation to time? How will you let them know?

7. How might you use the pocket planner?

8. What new insights do you now have about multitasking?

9. What insights or new questions do you have as a result of reflecting on the ideas presented in this chapter?

6

Effectively Working
With the Central Office
and Other Schools

Forging Success Through Collaboration

What I learned is that it's easier to ask for forgiveness than permission.

—A principal's voice

Schools do not operate in isolation but as part of a school district with a broad philosophy and set of goals and values emanating from the central office (Fullan, 2007). Indeed the interactions "of the district and the school can have a powerful effect on student achievement" (Marzano & Waters, 2007). Reality tells us that a strong relationship between the school and the central office is necessary to implement any major change over a sustained period.

It is not enough for a school to desire the change even if all the key human resources are in place at the school site. Funding and resources must be available, and the central office often allocates both. At a minimum, successful change necessitates the availability of inservice training, funding, and instructional resources for students and teachers. In fact, Fullan and Stiegelbauer (1991) have noted that "individual schools can become highly innovative for a short period of time without the district, but they cannot stay innovative without district action to establish the conditions for continuous and long term improvement" (p. 209). More recently, Fullan (2007) has noted the critical nature of lateral capacity building. That is, other schools across the district, state, and nation provide an invaluable storehouse of resources. Dwindling assets juxtaposed with federal and state mandates necessitate sharing ideas to build capacity to serve diverse student learners. Thus, lateral capacity becomes a moral imperative.

■ CAUGHT IN THE MIDDLE

Principals often find themselves caught in the middle between staff and the central office. Federal, state, and district guidelines, policies, procedures, and timelines must be followed while accomplishing the business of the school. This often involves sheltering teachers from outside interferences. Principals help teachers by finding out how the district is structured or governed. This enables them to represent the needs of the school. Schlechty (2001) reminds principals, "Learn to see yourself as a member of the district-level team as well as the head of your own team at the building level. Recognize that your school is not the only system you need to consider; it is part of a larger system. Other schools and other principals are not—or should not be—your competition" (pp. 213–214).

■ HOW IS THE SCHOOL DISTRICT GOVERNED?

Understanding governance can considerably enhance a principal's work life. Initially, principals must recognize that the relationship between a school and the central office will depend to a great extent on the structure of governance and size of the district. Developing effective strategies to work with the central office will depend on understanding how the district works. Concerning governance, there are many traditional and experimental decision-making models. For example, in one school district, the school may be largely autonomous, with control of the purse strings in the hands of a site-based counsel that includes a principal, parents, teachers, and community members. Another district may still make critical decisions in the central office with little input from the school site. What about the role of the elected school board? In most districts, school board members see their role as supporting and fine-tuning the broad policies of the district.

■ COMMUNICATION BETWEEN THE SCHOOLS AND THE CENTRAL OFFICE

Although gaining an understanding of the governance structure is important, a lot will depend on the personnel in the central office and schools and their mutual ability to communicate. Communication should be a two-way street, and the school principal can be the key to orchestrating an effective relationship with the district team. The central office views the principal as the primary contact person. Thus, from a practical viewpoint, it is easiest for a district office to say, "We need to get in touch with the Carver School; let's call the principal, Ms. Breyer." But the principal should not expect that it is the job of central office personnel to always initiate the contact. The principal's attitude must be, "It is my job to communicate proactively with the central office." Otherwise, the principal may hear from the central office only when something is wrong or when they have a new idea to be implemented without school input.

How can principals effectively initiate contact with the central office? Traditionally, central office personnel do not spend as much time in schools as they would like. Principals need to build occasions into the school calendar to bring central office personnel and school board members into schools. Invite them to major programs, and let them know when Senior Projects, Invention Week, or the Science Exhibition is taking place, or when the middle school is performing a play. Send them the dates of important events well in advance. Acknowledge their presence when they attend these events. Bring students to the central office to share their reports or math investigations. Send DVDs to the central office or coordinate webcasts so that personnel can watch real-time school activities.

Principals need to keep communication lines open with regard to key district meetings and new initiatives. They should either ask to attend the meetings themselves or send a school representative who has both expertise and practical knowledge. Furthermore, if a principal brings an important idea to a central office meeting, he or she will obviously have much more clout if the idea emanated from and has the support of teachers.

Communication also depends on knowing how the informal organization works, how things really get done. Fair or unfair, the image of the central office is often one of a bureaucracy that moves slowly and is dominated by red tape. How does one cut the time and red tape necessary to communicate an idea or jump-start a potentially rich innovation? Principals should consider these questions: With whom should you really speak? Who are the power brokers in the central office? Who "hangs together"? The idea is not to beat the system but rather to institute effective programs for students and teachers as quickly as possible. Engaging veteran principals or others who have worked in the school district for a long time can be the best way to find out how the informal organization operates.

Fortunately, many central office personnel are working hard to change the traditional bureaucratic image. Leaders are viewing the central office as service centers to improve student achievement and support teachers, principals, and parents. Schlechty (2001) advises central office personnel to remember that their "most important job is to create and manage systems that will enable principals and teachers to concentrate on the core business of schools, the creation of intellectual activity that students find engaging and from which they learn. Only secondarily, if at all, should you [central office personnel] see yourself as a supervisor" (p. 212). The central office in Long Beach, California, has tried to cut the red tape by streamlining the process for employing qualified teacher applicants. The school district tries to complete applicant physical examinations, fingerprinting, and paperwork in one day—and in one building. The rationale for consolidating the process is simple: "If someone has a bad experience when they come in here, we may lose a good teacher" (Johnston, 2001, p. 18).

School leaders must develop ways to slow down or eliminate an idea from the central office that may offer little prospect for student success. Deal and Peterson (1994), in *The Leadership Paradox,* describe the "bifocal principal" who needs to follow the "central office directives (yet) be creatively insubordinate" (p. 49). Also, principals should recognize that central office personnel are doing the same thing. The art of politely resisting an idea and hoping that it will go away is practiced on many fronts. This jockeying on the part of the school and the central office can be frustrating but also helpful because it keeps both sides on their toes.

It is important to build a relationship of mutual trust in which successes and failures are shared. Acknowledging failures may sound a little dangerous, but the alternative is to constantly worry about hiding mistakes. This makes for an unhealthy relationship. Additionally, principals are bombarded constantly with new ideas and innovations. Developing a strong relationship based on trust is critical to responding honestly when an idea emerges. If a principal is unable to express skepticism or a lack of knowledge about an innovation (e.g., What is Response to Intervention anyway?), it can be a very long, uncomfortable, and superficial relationship.

When central office personnel propose a new idea of worth or provide the support for a school-generated idea that is implemented successfully, it is the school leader's responsibility to acknowledge the role played by the central office. Central office staff need to know that they are valued by the school site and that they play an important role. Their efforts deserve to be validated. Central office personnel may not verbalize the idea, but they too often feel distant from schools. As one assistant superintendent noted, "How many articles and headlines have you read about central office leaders? I suspect you've read very few" (quoted in Grove, 2002, p. 45). When a school reaches out and recognizes the role of the central office, that act can greatly reduce the distance. So invite central office personnel to the key ceremonies that celebrate an innovation. They will remember this. The next time an idea develops within a school that has forged a warm and effective relationship with central office, implementation of a change just may come a little easier.

■ MANAGEMENT TIPS FOR WORKING WITH THE CENTRAL OFFICE

Based on the preceding ideas, the following tips gleaned from successful principals can be helpful in working with the central office:

1. *Request a district-level activities calendar* with key events identified by the district several months before a new school year begins. Post the appropriate dates in your office, on your calendar, and in the staff room. Ask the secretary to place the dates on his or her calendar. Color-code events and dates that will affect the school. Keep these in mind when planning school-level events. One principal developed such a timeline of events on butcher paper sheets in the staff room. Another used a software calendar program so new information could be added and the data used for planning.

2. *Create files on your computer or desk.* Establish folders for district-level projects and events by date. As you collect information or ideas, simply place them in the appropriate file.

3. *Plan ahead to participate in district projects, but expect surprises.* Assume that emergencies and unexpected events will pop up and drain energy from planned efforts. Although one should plan ahead, the plan will not be foolproof. The principalship is filled with unanticipated events. When you are unable to attend a meeting, ask the assistant principal or an appropriate faculty member to attend in your place.

4. *Keep the district informed.* Many principals send weekly e-mails containing information about activities at the school, with attached student writing samples or artwork, to the central office. Send copies of communications that the central office may ultimately need.

5. *Invite central office personnel* to celebrations, assemblies, class activities, and other school rituals.

6. *Read e-mails from the district carefully.* Save them electronically or as hard copies for one to two years. You never know when you will need them again! Share appropriate communications with grade-level or department teams or in the newsletter or bulletin. Back up all important electronic documents.

7. *Make presentations to the board of education* to keep its members informed about school-level activities. When appropriate, use students during presentations (but only if this concept is valued; in some systems, it may not be).

8. *Try to ensure that school-level personnel have representation on state or district committees* when the state or central office are going to make important curriculum decisions that affect your school.

Managing in these ways affords principals opportunities to stay visible and keenly aware of what is taking place in schools, the district, and the community. Networking in this way is a key skill of the effective leader. In addition, these actions and interactions will provide the school with significant information and resources to make effective decisions.

MAINTAINING A STRONG ■ RELATIONSHIP BETWEEN THE CENTRAL OFFICE AND THE SCHOOL

The tug-of-war between the school site and the central office has expanded and now includes the state and federal government. However, beyond standardized test scores, the federal and state governments cannot know the culture and precise needs of individual schools. Local context is critical. As Fullan (2007) observes, "To know what works in some situations does not mean we can get it to work in other situations" (p. 17). Those closest to the client often have the most relevant data on which to base decisions. The central office, then, may serve as a buffer or conduit between the local school and the large governmental agencies. The central office and the school need each other. As noted earlier, the central office can assist schools in various ways, including disseminating important information concerning state standards, frameworks, and benchmarks; sharing achievement data; helping with the hiring of administrators, teachers, and support staff; and setting policy for the district and schools.

To serve schools and teachers, central office personnel in the Arlington, Virginia, public schools take responsibility for assisting new teachers and teachers having difficulties, developing and implementing grants, meeting with citizen committees, organizing student art exhibitions and science fairs, conducting the textbook adoption and ordering process, and designing and conducting staff development (Grove, 2002). In Pittsburgh, Pennsylvania, central office supervisors work in schools to coach principals and principal trainees guided by the Educational Leadership Policy Standards. This initiative has invigorated central office leaders because "[this] newly flattened central office structure encourages midlevel supervisors to get out of the office and spend most of the week walking school halls and sitting in classrooms alongside the principals" (Samuels, 2008, p. 26).

District staff can link the ideas of the various schools to keep the schools in touch with one another, which is very similar to the role played by those organizing a consortium. And the various school sites can offer the district answers to questions about what is working. The school site is, of course, the laboratory in which important decisions can be judged as being on the right track or needing further work. In education, we often lament the fragmentation of the curriculum and the need for sustained coherence. The same point can be made regarding schools in a district. Too much fragmentation of information among schools within a district can easily lead to the weakening of human relationships and resource sharing that are so necessary in a learning community.

FORGING A SCHOOL AND ■ CENTRAL OFFICE PARTNERSHIP: PUTTING STAFF AND STUDENT LEARNING FIRST

The Fort Osage Story. In Independence, Missouri, at the beginning and end of each school year, building leadership teams from each school in the Fort Osage School District meet with a Central Office Team made up of the superintendent; assistant superintendents of educational services, personnel, and business services; and the director of special education. Together they discuss the School Improvement Plan that school site staff have developed. They dialogue about the following:

- goals
- the data that was used to develop each goal
- evidence that will be observable if the goal was accomplished

- needed resources
- responsible parties
- an Action Plan (steps to be taken to address each goal)
- how the goal will contribute to staff and student learning

This process creates an understanding of, and respect for, the unique needs and accomplishments of each school. It also provides a window into how the staff in each school conceptualize the school improvement process in relation to their daily work. The beginning-of-the-year conversations create a foundation of insights for school-level visits that central office personnel make throughout the year. At the end of the year, the closing conversations between the central office team and the building leadership teams provide vivid qualitative data about each school's accomplishments and challenges. Jeff White, assistant superintendent for educational services, reflecting on an end-of-year visit, exclaimed, "I am so jazzed about the high level of conversation that I just witnessed. The school is really turning around. It is evident that staff and student learning are thriving."

REFLECTIONS

This space provides a place for you to write down ideas that have been generated by this chapter, things you want to try, or adaptations of ideas presented here.

1. How is your school district governed? What are the organizational and individual sources of influence that need to be addressed in order to implement change?

2. How would you characterize your school's relationship with the central office? What are some strengths and weaknesses? Are there particular things you would like to change? Does the central office serve as a buffer or conduit for federal mandates?

3. Does lateral capacity building exist in your district? What are the activities that schools engage in to share expertise and problem solve?

4. What insights or new questions do you have as a result of reflecting on the ideas presented in this chapter?

PART III

Honoring the School's Mission

7

Understanding, Planning, and Implementing Change

We rarely recognize that changes in the nature of work also create losses that trigger powerful individual or collective reactions. The costs may not be immediately obvious nor reflected directly in tangible ways, but left unattended over time, pressure builds up and can become a silent killer in organizations—much like hypertension in the human body. The unresolved loss of title or office can cause personal maladjustments, such as depression or excessive drinking; the substitution of a computerized system for manual procedures can create uncertainty, confusion, and a loss of identity. Wholesale changes in an organization can dramatically affect overall morale, productivity, and turnover. Most often, however, we fail to link these effects to the real cause. We attribute the blame to personal or other intangible sources, rather than to changes in the work setting.

—Deal (1985, pp. 293–294)

■ CHANGE BRINGS LOSS AND RESISTANCE

The downside of change so eloquently described by Terry Deal (1985) is often neglected when school leaders present teachers with ideas that "must" be implemented. One's individual enthusiasm for the change may be quite tempered by the experiences of other faculty. Staff experiencing change may feel loss and insecurity and show resistance and confrontation. In fact, these behaviors should occur. Resistance, in particular, should be expected and can be very helpful in straightening out and improving the change process. Resistance will bring questioning and the need to examine the direction of the changes being implemented. In the end, if real change is to occur, organizational members must feel that the change has been effective and meaningful for them.

■ INFLUENCING INDIVIDUALS AND THE INSTITUTION

It is critical to go about change in a way that shows sensitivity to individuals affected by change and the institution that is transformed as a result of it. Thus the purpose of this chapter is to review significant aspects of change from individual and organizational perspectives to enhance the prospects for successful change to occur. The ideas discussed offer the best of what we know from research and practice to equip practitioners with basic information to develop thoughtful plans of action.

Initially and throughout the process, it is important to view change simultaneously from both individual and institutional perspectives. That is, it is important to see the trees and forest at the same time. Change takes place one individual at a time but, if effective, positively affects the whole organization. With this view in mind, this chapter begins by providing ideas to create a trusting environment—the first necessary step to implement effective change. The chapter then explores Michael Fullan's (2007) classical insights regarding change, reviews research-based stages that an institution should go through when implementing change, provides a meaningful framework for building individual support for change, and discusses levels of concern that individuals may experience when implementing change.

Principals should recognize the tremendous role they can play as change facilitators or obstructers. As Hall and Hord (1987) point out, "throughout our years of research and experience, we have never seen a situation in which the principal was not a significant factor in the efforts of schools to improve" (p. 1). More recently, Fullan (2007) has stated that "today, no serious change effort would fail to emphasize the role of the principal" (p. 156). Principals can make or break a school's effort to foster collaborative decision making or engage in a schoolwide professional development activity. A principal's willingness to listen and set up collaborative teams during faculty and parent meetings indicates a desire to share decisions and engage in change. Furthermore, if teachers indicate an interest in a professional development activity, such as peer coaching, the principal sends a clear message of support or opposition by how he or she responds to the initial idea and facilitates or obstructs the project. In subtle ways—such as where an item is placed on an agenda—as well as grand, explicit ways, a principal's actions influence change. Also, Fullan reminds us that change and progress do not always go hand in hand. In fact, rejecting change may be a bolder move for a school principal than pursuing what appears to be a "quick fix" solution.

BUILDING TRUST FOR SUCCESSFUL CHANGE   ■

Because change is holistic, every aspect of the organizational system has the potential to be affected. This underscores the importance of systemic thinking; that is, that changes in one part of the system have an impact on others. For instance, new graduation requirements or longer class periods may have profound effects on curriculum and teaching practices. Principals have a key role in preparing an environment where potential change initiatives can be rigorously examined by all staff members and, if appropriate, implemented.

One major factor in creating an environment for change is building a climate of trust in which risk taking and experimentation can occur. This is easier said than done, especially in cases where previously the norms in the building emphasized "playing it safe." Nonetheless, because change involves new ideas, new behaviors, new materials, and new ways of operating, people need a safe environment to feel comfortable embarking on a change journey. When implementing new ways of doing things, an individual's performance often gets worse before it gets better. We all have experienced this when learning a new move in a familiar sport, for example. Fullan and Miles (1992) describe this experience as the implementation dip: "Even in cases where reform eventually succeeds, things often go wrong before they go right" (p. 749). Therefore, trust—among individuals and within the culture of the school—is an essential ingredient in the change process.

In many change efforts, because the innovation requires new forms of working relationships among individuals (e.g., Professional Learning Communities, data teams), there has been greater attention devoted to building relationships versus focusing on a specific end, such as achievement, that performance actually decreases initially (Robbins, 1991a).

■ CONFLICT CAN CONTRIBUTE TO POSITIVE CHANGE

The environment must permit individuals to take risks and express different points of view. At Ford Motor Company, employees often comment, "Failure is the opportunity to begin again more intelligently." Hence failure becomes a source of knowledge. In the same way that failure comes to be viewed positively, the emergence of conflicting viewpoints often associated with a change effort can be positive as well. When different points of view are voiced, conflict often emerges along with lots of energy. This can actually fuel a positive change effort if conflict is harnessed to support quality results rather than be swept under the carpet or viewed as a negative. Thus, conflict can raise awareness of some aspect of the change that had not been considered before. This may have an important influence on the implementation of an innovation. In one school's change effort to move to grade-level teams, staff members had not considered the impact of teaming on specialists' positions. Conflict provided a source of knowledge that revealed a blind spot in the planning for teams.

An important quality of the expression of conflicting viewpoints is that there needs to be an orientation toward resolution rather than merely expressing a gripe. Conflicting ideas should be welcomed as providing valuable sources of information and insight to assist in planning for change or enhancing a change effort once it has begun. It has been said that if a change is "deep enough," it should be accompanied by conflict because it upsets the status quo.

Finally, another reason to accept conflict is that it brings differences of opinion out in the open. More damage is done when saboteurs operate beneath the surface through covert interactions to obstruct change efforts. This approach uses the unofficial or informal communication network in the school—the system through which information travels faster than the speed of e-mail (and holds more credibility!).

■ STRATEGIES TO PROMOTE TRUST

Because risk taking, experimentation, and voicing conflicting opinions are essential ingredients for change and because they thrive in a safe, trusting environment, attending to how to create such an atmosphere for change is an important first step. Yet this step can bring good or bad news. The bad news is that there is no recipe for successful change. However, that is also good news because it provides the opportunity to create a plan of action tailored to one's school. How change and trust building will be addressed at a school site depends on such issues as a school's history, student diversity, staff turnover, relationships among staff members, schedules and logistics, and degree of community support.

The following menu of options can help build trust:

1. *Walk your talk.* When words and actions are consistently aligned, credibility will usually follow. When one is credible, it is easier to believe in that person as a leader.

2. *Lead by personal example.* Leading by personal example provides an impetus for others to follow.

3. *Encourage people to talk about what it means to be trustworthy.* A simple activity that one can conduct at a faculty meeting is to ask individual staff members to list 10 behaviors that

contribute to one being perceived as trustworthy. Then groups of staff members get together, share their individual lists, and come to consensus regarding their top three items. Groups then report out their top three behaviors. The important attribute of this activity is that people spend time talking about what contributes to trust. How you spend time communicates what you value.

4. *Invite staff members to have input into collectively determining what the change will be and how it will be implemented.* Adults have a rich reservoir of experiences that begs to be tapped. Moreover, adults like to have a sense of control over what happens to them. Collective involvement about desired change and strategies for implementation can lend a sense of comfort, ownership, and security to those who will be directly affected by the change.

5. *Encourage consensus-building activities.* Consensus building enhances trust and facilitates change in that it provides opportunities for individuals to shape what happens at a site as a consequence of sharing individual viewpoints, facts, and opinions. A critical consensus-building question is: Can you live with it?

6. *Keep lines of communication open.* This helps dispel rumors and encourages dialogue and healthy interaction to engender mutual support. It also provides a forum for people to discuss the fears that often accompany change—fear of the unknown, losing jobs, and losing the familiar.

7. *Encourage disagreement.* Resistance usually stems from fear of being vulnerable or powerless. Information provided through resistance enables the facilitator of change to realize what will help people feel less vulnerable and more in control. Hence change can be approached more graciously when such factors are considered.

8. *Celebrate small and large successes.* People have a need to be acknowledged. This builds morale, recognizes individual deeds that contribute to organizational growth and accomplishments, and propels change. It is critical to be consistent with acknowledgment.

CLASSICAL INSIGHTS REGARDING ■ CHANGE AND CONTINUOUS IMPROVEMENT

Exploring the literature on change can build one's capacity to facilitate the change process. Michael Fullan's (2007) classic work, *The New Meaning of Educational Change,* includes many important insights that can inform and enhance one's practice. As you review the following points from Fullan, consider change efforts you have experienced. To what degree does each point explain the success or failure of the change effort?

1. Organizations must create the capacity for change and continuous improvement; the innovation is not the only goal.

2. Sustained change involves "lateral capacity building" (p. 56).

3. Successful leaders build teacher capacity, distribute leadership, and promote program coherence (e.g., specific learning goals, sustained over time).

4. Leaders set direction, "develop" people, and create collaborative communities; a key to change is that relationships improve.

5. Change is a journey in context—a process, not a destination.

6. Resisters have some good ideas.

7. Having a great passion for a change can get in the way if it means ignoring the ideas of others and the change process. Leaders need to be committed to the change process as well as the change.

8. Sometimes charismatic gurus hurt the process if they cultivate disciples rather than independent thinkers.

Finally, when one is intimately involved in a change effort, it is often easy to lose heart. Keeping Fullan's (2007) insights in mind helps us remember that change is not neat, but rather messy, most of the time. Yet change is inevitable and is a vital part of organizational and personal growth.

■ THREE PHASES OF CHANGE

In an ideal world, one would collaboratively plan prior to implementing change and consider the following question: Is the change consistent with the vision and mission of the school? Careful attention should be given to diagnosing needs, generating commitment, and developing an action plan prior to implementing change. One principal reflected, "I know that you can't walk in and change everything in one year. I found that out the hard way. You have to walk in and look things over critically and reflect on your priorities." Another, commenting on how much time the planning process took, said, "You just have to face the fact, as frustrating as it might be, that sometimes you have to go slow to go fast." Unfortunately, reality often does not permit us to look things over critically or to go slow to go fast. Often, mandates thrust an organization into an implementation stage without regard for a needed readiness stage in which understanding and commitment to the change might be built. By examining research-based observations in the RAND study of the phases that an institution should go through for successful change implementation (Berman & McLaughlin, 1978), individuals responsible for the innovation can work to ensure that the needed stages of the change process occur.

The RAND study "set out to characterize the process by which an innovation is translated into an operating reality within school districts" (Berman & McLaughlin, 1978, p. 13). The study uncovered an interesting phenomenon:

> Rather than a single process, several different ones could be observed for different innovations and also for the same innovation at different times in its evolution. Although all change agent projects evidently encountered a similar sequence of events and activities, three characteristic phases could be discerned within the overall process. . . . These phases roughly correspond to the project's beginning, middle, and end; but we did not use this simple terminology because neither beginning nor end makes sense in the context of a constantly evolving local educational system . . . and because instead of a chronological sequence "from beginning to end," the activities defining each phase overlapped one another. Instead, we call them *mobilization, implementation, and institutionalization.* (p. 13)

It is helpful to think about the change process associated with implementing an innovation in terms of these three phases. One example might serve to highlight some of the critical activities within each phase. Suppose a school was interested in examining block scheduling as a way to foster the development of students' academic and social skills and reduce behavioral problems.

In the mobilization phase, types of instructional strategies for the block would be studied. This could include readings, DVDs, and visits to sites where block scheduling is routinely used. Enthusiasm, commitment, dedication, and support for block scheduling would be rallied among stakeholders who would ultimately be affected by the decision to implement its use: teachers, parents, students, administration, and support staff. Planning efforts should include the development of a team of representative stakeholders. Plans would be made regarding needed resources such as professional development, follow-up, and implementation support.

In the implementation phase, professional development would be provided, follow-up would occur, and feedback would be solicited regarding the quality of training and support and the applicability of block scheduling to the classroom curriculum and student needs. Appropriate modifications would be made based on this feedback. "Review and refinement" sessions would be conducted. Typical follow-up sessions might include analysis of classroom observations, peer coaching, collaborative lesson development, and idea swapping and sharing.

The institutionalization phase is marked by acceptance or modification of the change project. Institutionalized change would occur if block scheduling became standard educational practice in the classroom and at the school level. Newcomers to the school would be taught block scheduling strategies, and these strategies would be modeled at faculty meetings and during professional development days.

Just as the organization goes through stages associated with the change process, so do individuals. The degree to which they receive support during this process will have a major impact on whether they will adopt a particular change.

A LOOK AT CHANGE FROM ■
THE INDIVIDUAL'S PERSPECTIVE

Federal and state mandates, district goals, advances in technology, new curriculum standards, and a number of other forces frequently require schools, and the individuals within them, to change. The invitation or, in some cases, the mandate to change often asks the organization and staff members to abandon long-standing, familiar practices in exchange for new ways of doing things. This phenomenon leaves people with a sense of loss, a longing to go back to the old ways of doing things, and a concern that being asked to do something differently implicitly means that what they had done before was not good. Frequently, a sense of denial emerges: "If we wait just long enough, this, too, will pass."

Individual responses to change differ. Some people welcome it; others greet it with fear or anger. Part of facilitating the change process involves understanding the individual's change experience. Organizations change only as the individuals within the organization change. Change is a highly personal experience. Essentially, it is an individual experience and takes place one person at a time. Personal meaning is one critical influence that ultimately determines whether a person is willing to change. If the change effort holds meaning for an individual, that person may be more likely to change. Teachers need to say and feel, "Yes, I can relate to this idea and see how it can improve student learning and make the job more exciting for me." People are more likely to adopt new behaviors when their own values and beliefs are consistent with the values and beliefs that undergird the new behaviors implied by the change.

Often, people are asked to change behavior before they have developed the new beliefs or values implicit in the change. This generates a feeling of discomfort. For long-lasting change to occur, individuals must first be provided with experiences through which they will develop the values and beliefs that drive the desired behaviors. Experiences change beliefs. Beliefs do not usually change without experiences. Many teachers have to experience positive results with students before adopting a new way of doing something. Unfortunately, teachers usually are asked to move on to the "next great thing" before having a chance to experience positive results and confidently internalize a new idea. An expert sixth-grade teacher, pleased with his emerging success teaching reasoning and problem-solving skills (per the National Council of Teachers of Mathematics), lamented that "we need to let teachers dwell on new ideas for 3 years, instead of 2 months or year" (S. Bachman, personal communication, April 2008).

To build interest and meaning for individuals who will be affected by change, the California School Leadership Academy, in Hayward, California, identified four factors that leaders can use to facilitate change. Each of the following factors in this framework should be considered before embarking on a change effort:

- Relevance—whether a change is relevant to one's life or work responsibilities
- Feasibility—whether people view the change as "doable" given other demands on their time and their philosophical beliefs
- Involvement—whether the individual being affected by the change has input into what the change will look like, sound like, and be like
- Trust—whether there is trust between the person being asked to change and the facilitator or initiator of the change

If staff members have collaboratively developed a vision that promotes quality teaching and staff and student learning, and if the proposed change is consistent with the vision, chances are it will be greeted with greater enthusiasm. It will be viewed as relevant, people will perceive it as feasible, it will have meaning because of the members' previous involvement with developing the vision, and an atmosphere of trust usually will have been established.

■ STAGES OF CONCERN

In addition to facilitating change by paying attention to creating individual meaning for the change process, change facilitators find it helpful to understand how individuals show their level of interest or concern for change. Hall, George, and Rutherford (1979) developed common characteristics that indicate one's interest or concern regarding innovative or change experiences. They emphasize that how people perceive and understand change will be dictated by their personality and experience. Some people may perceive a change as an outside threat, whereas others may view it as rewarding. The degree to which a concern may be assessed and responded to accordingly will facilitate one's understanding and experience of the change effort. Table 7.1, based on Hall et al.'s groundbreaking work, portrays these stages of concern.

One principal developed the chart shown in Table 7.2 after learning about these stages of concern to remind himself about how to respond to individuals' comments related to a change effort.

■ SOME FINAL THOUGHTS ON CHANGE

How change is perceived has a major impact on organizational response. Harold Storlien, former superintendent of the Medicine Hat School District in Alberta, Canada, advised us to look at all problems as challenges and opportunities. The principal can set a personal example by viewing change as an opportunity and encouraging risk taking and ownership on the part of teachers regarding the changes. This will create a climate of trust, which is essential for success. Key personnel in the process must constantly ask: Who do we need to inform? Who needs to know about what we are doing: Teachers? Parents? Principals? District personnel? Students? Community members? The media?

Inclusion of relevant groups is a critical factor in the change process. For example, the central office must be actively involved; there should be no surprises. The central office can supply the trainers, resources, time needed, and monetary support to implement the change. The whole

Table 7.1   Stages of Concern: Typical Expressions of Concern About the Innovation

Stage of Concern	Expression of Concern
6. Refocusing	I have some ideas about something that would work even better.
5. Collaboration	I am concerned about relating what I am doing with what other instructors are doing.
4. Consequence	How is my use affecting kids?
3. Management	I seem to be spending all my time in getting material ready.
2. Personal	How will using it affect me?
1. Informational	I would like to know more about it.
0. Awareness	I am not concerned about it (the innovation).

SOURCE: Hord, S., Rutherford, W., Huling-Austin, L., & Hall, G. (1987). *Taking charge of change.* Alexandria, VA: ASCD.

Table 7.2   A Principal's Responses to Concerns About Change

Stage of Concern	Response
6. Refocusing	Stimulate a discussion and provide a comfortable setting so teachers can discuss how this could be enhanced or improved.
5. Collaboration	Relate ways that individuals can collaborate and share ideas.
4. Consequence	Show how it might affect staff and students.
3. Management	Invite users to demonstrate how they manage the use of an innovation.
2. Personal	Share how it might affect student and staff learning.
1. Informational	Explain what "it" looks like in practice; provide examples.
0. Awareness	Provide information.

system must be involved for the project to succeed. Schools must revisit their mission and vision during the process and ask the following questions:

- Is the change on the right track?
- In what direction is the innovation going?
- If it appears to be going off track, is that okay?
- Is the project taking a direction that was unanticipated, but best?
- Has reality shown, based on actual classroom use, that the original plan was unrealistic?
- Do the new changes that appear necessary as a result of the initial experiments align with the mission and vision?
- Should the mission and vision be altered?
- Have the recommendations of the staff developers or previous examples of success of the innovation proved to be unworkable for this school? For example, a staff developer may recommend that student-led conferences with portfolios be implemented and required schoolwide after the training. Will that work for the staff?
- Should volunteers be enlisted to set examples and "massage" the project?

The ability level, human relations skills, and presentation strategies of staff developers brought into the school can obviously make or break the change effort. When staff developers are enlisted to start a program, are they operating on a level appropriate for the staff? Staff developers often know the ins and outs of an innovation and must remember that a staff member may know nothing about the proposed change. Staff developers must consider: If we listen, but respond at a higher level than is appropriate, then we are not addressing needs. The track record of the staff developers must be considered: Have they been involved previously with the school district? Have they talked with the key individuals such as the principal, teachers, district personnel, parents, and students who may be affected by the change? Eventually, plans should be put in place to develop teacher leaders as trainers, building capacity at the local site.

A phenomenon to be aware of, and plan proactively for, is a state of entropy or running out of steam that occurs about midcourse in a change effort. Many change agents plan ceremonies to acknowledge progress to date and to recall critical events along the way in order to generate enthusiasm and energy among organizational members to sustain progress in implementing the change. "Be aware of this reality, plan for it, but don't interpret it as losing the battle," commented one principal when discussing entropy. Rosabeth Moss Kanter (1997) offers a helpful insight with respect to the notion that if a change doesn't immediately produce results, it is tempting to move on to the next new thing: "The difference between success and failure is often just a matter of time: staying with the project long enough to overcome the unexpected developments, political problems, or fatigue that can come between a great-sounding plan and actual results. A basic truth of management—if not of life—is that nearly everything looks like a failure in the middle. At the same time, of course, the next project always looks more attractive (because it is all promise, fresh, and untried)" (p. 129).

Do not be overconfident if the process gets off to a smooth start; it may be an indicator that something is wrong. The change may have been implemented too fast. Or the staff members, in the beginning, may be holding back their opposition and just going along with a top-down directive. Phil Schlechty (2001) reminds us that "compared to sustaining change, starting change is relatively easy" (p. 39). He points out that this is why more changes are initiated in schools than are sustained. In writing about the challenge of sustaining change, he notes, "Two things sustain change: one is a leader or leadership group that acts as a change agent; the other is a system or group of systems that supports change" (p. 40). This explains why, when the school culture does not have the capacity to sustain a change effort, "the change rarely outlasts the tenure of the change agent" (p. 40). A key leadership task, then, is to study and then create those system conditions that will support and sustain a change.

One must provide rituals and ceremonies to dignify and deal with the loss of previously used methods when appropriate. Often, when a new program is being implemented, previous ways of doing things are discarded before time is taken to see how they may still have a function or perhaps be integrated with new practices. For example, if six-traits writing is implemented, are current approaches to writing just being junked and considered to be educational failures? How can the work of teachers who spent 20 years with the basals be dignified? Can an innovation be brought into a school with an acknowledgment of the elements of success of past practice? Is there a possibility that the old can be combined with the new instructional or curriculum strategy? For example, one principal reflected,:"There are some things that are working in that school and you need to work with people in the school who know what it has been like before. . . . If we did something last year that works, you need to inservice me. If it didn't work, we need to talk about how we can make it different."

For an innovation to succeed, the change and the mind-set for change must take hold in the workplace. If you want to know whether the innovation has occurred, do not just ask the superintendent or the principal or the teachers, visit the classrooms. Then visit the classrooms two years after the project was introduced. Are there now coaches in the school who can train new staff on the innovation? That is, has the change been institutionalized? How is the innovation working in other schools? How is the innovative practice (e.g., authentic assessment, differentiated instruction) being modified and improved? Are high school teachers talking with elementary staff about the change at districtwide functions? All personnel should be learning together throughout the system.

If the change is successfully implemented, eventual satisfaction should be observed throughout the system. The teachers should display satisfaction with the change, students will know of the change and talk about what has taken place, and site and district administrators will be a part of the process, as will parents. A key characteristic should be more schoolwide interaction. In the end, change must be systemic; all elements that are affected by the change must be involved.

Kurt Lewin (1951), the pioneer of Action Research, once said, "If you really want to understand something, try to change it!" Indeed, change is an all-encompassing experience that envelopes both the organization and its members, evoking a multitude of responses. The world is characterized by chaos, unpredictability, and change. The only way to keep up with the changes is by building change into the system. Guiding change so that it is successful is certainly an essential skill of an effective leader. On reflection, we should consider that the change process goes hand in hand with the notion of leader as learner. Indeed, the measure of a leader may well be his or her capacity to understand and work successfully with change—to stimulate it, shape it, nurture it, guide it, manage it, revise it, and keep the change journey going.

REFLECTIONS

This space provides a place for you to write down ideas that have been generated by this chapter, things you want to try, or adaptations of ideas presented here.

1. Think about a change effort that you are anticipating or in which you are currently involved. Which of the concepts presented in this chapter will be most relevant? Why?

2. What does successful change look like? What does poorly conceived/implemented change look like?

3. Review Fullan's (2007) classic insights regarding change and continuous improvement. Select the insights that are most relevant to your school. Consider posting them on a bulletin board near your desk or in the Teacher's Room.

4. Practice listening to individuals as they express concerns about a change. See if you can determine the stage of concern and an appropriate response.

5. What do you see as the two or three easiest traps that a school leader can fall into when trying to implement change? How can these traps be avoided?

6. What insights or new questions do you have as a result of reflecting on the ideas presented in this chapter?

8

Building a Vision and a Mission Together

The future belongs to those who believe in the beauty of their dreams.

—Eleanor Roosevelt

Are students, teachers, administrators, and parents hearing a consistent message about the school's purpose? How would students characterize their school? What would administrators, teachers, and support staff say? What do parents tell newcomers in the community about the school?

■ WHY HAVE A SCHOOL VISION AND MISSION?

The preceding questions all inquire: What does our school stand for? To answer this question with some clarity, a school must have a shared vision—a purpose that can be witnessed in the daily activities of the school. Stephanie Hirsh (1995/1996), executive director of the National Staff Development Council, explains, "A school vision should be a descriptive statement of what the school will be like at a specified time in the future. It uses descriptive words or phrases and sometimes pictures to illustrate what one would expect to see, hear and experience in school at that time. It makes reference to the facility, the curriculum, instruction, assessment, the staff and the community." The vision should be collaboratively developed and reflective of the stakeholders it serves: staff, parents, students, and community members. Special care should be taken to ensure that all students—special and regular education students, students of *all* cultures—be remembered, represented, and included in the vision.

"In contrast to a vision," Hirsh explains, "a mission statement is a succinct, powerful statement on how the school will achieve its vision. It provides guidance for actions on a daily basis. The mission statement answers: What is our purpose? What do we care most about? What must we accomplish? What are the cornerstones of our operations?"

There are as many definitions and descriptions of vision and mission as there are authors writing about the topic and schools trying to define their purpose. Although at first this may seem problematic, this may not be the case because the process of creating a vision and building a mission, which encourages participants to think about a school's purpose, may be more significant than an actual definition. For a vision or mission to be alive, the process must be a participatory one. Being involved in the process brings both ownership and commitment to the vision. Furthermore, it provides the opportunity for faculty members to discuss their values and beliefs related to schooling. For instance, in one high school, teachers talked about the fact that although student performance on high-stakes testing was important, given world affairs it was also important to educate the heart as well as the mind and to develop competencies such as empathy, perspective taking, and self-management.

When considering the vision- and mission-building process, one should keep in mind several ideas that have emerged from the literature on the characteristics of a powerful vision, especially for a learning community. A vision must be shared by the organization, and the organizational members must personally believe in the power of the vision as a force for creative, continuous improvement and as a force that can give personal meaning to their lives (Senge, 1990; Wheatley, 1992). It should be shared by those who are served by the school.

A school vision helps students, teachers, administrators, and parents have a sense of what is important in their particular setting. Knowing what is important helps those involved with the school make choices. It helps administrators set priorities, teachers construct lessons, and students find meaning in their work. A vision brings commitment throughout the system as people work together to create a school in which they personally are stakeholders. They believe in their work. In a Professional Learning Community, the vision and mission galvanize staff to act when it becomes evident that the vision and mission are not being realized. To illustrate when it becomes evident that a student is not learning, staff members committed to the question "How will we respond when a student experiences difficulty in learning?" will do "whatever it takes" to make a difference (DuFour, 2004, pp. 7–11).

The principal should play a major role in transforming the values and beliefs of the school into a vision. In fact, Roland Barth (2001a) defines leadership as "making happen what you believe in" (p. 446). This is accomplished through both symbolic and expressive leadership behaviors. From the symbolic perspective, a principal models and focuses individual attention on what is important. From the expressive side of leadership, principals, talking with teachers, help crystallize and communicate the rationale for a vision and mission and generate shared discussions about what is important in the school. This attention to the meaning of a school leads to the development of a mission statement grounded in the collective beliefs of the staff. The process creates a commitment to shared direction and the energy to pursue it. The shared meaning helps create a team orientation: "Yes, we are working together!" Teachers can be confident that colleagues are working on the same key principles with students related to academic or social goals on each grade level. Interestingly, when school beliefs and values are internalized, teachers function more freely and effectively—with less supervisory intervention—because they know what is important in that particular school setting (Grimmett, Rostad, & Ford, 1992).

Given the many external pressures and expectations put on schools, staff must remain focused on pursuing the vision lest they risk veering off in one direction after another. Unless staff members have a clear direction, they may be spinning their wheels under the false impression that they are productively moving ahead.

A vision helps members of an organization identify what is important and avoid spending time on what is not. In reviewing the history of management, Drucker (1992) notes that we fail to work "smarter" and only ask "*How* is it [the job] done?" instead of "*What* is the task?" and "*Why* do it?" (p. 97). When our mission is clear, we know what the task is and why we should do it. Thus a school leader, in a setting where a shared vision and mission exists, should be able to answer questions such as the following:

- What kinds of social skills are important to the culture of the school?
- Do the results of teaching and learning have meaning in the workplace once students complete their schooling?
- What are the best teaching strategies and schoolwide traditions to accomplish the intended outcomes?

Peters and Austin (1985) stress that effective principals are "obsessed" with outcomes that represent the beliefs and values of the school. They function as a galvanizing force that propels collective actions toward their accomplishment.

■ SCHOOL ACTIVITIES THAT HIGHLIGHT THE MISSION

The mission should consistently emphasize commitment to students, demonstrated in both talk and actions. During the school day, effective principals discuss educational issues, not Saturday night's faculty party. Successful principals serve as models for teachers, work closely with them, and engage in conversations about teaching, learning, and students. Committed principals ask about students: "Is Manuel improving in math?" "Has Stacey's home situation settled down?" "How has Bobby adjusted to his brother's jail sentence?" They ask teachers: "Is there something I should be doing that I am not?" "How might I support you in pursuing the mission of our school through classroom and schoolwide activities?" Bennis and Nanus (1985) emphasize that getting "the message across unequivocally at every level is an absolute key" (p. 43). The message—the school mission—should be reiterated as often as possible: orally, in e-mails, during faculty meetings, at parent gatherings, and when working in classrooms with students.

At one middle school, students take a homework folder home every evening. The mission is printed on the inside cover. Sixth and seventh graders must have signatures from parents indicating that homework has been completed. Students in the eighth grade carry the same folder but sign nightly for themselves. Often a slogan is developed that encapsulates the mission. This short version of the mission might appear on stationery, binders, or T-shirts to remind everyone of the mission.

The most effective way to communicate the mission is by personal example. A principal should spend time with students (low, medium, and high achievers) when possible, know their names, and join in celebrating student achievement and good citizenship. To illustrate, principals should use their offices to hear third graders read and share lunch with the middle school student government, the high school National Honor Society, service clubs, or the varsity basketball team. Principals should spend time on the playground, in halls, and in classrooms. The vision or mission can be reiterated through student recognition assemblies, complimentary notes to teachers, parent nights, bulletin boards that display student work in prominent places, and positive calls home to parents.

A note to faculty on the last day of school can emphasize the mission:

Dear Staff,

On this last day of classes, I just want to reaffirm how much I appreciate your professionalism and dedication to our students.

Reflecting on this year, I can't help but think—extending my thoughts back to last August—that we brought 10 new teachers into our elementary school program, yet we quickly became one unified, professional group. This is a tribute to all of you and our mutual desire to work as a team in the best interest of our kids.

Reflecting back on your expectations for the class, how did you do on your legacy (with the class)? What was the most e_____ _____ _____ ____Will it change next year or remain the _____ _____ _____ _____ e our elementary school mission: let's _____ _____ _____ _____ care.

Thank you for your support _____ _____ _____ _____ dent. Have a special summer.

_____ _____ nnie

[Handwritten note:]

Mission Visibility

- *oral*
- *email*
- *special events*
- *faculty meet.*
- *parent meetings*
- *student meetings*

When discussing school culture _____ _____ _____ _____ ples of activities that can contribute to streng_____

School traditions such as alumni _____ _____ _____ _____ er- ings, and yearly recognitions of me_____ _____ _____ _____ ld a shared sense of community an_____ _____ _____ _____ ls, academic awards banquets, and c_____ to celebrate the granting of tenure to teachers can solidify the values of teachers and others, signal school purposes, and provide a social event to tighten collegial bonds.

It is important to analyze whether these traditions match the school's mission or contradict it. For example, one principal noted, "We were emphasizing collaboration and teamwork. Yet I realized we still had a 'Staff Member of the Month' award!"

To clarify what a school stands for, faculty groups, students, and parents work with the administration to build a school philosophy statement. The process will be slightly different in each school. But as mentioned previously, the process aspect of this activity often is more important than the result. Specific schoolwide, departmental, grade-level, or class goals derived from the mission statement will have stronger roots and a clearer mandate because of the mission-building and goal-setting process. The process and written results also help keep the school leaders accountable.

Let us examine the end result of this process and then explore how a mission statement can be created by school groups. The following document, the philosophy statement of the American Embassy School, helps all involved to see the school vision:

The American Embassy School Philosophy

We believe in the dignity and worth of each student and recognize the importance of their responsibilities to their fellow citizens in the world community.

We believe that all youth should have equal opportunity for education consistent with their individual capabilities and with their personal and social needs.

We believe that change is a constant factor in life. Therefore, education should encourage in students the development of personal values and thinking processes which will facilitate their ability to adapt to a changing society.

We believe that learning is an unbroken activity, continued throughout an individual's life span. Therefore, education should foster independent thinking, exploration and experimentation as a lifelong process.

Based on this philosophy statement, the following goals of the American Embassy School, Elementary Division, were written by the teachers, administration, parents, and school board:

Guided by the general goals of the American Embassy School, the elementary school will:

- Establish a firm foundation in the core curriculum of Reading, Language Arts, Mathematics, Social Studies, and Science
- Enrich the curriculum through age-appropriate exposure to subjects such as Physical Education, Art, Foreign Language, Music, and Technology
- Enable students to gain an understanding and appreciation of India and global issues
- Provide an environment that celebrates and promotes maximum growth and development of children
- Instill an interest in and an eagerness for learning, permitting children to realize their fullest potential
- Recognize and respond to the individual intellectual, aesthetic, physical, emotional, and social developmental patterns of children
- Develop a program of active, student-centered learning based on a progression from concrete to more abstract thinking

■ JOINT ADMINISTRATIVE AND FACULTY MISSION STATEMENT

An interesting variation on developing a schoolwide philosophy statement is for the administrative and teaching staff to create a joint mission statement to define their role as professionals. The following mission statement was developed on a voluntary basis by interested administrators and teachers during several sessions (including Saturday mornings). The statement was shared with the whole administrative and teaching staff for final approval:

The professional staff of the American Embassy School strives to offer the best educational program possible in order to develop the mind and character of each student.

1. Based on the goals of the school, the professional staff determines how to make curriculum and instruction meaningful.

2. Within available means, we prioritize and manage resources and programs to provide the best education possible for our students.

3. We work to effectively communicate goals, objectives, and strategies to parents, students, and each other.

4. We are committed to ongoing professional development for the benefit of our students, ourselves, and each other.

Slogans keep the mission statement alive in the eyes of organizational members. "AES—Where children are challenged in caring classrooms" or "Every person is a learner" can signal to faculty what is important in a particular school setting. In a workshop with the support staff, the slogan "AES—Where every family will always feel welcome" served as a catalyst to institute family friendly procedures for registering students.

■ MISSION-BUILDING ACTIVITY

Although there are several ways to acquire a mission statement—borrowing one, buying one, synthesizing one—the most powerful strategy is to create one. The following technique represents one approach to developing a mission based on the collective visions of the staff, students, and parents. This approach has been used successfully throughout the United States, Canada, Europe (including Great Britain), and Asia.

Materials needed:

- chart paper
- tape
- markers
- large Post-it notes
- index cards

Steps:

1. Explain what a mission statement is. For example, "a mission statement describes the purpose and beliefs of an organization and communicates a vision of what the organization stands for, what its members believe, and what ends will be accomplished in keeping with the purpose and beliefs. It serves as a galvanizing force for action."

2. Build a rationale for a mission statement. This step might include explaining why mission statements are helpful (shared sense of purpose, common direction, energizer) and examining mission statements from other organizations. During this examination, the staff could be asked to analyze the values that seem to be implicit in the mission statement. Identify how a mission statement influences a staff member's life.

3. Invite the staff to take part in the development of the mission statement. Explain that this is an opportunity to synthesize individual staff members' dreams or visions into a statement reached through consensus. This statement will represent the ends to which all within the organization will strive for and commit to.

4. Ask staff members to think for a moment about the place where they would like to send their own very special child to school. How would the child be treated? What would his or her experiences be like? How would he or she feel? Have staff members describe their thoughts on Post-it notes.

5. Now ask them to think about the place where they would like to go to work every day. What would it be like? How would they feel? How would people interact? Have them write these ideas on Post-it notes.

6. Have staff members take their two Post-it notes and fuse them into one. Write these thoughts on an index card.

7. Individuals then meet in table groups of four to six and share their index cards. After they are all read, each table group uses markers and chart paper to create a composite of the individual cards to which all in the group can agree.

8. Pairs of table groups meet and share their charts. They synthesize their two charts into one.

9. Continue the process until the entire group creates one chart that represents the shared visions for the mission of all in the room.

10. If parents and representative students have not been involved in this process, this same procedure may be repeated with them and the products of their work brought to the faculty. The staff could incorporate these charts with the faculty work ones that they created.

11. At another time, a contest could be held and the staff could work together to create a slogan that would encapsulate the mission statement. A mission statement alone, however, will not stay alive unless specific goals are created to accomplish the essence of the mission.

■ DEVELOPING YEARLY SCHOOL IMPROVEMENT GOALS TO ACCOMPLISH THE MISSION

Another excellent exercise to keep the school vision and mission in mind is to develop annual goals, an essential component of School Improvement Plans. Although each state or school district may have specific guidelines, the following process, modified to address each context, can be used to successfully develop goals and/or School Improvement Plans.

The process starts in the spring of a school year, looking toward the following year's opening of school. The teaching staff look at the previous year's goals and divide into about five groups of teachers across grade levels, subject areas, and friendships. (For the first year, initial goals can be set up using the topic headings such as those listed in the example that follows.) Each group reviews the goals to get the ideas flowing and then answers three questions: What are our major successes this year based on the goals? What are some areas that we still need to improve? What are the recommendations for next year? When the groups reassemble, they listen for common points. (A recorder word processes the common points or posts these ideas on butcher paper.) When three or four groups make the same point (e.g., effectively using common assessments, integrating technology), the teachers know that they are on to something. This energizes and begins focusing the staff for the next year. The faculty fine-tunes the goals during the first month of school and receives individual copies of the final document. The goals should be revisited often during the year by sharing experiences during faculty meetings and professional development days.

Again, it is important to stress that the process of writing specific school goals helps keep the principal and staff accountable. The goals become the "checklist for success" for that year, and ultimately the entire staff is responsible for implementing the goals.

Elementary School Goals

A. Student Expectations

   1. Focus on student responsibility to promote academic and social independence and acceptance of consequences. Stress student courtesy, caring, and tolerance.

   Implementation:

- Tailor the school rules to promote your classroom goals.
- Hold recognition assemblies with special themes (e.g., proper nutritional habits).
- Use "Citizens of the Week" awards to emphasize specific school goals.
- Stress the importance of positive behavior on the school buses.

   2. In the classroom, maintain high expectations and challenge each child.

   Implementation:

- Encourage independent, critical, and divergent student responses.
- Encourage the use of learning centers and enrichment resources or strategies.

3. Raise faculty and student consciousness concerning environmental issues.

   Implementation:

   - Model recycling, energy conservation, and "less is more" themes.

B. Curriculum and Instruction

   1. Promote the new language arts program.

      Implementation:

      - Stress the integration of the language arts.
      - Emphasize content area writing.
      - Recognize the importance of public speaking.
      - Increase the use of Internet and other reference material.

   2. Continue the curriculum review process.

      Implementation—Science Committee:

      - Principles adopted by the Science Committee emphasizing NSTA Standards will be shared with the faculty to make appropriate curriculum decisions.

      Implementation—Reading Committee and Fine Arts Committee:

      - Committees review important curriculum standards and plans for implementation.

   3. Mathematics: Further work with NCTM Standards.

      Implementation:

      - Conduct a math investigation at each grade level.
      - Provide workshops for new staff on NCTM Standards.

   4. Raise consciousness concerning curriculum connections in all subject areas.

   5. Social Studies: Continue refinement of global studies curriculum.

      Implementation:

      - Increase communication for regular classroom lessons on global studies in Grades 2–4.
      - Curriculum resources should be easily available to all teachers.
      - Work on timeline for semester reports (in Grades 3–5) to avoid overload in library and end-of-year pressures.

   6. Place special emphasis on importance of curriculum pacing in all subject areas.

   7. Pilot Telecommunication Technology Project.

   8. Continue to challenge students with appropriate teaching strategies.

      Implementation:

      - Refine questioning and feedback strategies to diagnose student needs and provide appropriate resources.

C. Professional Development

   1. Expand peer coaching activity to include a variety of reflective teaching activities.

   2. Teachers' Center: Continue to expand use.

(Continued)

(Continued)

Implementation:

- With significant number of new staff, assist them to maximize use.
- Highlight professional journal articles with all staff.

3. Portfolios: Extend student options and teacher involvement.

Implementation:

- Develop a buddy system to support teacher dialogue about portfolios.
- Expand the portfolio project to include more science and math options.
- Continue to develop core staff with portfolio expertise.

4. Teacher Professional Growth: Pursue a variety of ways for teachers to assess their growth (e.g., digital videos, teacher portfolios, various observation instruments) and move toward exploring Professional Growth Plans.

5. Faculty meetings: Increase teacher input and participation.

Implementation:

- Provide time for teachers to share ideas and success stories.
- Increase cross-grade-level exchanges.

D. Assessment

1. Experiment with a variety of formative and summative assessments of reading and math.

2. Update report card categories to reflect curriculum changes.

3. Early Childhood Education Center: Systematically use High Scope curriculum and assessment instruments to observe students and tailor the curriculum to individual needs.

E. Parent–Teacher Relations

1. Increase communication with parents through the monthly coffees.

Implementation:

- Assist more non-English-speaking parents who attend coffees.

2. Emphasize effective proactive communications with all parents.

F. General

1. Increase communication between specialist and regular classroom teachers.

Implementation:

- Both groups of teachers should take initiative regarding communication.
- Use daily "Look Book" e-mail to inform specialists of field trips.
- Increase involvement of specialists in grade-level meetings.

Leaders emphasize that what a school stands for should be celebrated and not become simply an idea that gets lost in a dusty file. Individuals working in a school should work to agree on what their school represents. In fact, to take the idea a step further, many educational professionals are now writing professional and personal mission statements to help them take greater ownership of their day-to-day school activities and personal lives. This also helps school leaders keep on track by fostering constant reflection about their personal and professional work and experiences.

Much of what we have stated is encapsulated in the words of Peter Drucker (1992), the giant of 20th-century management theory:

> What distinguishes the leader from the misleader are his goals. Whether the compromise he makes with the constraints of reality—which may involve political, economic, financial or people problems—are compatible with his mission and goals or lead away from them determines whether he is an effective leader. And whether he holds fast to a few basic standards (exemplifying them in his own conduct), or whether "standards" for him are what he can get away with, determines whether the leader has followers or only hypocritical time-servers. (p. 121)

REFLECTIONS

This space provides a place for you to write down ideas that have been generated by this chapter, things you want to try, or adaptations of ideas presented here.

1. Given the school in which you work, consider how a mission statement and slogan might be created.

2. Should the mission statement be chiseled in stone, or should it be a flexible document? Explain.

3. Write a brief mission statement that exemplifies your vision of the good school. Provide two or three examples (paint an image) that show how the vision is realized in the day-to-day school activities.

4. What insights or new questions do you have as a result of reflecting on the ideas presented in this chapter?

PART IV

Working Together to Build a Learning Organization

9

Enhancing Teacher Growth Through Supervision and Evaluation Practices Designed to Promote Student Learning

I ask teachers, before observing, "How will you know that all students are engaged? How are you going to promote their engaged behavior? What kind of samples of student work do you want to bring to our postobservation conference?"

—A principal's voice

■ ISSUES AND DILEMMAS

If schools are to be regarded as learning communities, everyone in a school must engage in the study of what constitutes learning. Our vision of lifelong learning for students can hold greater meaning if teachers and administrators have an ongoing conversation to improve their performance. Yet in many schools, teachers feel intimidated when principals walk into their classrooms and are especially fearful of the observation and conferencing process. This is a clear indicator that the traditional administrative evaluation process has failed. Ideally, principals should frequently visit classrooms to see, share, affirm, and celebrate the important work of schools. Interestingly, teachers often resent the glowing written recommendations from principals who never seriously observed in their classrooms. This tells us that teachers feel "cheated" about the assessment of their performance and the missed opportunities for professional growth and instructional conversations that could have been fostered by the principal.

Beyond the anecdotal evidence that administrators should visit classrooms to support teachers and celebrate learning, research demonstrates that student achievement is related to intentional classroom visits by the principal and a principal's knowledge of and ability to assist teachers with regard to curriculum, instruction, and assessment. Kathleen Cotton's (2003) influential work, *Principals and Student Achievement,* concludes that successful schools employ instructional leaders who observe classes and provide feedback to teachers while monitoring student progress data in a collaborative culture that supports continuous improvement. Marzano, Waters, and McNulty's (2005, pp. 52–61) research on 21 responsibilities of school leaders reinforce Cotton's findings. Responsibilities directly relating to instructional leadership include the following:

- intellectual stimulation (i.e., encouraging collaborative staff dialogue with cutting-edge ideas to support innovative change)
- involvement in curriculum, instruction, and assessment (i.e., hands-on involvement with teachers in classrooms)
- knowledge of curriculum, instruction, and assessment (i.e., an understanding of research and Best Practice to inform teachers)
- monitoring/evaluating (i.e., providing feedback and guidance to teachers concerning data related to student achievement)
- visibility (i.e., showing up in classrooms and other school venues on a daily basis to support teaching and learning)

As noted in Chapter 2, Deming stresses that when employees are having problems, management must learn to take responsibility, for the system is likely failing the employees. Deming opposes performance evaluations, merit ratings, and annual reviews (Walton, 1986, pp. 90–92). Although we maintain that practical considerations relating to schools and current district, state, and national educational polices make it difficult to fully embrace Deming's view on evaluation, we strongly believe that the dialogue he stimulated in education may have a profound impact on schools and the literature about schooling (e.g., English & Hill, 1994). Moreover, Deming stresses that the old administrative paradigm of intimidation and control lent itself to *snoopervising* and caused bitterness on the part of teachers as principals told teachers what they were "doing wrong." That model has no place in schools functioning as learning-focused communities. Thus we need to move away from operating on fear so the notion of growth can be built in from day one. It is important that principals communicate with teachers that supervision and evaluation processes are intended to build their capacity to promote student learning. Risk-taking behavior cannot flourish in an environment of intimidation.

In this chapter we discuss essential ingredients for successful supervision, effective instructional strategies, brain-compatible practices related to cognitive science, clinical supervision strategies, tips for conferencing and observing, the use of walk-throughs for generating authentic feedback, guidelines related to evaluation and legal concerns, and final thoughts on supervision and evaluation.

Supervision is providing support for teachers so they become the best they can be. Implicit in this definition is the development and refinement of a knowledge base and craft practice regarding effective teaching and learning. Supervisors provide resources and promote informal and formal conversations with and among teachers to affect curriculum, teaching, assessment, student learning, and professional development. For example, recommending a professional journal to a teacher or sharing an article with the staff may be an important contribution made by a school principal. Additionally, providing support for interdisciplinary planning, assisting teachers in developing an advanced-placement high school course, or facilitating a professional forum on assessment based on state standards are all activities that can be supported directly or indirectly by the school leader in an effort to foster professional growth.

■ ESSENTIAL INGREDIENTS FOR SUCCESSFUL SUPERVISION

To maximize the impact of supervision, principals must develop an honest, caring, and trusting relationship with teachers. Implicit in the process of supervision is the notion that adults have innate needs and desires to improve, grow, and learn. These desires are essential characteristics in a healthy school culture. The early foundational research of Herzberg, Mausner, and Snyderman (1959) and Maslow (1954) demonstrates that as lower-level factors such as physiological needs and safety are satisfied, motivation comes from "finding one's niche," the work itself, and the sense of achievement. These, in turn, foster the development of self-esteem that allows risk-taking behavior so that teachers become motivated to stretch and grow. Additionally, teacher needs for assistance vary depending on one's life stage, teaching skills, gender, personal events, career expectations, and commitment to the job. Principals must honor and address these individual needs to help teachers develop professionally and personally (Glickman, Gordon, & Ross-Gordon, 2007).

As principals actively learn from the teachers and students around them, and acknowledge that learning, everyone in the school becomes empowered with the knowledge that his or her ideas are influential. This notion can help create a risk-taking climate in the school. If we really mean that the leader is a learner, then the principal should expect to learn a great deal through the supervision and evaluation process—especially related to the particular context of a teacher's classroom decisions (e.g., Why that decision, at that moment?). This gets into the ecology of individual classrooms and gives special meaning to each teacher decision and classroom event. Furthermore, the leader-as-learner model can be transferred to the student as teachers show students that, as teachers, they are learning every day.

The ideal dialogue between principals and teachers can, in some ways, be seen as analogous to the process of scientific discovery. When old ideas are found to be ineffective or "mistakes" are discovered, the scientific community celebrates because an advancement has occurred. We need to celebrate responsible risk taking and "mistakes."

A postobservation conference with an experienced kindergarten teacher effectively illustrated this process. The lesson objective was to help students identify a variety of animal coats (e.g., skin, fur, scales, feathers) and recognize how the coats protect the animals. The teacher opened the lesson by showing a variety of animal coats and had the students touch them. She then asked the following question: "What do you think the fur and feathers do in the rain?" The kindergartners answered: "Get wet!" The answer she expected was: "The coats or coverings protect the animals." The students did not see protection at all—they saw a lot of wet animals!

The principal listened carefully as the teacher expertly analyzed her lesson. This experienced teacher noted that regardless of how long one teaches, "we tend to focus in on the lesson objective from an adult's viewpoint instead of thinking about what a child might say." As a supervisor, the principal was fortunate to be on the listening end of this conference as the teacher expressed an insight of universal meaning for all teachers.

A discussion of supervision would be inadequate without providing a model of evaluation that can be used in schools. However, an important issue should first be addressed. Practitioners are constantly advised to separate supervision from evaluation. Although conceptually it may be ideal to separate the formative and summative process (e.g., supervision and evaluation), the political reality and the day-to-day interactions between teachers and principals make this an unrealistic aim. Reality, for the principal practitioner, is that you can never fully separate supervision and evaluation. A helpful way to conceptualize the interrelationship between supervision and evaluation is to think of supervision as the formative process that allows for several "dress rehearsals." The evaluation is the summative process in which institutionalized state and district guidelines are used to assess teacher performance. Although most supervisory textbooks remind us that the formative process is descriptive and nonjudgmental, again, reality reminds us that it is almost impossible to avoid a degree of summative interpretation; we all seek to know if we are successful when teaching. Figure 9.1 demonstrates the interrelationship between these two concepts.

It is important that the supervision or evaluation process is nonintimidating and emphasizes the growth orientation of both functions. This idea can be shared with the entire faculty at the beginning of the year as well as during individual conferences with teachers. Most teachers are good to excellent, but we constantly talk about the problems of firing 5 percent. Certainly, it is important to uphold standards of excellence. After assisting a marginal teacher, if no growth occurs within the allowed time period, the principal should document the teacher's lack of progress and seek nonrenewal using a legally defensible approach. For the most part, these cases tend to represent a small percentage of the staff (see Guidelines Related to Evaluation and Legal Concerns later in this chapter). We need to focus on the other 95 percent and keep them motivated and excited about their growth.

Even champions need coaches, and educators need to continually provide feedback to all teachers, including the best ones. As Blanchard and Johnson (1983) stress in *The One Minute Manager,* "Feedback is the Breakfast of Champions" (p. 67). Principals need to keep that idea in mind. Principals can model this notion by asking teachers for feedback regarding the effectiveness of the principals' supervisory practices.

By emphasizing the theme of growth, the supervisory climate is enhanced and the entire school takes great strides toward becoming a community of learners. One principal reported:

> One of my most productive conferences was with an expert teacher who was trying specific cooperative learning techniques for the first time. My job with her was just as important as with the marginal teacher. I needed to do what I could to provide meaningful data, ask questions to foster reflection and analysis, and to keep her motivation high. What she gained in her experiment with cooperative learning was a clinic for both of us on what should be included in a good cooperative learning lesson. I gained insight into what supervisory approaches were helpful. I won't have to worry about burnout with that teacher for a long time, because she was engaged and motivated by the learning process related to the implementation of cooperative learning and the opportunity to reflect and analyze the lesson and its effects. Furthermore, her enthusiasm will hopefully stimulate other members of the staff, and her students!

Figure 9.1   Formative Assessment and Summative Evaluation Continuum

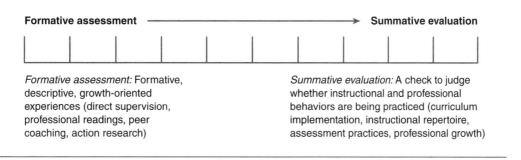

Formative assessment ————————————————→ Summative evaluation

Formative assessment: Formative, descriptive, growth-oriented experiences (direct supervision, professional readings, peer coaching, action research)

Summative evaluation: A check to judge whether instructional and professional behaviors are being practiced (curriculum implementation, instructional repertoire, assessment practices, professional growth)

A critical role of principals is to help teachers fine-tune their professional skills. A key is to encourage teachers to reflect on what is taking place in their classrooms, in relation to instructional and curricular decisions. Although we cannot assume that all teachers are equally reflective and thoroughly engaged in a professional development journey, most are. Those who are not can be assisted by the principal's direct supervision or work with teacher leaders and/or coaches. As progress occurs, the principal responds to the teacher's growth by offering a differentiated menu of professional development activities from which to choose. Only time will tell whether the teacher will become an outstanding educator, but an indication of growth will certainly be the complexity of discussions about teaching, learning, and assessment with the principal and other colleagues (Glickman et al., 2007).

It is a principal's responsibility to facilitate and expose teachers to a variety of useful, relevant instructional ideas. In this role, principals can foster teachers' reflective practices to help them analyze their teaching and interactions with students. At other times, teachers may request direct intervention from the principal. One teacher noted: "What if I am missing something that is really a problem in my teaching? How will I know if I cannot determine that as an area of weakness in myself?"

Beyond the classroom, establishing a professional DVD and video library of effective techniques, teaching episodes, and important topics for discussion can also help. Showing episodes during faculty meetings or encouraging individuals or groups of teachers to view and share ideas can help professionals reflect on their decisions. As Glickman et al. (2007) suggest, in addition to direct assistance, individuals grow as a consequence of "curriculum development, professional development, group development and action research" (p. 9).

A workshop for teachers who are new to a school, reviewing the philosophy behind the school supervision process, can certainly help provide the rationale and reduce teacher anxiety about the process. Moreover, principals who implement a new system owe the staff an explanation about it. Also, longtime teaching veterans in a school can often use a refresher concerning how evaluation, formative assessment, and professional development are related, and the principal can benefit significantly from staff comments during a faculty meeting or workshop on how the process is going.

■ EFFECTIVE INSTRUCTIONAL STRATEGIES

The link between supervision and effective instruction should be an inextricable one based on solid research. That is, the supervision and evaluation process should be driven by an understanding of cognitive science, how the brain processes information, and the necessary elements that contribute to learning. This focus on brain-compatible learning also broadens traditional notions of supervision and evaluation by including an affective dimension. Research on brain functioning seems to indicate, for instance, that when learners feel at risk, their capacity to learn is reduced considerably because much of the mind's focus is turned to the task of establishing a sense of well-being. Therefore, the learning environment and the attitudes and perceptions toward learning tasks should be included in any supervisory or evaluation focus.

Although many teaching strategies exist, it is helpful to examine some general themes that often characterize core elements of effective instruction. Cognitive science, enriched by recent research related to "the social and cultural contexts of learning" (Bransford, Brown, & Cocking, 2000, p. 8) has enabled educators to gain a greater understanding of important principles that can lead to enhanced student learning. Constructivist learning is certainly an essential feature of the science of learning, but Bransford et al. caution educators to take a balanced position, considering the complexity of teaching:

A common misconception regarding "constructivist" theories of knowing (that existing knowledge is used to build new knowledge) is that teachers should never tell students anything directly but, instead, should always allow them to construct knowledge for themselves. This perspective confuses a theory of pedagogy (teaching) with a theory of knowing. . . . [However] there are times, usually after people have first grappled with issues on their own, that "teaching by telling" can work extremely well. (p. 11)

Based on this balanced approach to teaching and learning, Bransford et al. (2000) suggest that three major principles have far reaching implications for teaching:

1. Students come to the classroom with preconceptions about how the world works. If their initial understanding is not engaged, they may fail to grasp the new concepts and information that are taught, or they may learn them for purposes of a test but revert to their preconceptions outside the classroom.

2. To develop competence in an area of inquiry, students must: (a) have a deep foundation of factual knowledge, (b) understand facts and ideas in the context of a conceptual framework, and (c) organize knowledge in ways that facilitate retrieval and application.

3. A "metacognitive" approach to instruction can help students learn to take control of their own learning by defining learning goals and monitoring their progress in achieving them. (pp. 14–18)

The practical application of these important findings is demonstrated below by considering how teachers prepare students for learning and use brain-compatible teaching strategies to maximize student learning. These concepts and strategies are essential tools for supervisors who serve as instructional leaders.

Preparing the Student's Mind for Learning

The minds of the learners first need to be prepared for the learning that is about to occur. This requires a meaningful focus of the learners' attention. Once this happens, it is important that an outcome be stated so that students will know where the lesson is headed. Even with a discovery lesson, a general outcome can be stated (e.g., "By the end of this lesson, you will be able to solve this mystery!"). To begin instruction at the appropriate level of difficulty and resolve any preconceived misconceptions about what is to be taught, it is helpful to assess what students already know about the topic of the lesson and what they would like to know.

Because the mind stores information according to whether it perceives that there is a future purpose, it is helpful either to provide a meaningful purpose or to engage students in identifying the possible reasons for the lesson. Furthermore, if there are prior learnings that may assist the students in this lesson, they should be recalled as well.

Instruction

Instruction usually consists of three parts: input, modeling or demonstration, and active involvement or rehearsal. Input can be provided in several ways. The teacher may provide information, perform an experiment, show a DVD, assign a reading, or construct a model. Or input may be provided by students, such as explaining a math investigation to the class. Following this, it is helpful to provide a demonstration or model so that the learners can see what was introduced during the input phase. Finally, students should be provided with an opportunity to rehearse what has just been taught and modeled. The key to the rehearsal is that students should be able to demonstrate to the teacher that they comprehend the intended input and, as appropriate, that they can either recall the information or perform the task.

Practice

To develop fluency and accuracy, and to promote long-term remembering, students should practice the new learning under the teacher's guidance in the same manner that the skill ultimately will be assessed. When students have demonstrated that they can perform the skill independently, they should be encouraged to practice in a way that can be retrieved and recalled during assessment. Teacher guidance is essential to ensure perfect practice. (Errors practiced are difficult to eliminate.) This increases the likelihood that students will store or internalize correctly the information that has been taught. Students need opportunities to revisit previously taught content so that this content remains vibrant and accessible over time.

These core elements can be helpful as part of the framework for discussing lesson plans, observing a lesson, and assessing the extent to which the teacher accomplished his or her desired goals, based on student understanding, using work samples as evidence of understanding.

■   BRAIN-COMPATIBLE TEACHING PRACTICES

In addition to the elements discussed previously, the following 21 brain-compatible teaching practices offer teachers specific strategies to maximize student learning:

- Immediately engage the attention of learners when they come into the classroom. The activities need to be of high interest and anchored in benchmarks or standards. They can be used to build readiness for a lesson about to be taught or review a previously taught concept. (The brain remembers best what comes first, and next best what comes last. Information lingers in the sensory memory only three-fourths of a second. Then information is either forgotten or sent to short-term memory. If the teacher doesn't engage the attention of the learners, something else will!)
- Routinely post lesson outcomes, benchmarks, or standards in a specific place on the chalkboard so students can refer to them. An agenda for the day and homework assignments should also have a regular place on the board. (Advance organizers trigger attention and are linked to promoting memory.)
- Use state standards to design curriculum and instruction and assess student work. (Research indicates that high-performing, high-poverty schools implemented this practice with notable results. Making the brain aware of performance targets increases attention.)
- Involve students in active learning experiences that engage a variety of learning channels: auditory, visual, kinesthetic. Seek ways to structure activities so that students may have an opportunity to use a variety of intelligences (visual-spatial, mathematical-logical, verbal-linguistic, musical, bodily-kinesthetic, interpersonal, intrapersonal, naturalist; Gardner, 2006). (Individuals remember only 10–20 percent of what they hear. Active involvement focuses attention and increases the probability that students will remember what they have "rehearsed.")
- Engage students in learning tasks such as experiments or experiential activities that require them to actively construct meaning. (The brain actually forms new neural connections when it is actively engaged in "meaning making" based on experiences.)

- Chunk curriculum content appropriate to the developmental age of the learner. (The capacity of short-term memory appears to develop with developmental age. This has major implications for the design and delivery of curriculum.)

- Change activities at least four or five times within the context of a lesson. For example, students may first be actively engaged in a warm-up activity, report out, experience direct instruction, create a graphic organizer to summarize learnings, stand, pair and share their work (with other students), and respond to a prompt in their learning journals. (The more firsts and lasts within a lesson, the more memorable its content.)

- Provide opportunities for meaningful "rehearsal" or practice after initial content has been introduced. Periodically provide review activities to distribute rehearsal opportunities over time. (The more opportunities a student has to meaningfully rehearse, the greater the chance that information will move from short-term to long-term memory. Providing rehearsal opportunities using a variety of learning channels will maximize the probability that long-term retention will occur.)

- Structure opportunities for movement during learning experiences. (Movement provides oxygen to the brain, increases attention, and, in some cases, integrates communication between the right and left hemispheres.)

- Seek opportunities to integrate the curriculum. For example, in the well-known *Dear America* series, students read autobiographical accounts written by fictional characters based on actual historical events. So history comes alive in a language arts context. (Subjects are not found in isolation in the real world. Long-term memory stores information in networks of association. The more associations or connections a student has with a particular fact or concept, the more easily that information can be recalled.)

- Use humor related to content. For example, concepts may be taught using a cartoon lecture. (Humor increases retention up to 15 percent!)

- Engage students in a variety of tasks that require higher-order thinking skills. (Analysis, synthesis, and evaluation tasks require students to access and use remembered information to foster new neural connections in the brain.)

- Provide for a variety of flexible grouping contexts that engage students in working with different classmates. (Much learning occurs through social interaction. Students can receive instruction appropriate to their learning needs and pace in small-group settings. As students master academic content, they simultaneously develop skills in working with and appreciating others. For many students, a small-group setting reduces anxiety. According to brain researchers Caine and Caine [1991] the brain functions optimally in a state of *relaxed alertness.*)

- Assign and grade relevant homework that extends rehearsal opportunities and reflects how content will ultimately be assessed. (Students learn more when they complete homework that is graded, commented on, and discussed by their teachers.) Whenever possible, engage students in developing rubrics to assess their work. This increases their awareness of key attributes of quality work and lends credibility and authenticity to the grading process.

- Match instruction and assessment practices that are consistent with how standards and benchmarks ultimately will be assessed and the setting in which assessment will occur. (Research on state dependence indicates that content will be most easily recalled when it is assessed under the same conditions as when it was originally learned.)

- Use authentic assessment measures. Engage students in applying new and recent learnings in a real-world context. (The brain remembers based on what is embedded in a particular context. For example, to remember what they had for dinner last Saturday night, most people will have to first remember where they were.)

- Provide opportunities for students to summarize their learnings in written or verbal form and communicate them to others. (Summarizing strengthens neural connections. When students rehearse through reciprocal teaching, retention is enhanced 65–90 percent!)
- Monitor and invite students to monitor their own progress. (Self-monitoring and feedback can be sources of intrinsic motivation and may increase attention and focus.)
- Select assignments that are challenging and interesting. Provide a support structure to help students achieve success in a psychologically safe environment. (The brain learns best in an atmosphere of *high challenge and low threat;* Caine & Caine, 1991.)
- Create a learning environment where students perceive that they are (1) safe from physical, verbal, or psychological harm; (2) free to experiment and take risks when learning; (3) connected in their relationships with others, including the teacher and other students; and (4) valued members of the class. (Sylwester [1995] notes that "emotion drives attention which drives learning and memory" [p. 72]. If students feel safe and cared for, if teachers and others are responsive to their needs, students' ability to focus and learn will be enhanced.)
- Encourage parents to stimulate their children's intellectual development and to provide a caring, responsive climate in the home. For instance, teachers can ask parents to help their children rehearse a presentation to be given in class or discuss the results of a recent class science experiment. (Environment plays a key role in brain development and intelligence. Verbal interaction with children, for example, has a direct impact on language and vocabulary development. A caring, responsive climate contributes to the development of a child's sense of self-esteem.)

In addition to these 21 practices, Marzano, Pickering, and Pollock (2001) have identified nine powerful research-based instructional strategies. These strategies can make a significant difference for students if employed effectively. The nine strategies apply to all subject areas, all grade levels, and all socioeconomic groups. These strategies include comparing and contrasting; summarizing and note taking; reinforcing effort and providing recognition; homework and practice; nonlinguistic representations; cooperative learning; setting objectives and providing feedback; generating and testing hypotheses; and questions, cues, and advance organizers. These strategies could be reviewed during the supervisory process to support teachers in planning instruction, or as part of a small-group or faculty-wide staff development initiative.

■ INCREASING TEACHER AND ADMINISTRATIVE REFLECTION THROUGH CLINICAL SUPERVISION

A four-step variation on the clinical supervision model can be used to implement an examination of these teaching and learning strategies. With this model, the emphasis moves from the sole concentration on observable teacher behaviors to more important conversations and reflections about planning, teaching, learning, student work, and assessment. Thus the model serves as a catalyst for talking about teaching and learning. A critical part of this model is the preobservation conference that precedes the teaching. As Costa and Garmston (1991) have stated, "a good preobservation conference is worth six observations." The preobservation conference provides an opportunity for the teacher to unpack the thinking behind the planning process. It also provides a reference point to compare expected and actual outcomes in the postobservation conference.

1. The Preobservation Conference

Usually the teacher will choose a lesson, the key points to be observed, and the desired type of data-gathering method. There needs to be a focus on building rapport, trust, and self-esteem. Listening to the teacher during the conference is a key supervisory objective. If the teacher talks more during the conference than the principal, declare the conference a success. Why? Because the teacher is talking and thinking about the teaching and learning processes. Principals have to get away from the notion that it is their role to "run" the conference. However, this does not preclude asking effective questions to stimulate discussion. Possible questioning topics may relate to student work samples, addressing standards, brain-compatible learning, diversity, equity, students with disabilities, English Language Learners, problem solving, engaging all students, the complexity of group work, and valuing teacher decision making. One experienced principal often tells teachers during preobservation conferences, "I value your ability to make instructional decisions on the spot." Specific questions may include: What are your expectations for students? When teaching, how do you know that students are engaged? How do you know they are progressing? How do you know that the standards are being achieved? How are you coping with the standards and specific challenges of special needs students? The more specific the preobservation conference discussion, the more fine-tuned the lesson is likely to be. As the lesson unfolds, data is gathered based on the focus identified in the preobservation conference. This provides feedback for analysis that will occur in the postobservation conference. Figure 9.2 is an example of a preobservation form that teachers can use to focus the preobservation conference and lesson.

2. Observation

Traditionally, this has been the key step. The supervisor must work to reduce a teacher's anxiety about this step and stress that the primary purpose of the observation is to provide data from instructional episodes and student work samples for discussion during the postobservation conference. Students may be informed about the observation so that they can see that adults also continue to grow. For example, "Mrs. Johnson will be coming in to watch our class today. She'll be interested in discovering what helps us learn." With the popularity of principal and teacher walk-throughs, a visit from the principal is no longer an unusual event in many schools. During this step it is crucial to observe teacher behaviors, students, and student work samples. Schlechty (2001) advises, "Rather than observing the classroom to see how the teacher is performing, the principal observes the classroom (and perhaps interviews students and reviews assignments as well) to determine the extent to which students are engaged, persist, and experience a sense of accomplishment and satisfaction as a result of what they are asked to do" (p. 144).

3. Reflections on the Observation

With this four-step model, solitary reflection is essential and critical to the success of this process. If a supervision model is used that includes pre- and postobservation conferences, then it is vitally important that the teacher has an adequate opportunity to analyze the lesson before the postobservation conference.

Along with student work, the principal should provide the type of data requested by the teacher. The teacher may then review the principal's script-tape (e.g., written play-by-play of the lesson) and examine the principal's diagram of the verbal flow during the lesson, an analysis of questioning strategies, a digital video or audio recording, or the principal's summary of the lesson. The principal will need time to prepare the observational material for teachers if both descriptive and interpretive data are needed.

Figure 9.2   Preobservation Conference Form

PREOBSERVATION CONFERENCE FORM

Teacher's Name _____ Today's Date _____

Subject _____

1. Lesson Objective: What do you want the students to know and be able to do as a result of this lesson? (If appropriate, please bring student work samples to our postobservation conference to support the objective that emerged during this lesson.)

2. How does this lesson "fit" into the subject curriculum? Are there particular state or district standards or benchmarks that will be addressed by this lesson?

3. What background knowledge/skills do the students have for this specific lesson or the major topic/unit that includes this lesson?

4. Do you anticipate any particular difficulties that the class or special needs students may encounter during this lesson?

5. Would you like me to observe any particular students during the lesson or ask students specific questions about their learning?

6. What will be the key aspects/steps of this lesson? What activities will the students engage in during the lesson to meet your expectations? Let's remember that the lesson may include surprises that we could not have anticipated that may alter the sequenced steps of the lesson. (If you prefer, attach your lesson plan to this form.)

7. What teaching strategies/techniques/issues and student learnings do you want me to concentrate on during the observation for discussion during the postobservation conference? Suggested areas for feedback include teacher decision making, motivation, student work evidence, use of rubrics, student voice, providing feedback to students, reinforcing students, student participation, equity in the classroom, respecting diversity, tapping into preexisting knowledge, constructivists techniques, addressing standards, domain-specific concepts, lesson sequence/logic, questioning strategies, traditional and alternative assessment strategies, opening or lesson closure, logic or difficulty of ideas, pacing, checking for understanding, atmosphere in the classroom, classroom management, clarity, higher-level thinking, problem solving, modeling new learning, use of technology, variety of activities, "out of the box" teaching techniques, organization of the lesson, creativity and imagination in the classroom, risk taking, student discovery of ideas, lab procedures, engaging all students, cooperative learning, peer support, use of instructional resources, teacher-centered behaviors, student-centered lessons, brain-compatible learning, multiple intelligences, and addressing special needs students. What have I missed that you would like feedback on? (It is recommended that only two or three strategies, techniques, or issues are selected for the observation and for discussion during the postobservation conference.)

8. What else do we need to discuss?

Date, room, and time of lesson _____

Please fill out this preobservation form before or, if necessary, during our conference. Your comments on the form will provide the basis for the preobservation conference, the observation, and the postobservation conference. I look forward to visiting your class and to our discussions!

Another approach is to provide the descriptive data to the teacher immediately following the lesson without any interpretive supervisory comments so that the teacher may analyze it before the postobservation conference. The teacher, however, should be invited to reflect on the lesson and make observations before examining the data. The teacher analysis of the lesson may include a wide range of comments, such as why spur-of-the-moment decisions were made or what surprises occurred during the lesson. It may also include a comparison between the reflective interpretive data and the descriptive observational data.

4. The Postobservation Conference

The goal of the postobservation conference is to encourage the teacher to reflect on his or her decisions related to student learning (e.g., What happened as expected? What happened differently?). The teacher should have an opportunity to verbalize a comparison between his or her recollections of the lesson and the actual data from the observation.

Again, the teacher should dominate the discussion and, in most cases, decide where to go next. Interestingly, when trust is established, teachers prefer to take the initiative in stating that a lesson was successful or did not go well. When the teacher spots a problem, he or she takes ownership and is in the driver's seat in recommending ways to fine-tune a teaching strategy. As a conference facilitator, it is critical that the supervisor remain focused on the topics agreed upon during the preobservation conference unless behaviors occurred during the lesson that were unacceptable. Moreover, the conference can provide the opening for the next observation or another professional growth activity.

■ TIPS FOR CONFERENCING AND OBSERVING

Obviously, the preceding supervision model has many variations and depends greatly on the experience of the teacher, the experience of the principal, the context of the school and students, and, most important, on the relationship between the supervisor and the teacher. The tips that follow are intended to generate additional ideas to enhance the supervisory process.

Using the Student Learning Nexus Model. It is always helpful for supervisors to have a model related to teaching and learning to help them see the global complexities of a lesson or series of lessons. The Student Learning Nexus Model (Figure 9.3) can be used as a compact framework for principals, coaches, teacher leaders, and central office personnel when considering aspects of instruction, curriculum, assessment, and the classroom environment as they relate to student learning. The model also can facilitate dialogue between supervisors and teachers during a clinical supervision conference or among teachers using cognitive coaching and/or peer coaching strategies. Note that each component of the model is interrelated and aligned with the other components. Thus, if a district has a first-rate group of teachers but a curriculum that lacks coherence, then meaningful and successful student learning is unlikely. Supervisors, teachers, and district administrators should feel free to add components to the Student Learning Nexus Model to meet local contextual needs. In essence, this model is intended to enrich the conversation about teaching and learning.

Use student work. Using student work during supervisory conferences helps teachers connect their planning and teaching efforts with the outcomes students produce. Invite teachers to bring student work from the lesson when discussing the lesson outcomes. This provides evidence to discuss: What did the students do? What did they accomplish? Were the objectives reached? Were students engaged in meaningful work? In most cases, this is very satisfying for the teacher and gives the principal a feeling for what is taking place in class. One experienced principal recommended

Figure 9.3 Student Learning Nexus Model: Balancing Instruction, Curriculum, and Assessment in a Healthy Environment

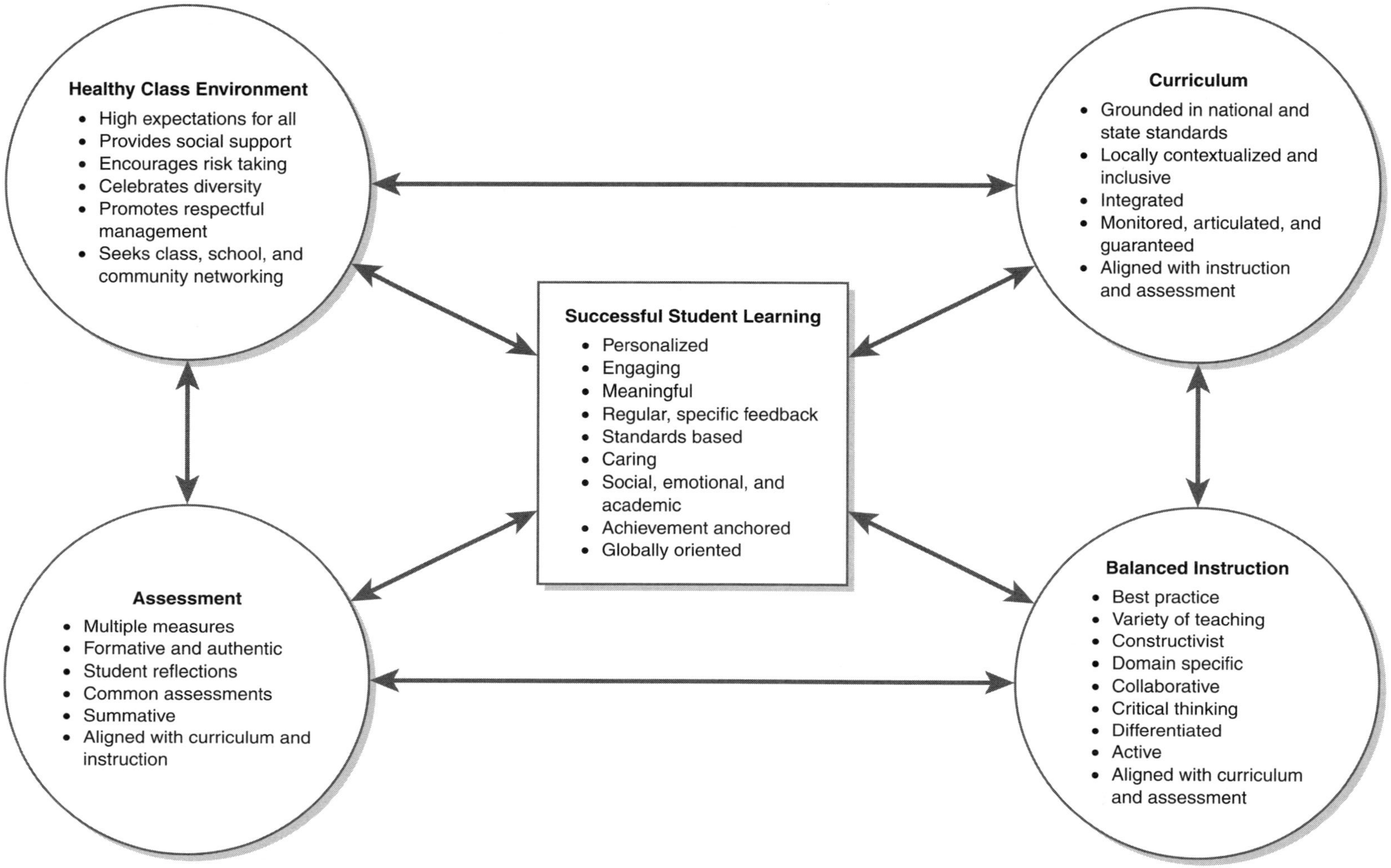

Curriculum
- Grounded in national and state standards
- Locally contextualized and inclusive
- Integrated
- Monitored, articulated, and guaranteed
- Aligned with instruction and assessment

Balanced Instruction
- Best practice
- Variety of teaching
- Constructivist
- Domain specific
- Collaborative
- Critical thinking
- Differentiated
- Active
- Aligned with curriculum and assessment

Successful Student Learning
- Personalized
- Engaging
- Meaningful
- Regular, specific feedback
- Standards based
- Caring
- Social, emotional, and academic
- Achievement anchored
- Globally oriented

Healthy Class Environment
- High expectations for all
- Provides social support
- Encourages risk taking
- Celebrates diversity
- Promotes respectful management
- Seeks class, school, and community networking

Assessment
- Multiple measures
- Formative and authentic
- Student reflections
- Common assessments
- Summative
- Aligned with curriculum and instruction

addressing the following issues and questions during a postobservation conference related to student work:

> Remember, all those wonderful activities may not show meaningful work. Prudently ask, during appropriate conferences: What is the point of the lesson? What are the "learnings"? Do the student products reflect the lesson objectives? Let's look at a range of products, good products, unsatisfactory products. What are the rubrics? Are aspects of the student work reflective of state assessments? Keep in mind that the products at the postconference will show if quality work has been going on all year, not just during the two or three conferences.

Digital videos. If a teacher records a lesson for an observation, consider recording only part of the lesson: the opening, the student group work, the teacher modeling, the questioning, or the closure. A 10-minute video will easily lead to a 45-minute conversation.

Using handheld or laptop computers to collect observation data. Increasingly, technology has enabled supervisors to conveniently gather classroom observation data and quickly share the information with teachers by using handheld or laptop computers. These instruments can be used during traditional observations or during walk-throughs. Software programs have been developed to collect classroom data on topics such as student responses, Bloom's Taxonomy, time on task, teacher patterns of movement, wait time, inappropriate student behavior, quality of teacher directions, and observed behaviors during walk-throughs. Companies supporting these technologies stress that state and district terminology and evaluation criteria can be entered into the programs to customize the resources for local use. As with any new technologies, it is important that school leaders first pilot techniques to minimize glitches before the instruments are used on a regular basis. Also, teachers need to be informed during faculty, department, or grade-level meetings about any new observation and data-gathering systems that will be implemented.

Include student input. Students can add an important dimension to the evaluation process. One principal recorded the preobservation conference, lesson, and postobservation conference with an experienced member of the staff. The teacher was helping the principal refine his conferencing techniques as he provided feedback on her teaching. The lesson was on dividing fractions. The teacher was very disappointed with how she began the lesson, and she shared this sentiment with the principal and her students after the lesson. She felt that their difficulty during the lesson was due to a lack of clarity on her part. The students told her that she was "way off" regarding her feelings about the lesson and that this particular lesson was one of the most challenging and interesting lessons of the school year. The students explained that the lesson really made them think, helped them actually see how to get the answers, and made them realize that more than one correct answer was possible. That experience helped the teacher and supervisor reflect on how difficult it is to assess lesson success.

■ WALK-THROUGHS, SNAPSHOTS, OR DRIVE-BYS

In our book *If I Only Knew: Success Strategies for Navigating the Principalship* (Alvy & Robbins, 1998), we suggest using brief classroom visits as an excellent strategy to celebrate student and teacher success and affirm that the classroom is the center of a school. The popularity of walk-throughs is a welcome addition to the supervisory landscape as the strategy has helped to reduce teacher isolation while also providing leaders with an opportunity to celebrate classroom success and monitor whether schoolwide initiatives are being implemented. As noted earlier in the chapter, research strongly supports the notion that intentional principal visibility is related to student success.

However, a couple of cautionary notes are worth mentioning concerning walk-throughs. First, many teachers are uneasy about walk-throughs and see the event as a "drive-by" visit that might be used during the evaluation process. Quite rightly, teachers are concerned about a "bad teaching moment" having far-reaching implications. Thus, it is critical that district and school leaders explain to teachers the rationale for walk-throughs and how the process can be used effectively as another way of gathering information about classroom episodes and the culture of a school. Skretta (2007) suggests talking "with teachers beforehand about the importance of informal observations so they are not alarmed by your presence and do not assume that your visit is for student disciplinary reasons" (p. 21). Second, supervisors need to keep in mind that a walk-through is a snapshot of a classroom moment. Supervisors do not remain in the classroom for an extended period, thus they are likely to miss the ebb and flow of a lesson, a teacher's pacing and sequencing, and a student's deliberate understanding of a concept. These cautionary points do not diminish the power of a walk-through, but like any technique it has benefits and flaws.

A benefit of walk-throughs is that the technique can be used in several ways. The following options should be considered:

- Supervisors conducting walk-throughs should plan visits at different times during the day to see a variety of subjects taught and to get a feel for how the school "rhythm" may change during the course of a day. It is important that walk-throughs are scheduled on the supervisor's calendar, otherwise they will likely not occur.
- Principals should consider conducting walk-throughs with teachers. Together they can observe classes and discuss important student and teacher behaviors.
- Consider using walk-throughs to support schoolwide initiatives. Thus, if higher-level thinking techniques are being emphasized, the walk-through participants can look for related strategies.
- Teacher leaders and coaches can conduct walk-throughs with new or student teachers to point out effective strategies.
- Middle or high school departments and elementary grade-level teams can schedule walk-throughs to observe department or grade-level techniques or new strategies being piloted. Skretta (2007) recommends "leveraging the strengths of individual teachers for professional development of the entire faculty" (p. 21). Principals can encourage these activities by offering to substitute teach or hire a substitute teacher if funding permits the option.

The long-range potency of the walk-through is described by Granada and Vriesenga (2008) as they reflect on the success of the technique at East Jessamine High School in Nicholasville, Kentucky:

[The] teachers and students had to adjust to having an administrator in their class-rooms frequently. The administrators wondered how instruction would be affected. Within about six weeks, that question was answered as their presence in the classrooms became the norm. Before the walk throughs were implemented, instruction stopped any time an administrator entered a classroom so that the teacher could see what the administrator needed. Now when an administrator enters a classroom at East Jessamine, he or she rarely even gets a glance. A student may look over occasionally and smile or wave, but instruction and learning flow smoothly. Often students are unaware of the administrators' entry or exit. Some freshmen students told their teacher, "The principals are like ninjas, in and out silently." The administrators, in essence, had faded into the background. (p. 26)

■ GUIDELINES RELATED TO EVALUATION AND LEGAL CONCERNS[1]

The legal guidelines related to evaluation are really for only 2 percent of the faculty, but 100 percent of the headaches.

—A principal's voice

Although this chapter certainly emphasizes the professional growth component of supervision and evaluation, there are times when quality assurance necessitates nonrenewal of faculty who, based on their teacher performance, are not meeting the needs of students. Although it is impossible to provide specific legal guidelines that will meet the particular expectations for each state concerning work with marginal teachers and possible nonrenewal, the following broad guidelines can serve as a starting point for principals:

- Pay attention to deadlines! Keep track of observation dates, due dates for written summaries of observations, and employment status deadlines. Concerning dates, know whether the deadlines relate to specific school work days or all calendar days, including weekends, holidays, and other nonteaching days. Deadlines will likely be different for new teachers, tenured teachers, and marginal teachers on probation engaged in an assistance/improvement plan.
- Know the union contract inside and out. For example, are there restrictions on how you can use announced and unannounced observations? Are short observations, walk-throughs, or drop-ins permitted as part of the documented evaluation process?
- Know the district instruments for evaluation and observation. There may be different instruments for new teachers and experienced teachers, for successful teachers on professional growth plans, and for marginal teachers on assistance/improvement plans. Find out whether your own customized observation instruments or forms are acceptable or if district guidelines mandate specific instruments and forms based on district and union agreements.
- Document, document, and document. A paper trail must be maintained if nonrenewal may result based on classroom performance. The documentation should be tied to specific state or district expectations for teacher competency. Make sure the documentation is specific, professional, and includes dates and responses. Assume that notes and related e-mails could be made public.
- If it looks like a marginal teacher will be placed on a timeline for improvement with possible nonrenewal of a contract, then the specific teaching problem should be documented (described) with precise language that provides a rationale concerning why the behavior is detrimental to student learning. A clear and explicit explanation of instructional performance expectations should be presented with recommendations or suggestions for improvement.
- A plan for improvement and/or assistance should be based on state laws, providing an adequate warning and timeline for improvement (e.g., 90 days on probation). Although the union contract must be in compliance with state law, it may be more restrictive than state law. Again, know the state laws and the union contract. The improvement plan should clearly indicate the problematic behavior and suggested remediation interventions (e.g., mentoring, workshops, teaching strategy DVDs, observations of colleagues, conferences). Of course, the principal must follow up and document whether progress has occurred.

- Often, school district lawyers offer state legal workshops for principals concerning working with marginal teachers and legal issues related to nonrenewal. Although it is critical to attend these workshops, they do not substitute for quality supervision and professional development. Always stay in touch with district administration and legal counsel when nonrenewal is an issue.

Finally, it is important to note that even when working with marginal teachers, one must always hope that the result will be successful for both students and teachers. As Tucker (2001) notes,

> every administrator committed to taking his or her school to the next level of excellence should provide assistance to struggling teachers. They have an ethical obligation to do so because successful remediation affects many people. Students and their parents benefit because it ensures a quality educational experience. For teachers, remediation reflects the school system's concern for its teachers' professional development. Dedicated administrators know that whole-school improvement won't happen unless everyone performs well, and helping each teacher do so is an integral part of an instructional leader's role. (p. 53)

FINAL THOUGHTS ON ■ SUPERVISION AND EVALUATION

Certainly, an effective supervisory process makes a principal a better evaluator when summative evaluations are required. With a good process, there should be few surprises. Teachers most often respect the process because the principal is familiar with their teaching style, has engaged in conversations with them on teaching, and has seen student performance and work in their classrooms. Probably the most valuable part of the process of helping the principal reflect for the summative evaluation is the teacher's analysis of his or her own performance and assessment of student progress, because the analysis reveals much about one's desire and ability to understand the classroom and grow as a professional.

The teacher evaluation process should assess the extent to which a teacher meets the standards identified by the state and/or local system. Ideally, these standards should be developed collectively by teachers, administrators, and the board of education and be based on a working knowledge of what fosters learning. Although the evaluation instrument may be based on state expectations, these are usually minimal standards for quality assurance that can be extended for growth. However, as Best Practice strategies are being implemented, one hopes that summative evaluation instruments will rise above minimum expectations. A comprehensive evaluation instrument can provide the professional community of educators with a strategy for engaging in dialogue about growth:

> A framework for professional practice offers the profession a means of communicating about excellence. Educators have learned the value of a common vocabulary to describe teaching. Because of Madeline Hunter's work, most educators know what is meant by "anticipatory set," "input and modeling," and "teaching for transfer." Now, as our understanding of teaching expands, we need a vocabulary that is correspondingly rich, one that reflects the realities of a classroom where students are engaged in constructing meaning." (Danielson, 1996, p. 5)

It is important to note that Danielson's (1996) four domains of instructional practice (planning and preparation, the classroom environment, instruction, and professional responsibilities) provide a wonderful framework for a dialogue about the classroom experience and teacher growth.

Together, the supervision and evaluation processes work to focus both the teacher and the principal in an examination of what contributes to learning for both students and staff. Collectively, these processes can and should support the school's vision of professional growth and student learning.

NOTE

1. The authors wish to thank Sharon Jayne, Les Portner, Billie Gehres, and Jay Walter, four recently retired Washington State school administrators, for their assistance concerning these legal guidelines.

REFLECTIONS

This space provides a place for you to write down ideas that have been generated by this chapter, things you want to try, or adaptations of ideas presented here.

1. What are your thoughts regarding the broad definition of supervision provided in this chapter? For example, do you think the definition is realistic?

2. What would be the various considerations when observing and conferencing with the new teacher? The experienced teacher? What other teacher profiles should be considered?

3. How do you feel about supervising teachers, specifically about their teaching?

4. What would be two or three of your individual goals as a supervisor?

5. For the veteran principal, how have you grown as a supervisor? What areas do you need to strengthen?

6. What are we doing for our best teachers to keep them at the top of their game?

7. If walk-throughs are used in your district or school, do you think the strategy is being used effectively? Why or why not? Do you have other ideas for maximizing the use of walk-throughs?

8. What insights or new questions do you have as a result of reflecting on the ideas presented in this chapter?

10

Maximizing Feedback
About Teaching

*Differentiated Professional
Growth Options*

Thinking improves when people interact with each other, when they break routine by experimenting, when they observe others at work, and when they assess and revise their own options. A cause beyond oneself becomes the norm, and the school becomes successful.

—Glickman, Gordon, and Ross-Gordon (2007)

REFLECTIONS ON FEEDBACK ■

Invited feedback about teaching provides teachers with data about the use of particular curricular, instructional, assessment, and classroom management practices and their consequences. The data provide a lens through which teachers can reflect and examine their own behaviors in relation to their impact on student learning. It also provides the basis for a dialogue among colleagues about the thinking involved in planning and delivering instruction. Through the process of receiving feedback, teachers determine what they might do differently if they taught the lesson again. This analysis fosters professional growth, instructional excellence, and, ultimately, student learning.

Traditionally, other than from student to teacher, feedback about instruction has occurred during supervision. Glickman et al. (2007), when addressing the topic of supervision, referred to a "super vision" of effective instruction. This play on words provides a helpful perspective on supervision and its ultimate capacity-building capability. Supervision is a growth-oriented process designed to enhance instruction, curriculum delivery, and assessment practices, primarily as a result of feedback based on classroom observation. Over time, it contributes to developing the teacher's thought process about teaching. Ultimately, it should result in enhanced learning for students.

■ MOVING TOWARD COLLABORATIVE FEEDBACK

In the past, the supervisory process has been conceptualized as occurring between a principal or supervisor and a teacher. However, with the focus on the school as a Professional Learning Community, many have raised the question about whether the supervisory process should be collaborative as well, to complement the cooperative goal structure of the school. The notion here is that teachers, working closely with students on a daily basis, have the capacity to provide one another with meaningful feedback that ultimately impacts student learning.

Proponents of this belief point to the fact that, in some settings, the individualistic nature of supervision occurring only between principal and teacher is inconsistent with the conceptualization of the school as a learning community where shared discussion and analysis of teaching and its consequences are a treasured part of daily life. There is much evidence to show that, given the numerous demands on the principal's role, there is limited time for supervisory visits. Hence, with the exception of classroom visits that may occur during Leading and Learning by Wandering Around, in many settings meaningful feedback about teaching becomes rather spotty. If teachers have the option of seeking feedback from other sources—colleagues, students, parents, and self, in addition to the principal—the process of continuous improvement based on frequent opportunities to receive feedback will be enhanced. Furthermore, a collaborative process provides an avenue through which to tap the rich knowledge base about teaching that exists in individual classrooms.

However, in spite of the powerful argument for a collaborative approach, some teachers express a desire to maintain the option of receiving the more traditional form of supervisory feedback from one's immediate supervisor.

Together, these points of view about traditional and collaborative practices have led to the accommodation of both in the development of a system of differentiated professional growth options. This approach is timely. Since most principals are requesting that teachers differentiate learning experiences for students, it is important for modeling's sake that principals offer teachers differentiated learning experiences rather than one-size-fits-all professional development.

■ DIFFERENTIATED PROFESSIONAL GROWTH OPTIONS: HOW THE SYSTEM WORKS

The process of providing differentiated professional growth options involves teachers and administrative staff developing professional growth goals for themselves and determining, from a menu of options, how they wish to pursue these goals. The ultimate outcome of this process should be to enhance individual staff members' collective capacity to foster high levels of student learning. The menu might include the following options:

- Clinical supervision
- 360-degree feedback
- Cognitive coaching
- Conversations about student work
- Audio or video analysis

- Drop-in visit
- Archaeological dig
- Data talk
- Program planning and delivery analysis
- Reflective journals
- Portfolios
- Peer coaching
- Problem solving
- Action Research
- Study groups
- Lesson study
- Professional book talks
- Individual professional growth plans
- E-learning, webinars, podcasts

In some settings where a high degree of trust exists, these professional growth goals are shared so that staff members become aware of others' interest areas and can support one another. This can become the basis for shared work and networking. In other settings, principals may share their goals with the staff and then meet individually with teachers. Depending on the system and its policies, principals usually have the final decision-making power in the process of determining how goals might be met. In the instance when a staff member needs more direct guidance, this should be provided, especially for nontenured or at-risk staff.

The differentiated approach fosters positive attitudes and perceptions about teacher-initiated professional growth and creates a schoolwide focus on what contributes to cognition and the development of affective skills. As faculty members experience an environment where reflection, professional dialogue, collaborative study of teaching, and self-analysis become treasured values of the occupational culture, they experience learning about learning and learning about themselves. Collectively, these insights help sensitize staff to the need to replicate, in the classroom for students, those same conditions they have personally experienced.

■ SOURCES OF FEEDBACK: CATEGORIES AND APPROACHES

There are several sources of feedback: supervisor, principal, peers, self, consultants, parents, and students. To address professional growth goals, one may select from a combination of these. The following paragraphs detail a variety of approaches to providing feedback. Who engages in each of these is largely a decision of the person defining how his or her professional goals will be addressed. The professional growth goals should be grounded in how one's current skill set impacts student learning.

Clinical supervision. This approach, described in detail in Chapter 9, involves a preobservation conference, observation, reflections, and postobservation conference. Discussion and analysis of teaching should be based on a common framework of language, such as the Hunter Model, or brain research, using the information-processing model. The goal of this process is to assist and support teachers as reflective classroom decision makers.

360-degree feedback. This type of feedback allows staff members "to gather data about themselves from multiple sources in their circles of influence. The fundamental premise is that data gathered from multiple perspectives are more comprehensive and objective than data gathered from only one source" (Dyer, 2001, p. 35). The raters might include superiors, subordinates, peers, parents, students, and community members. The individuals being rated by others also rate themselves. With 360-degree feedback, staff members have the opportunity to compare their views of themselves with the views that others have of them. Karen Dyer, manager of the education sector of the Center for Creative Leadership in Greensboro, North Carolina, writes, "The feedback is powerful because these data identify behaviors that leaders (and other staff members) can work either to strengthen or to diminish. In addition, 360-degree feedback assists them in comparing their performance to stakeholder expectations. The school district can also measure behaviors and characteristics that relate to the values, beliefs, goals, and strategies of the organization. . . . Crucial to using the 360-degree process is trust." Hence, to ensure overall quality, effectiveness, and integrity, Dyer suggests that five key factors be addressed in the 360-degree feedback process:

- Feedback is developmental, not evaluative.
- A coaching or mentoring session accompanies feedback.
- The development of a goal or action plan follows feedback.
- Feedback data belong to the receiver.
- The process is confidential. (p. 36)

One teacher who chose this approach reported that the data she received from students, regarding which of her instructional behaviors helped them learn best, provided a compelling case for her to continue differentiating instruction.

Cognitive coaching. This is a nonjudgmental process built around a planning conference, an observation, and a reflecting conference. It is not dependent on a common language. Rather, it involves using clarifying questions, pressing for specificity, reframing, and other communication tools so that colleagues who don't share a common language can still communicate. Anyone in the educational setting can become a cognitive coach—teachers, administrators, department chairs, or support personnel. A coaching relationship may be established between teachers, administrators and teachers, and/or administrators and fellow administrators (Costa & Garmston, 1994, p. 2).

In some districts, cognitive coaching skills are being used by school secretaries, counselors, bus drivers, aides, students, parents, playground supervisors, and cafeteria workers to enhance communication and establish trusting relationships. The goals of cognitive coaching, according to Costa and Garmston (1994), are "establishing and maintaining trust, facilitating mutual learning and enhancing growth toward holonomy [which is defined as] individuals acting autonomously while simultaneously acting interdependently with the group" (p. 13).

Conversations about student work. Conversations about student work engage small groups of teachers in examining the work they design for students and the results of that work. Phil Schlechty (2001), noted author of *Shaking Up the Schoolhouse,* notes, "Teachers do not cause learning. . . . Rather, they design activities for students from which students will learn" (p. 83). Schlechty believes that when work is "designed right" and when the "right content" is addressed in the work offered to students, students learn. Hence, he says, "The primary source of variance in student learning is the quality of the work the teachers and the schools provide to students" (p. 84).

In conversing about student work, teachers usually follow a protocol. There are a variety available. Schlechty (2001) presents 10 design qualities that are likely to make schoolwork more meaningful and engaging. The design qualities are Content and Substance, Organization of Knowledge, Product Focus, Clear and Compelling Standards, Protection from Adverse Consequences for Initial

Failure, Affirmation of the Significance of Performance, Affiliation, Novelty and Variety, Choice, and Authenticity (p. 107). Teachers in one district used these qualities as the basis for collaborative planning of student assignments and reflection after the assignments were given and student work collected. They noted the positive impact this process had on staff and student learning.

Audio or video analysis. This involves an individual recording him- or herself, reviewing the recording either alone or with colleagues, and reflecting on the thinking, behavior, and outcomes derived from the performance.

Drop-in visit. This activity usually occurs when an individual drops in to a classroom meeting or presentation and leaves a note containing an observation or probing question.

Archaeological dig. The "dig" involves examining artifacts from lessons, professional growth activities, programs, meetings, or other events and having conversations about them. The goal of the dialogue is to stimulate reflection and thinking about practice.

Data talk. This activity engages the teacher and teacher-chosen colleagues in analyzing disaggregated data and dialogue about which instructional and curricular practices are working well and which need to be changed. The goal is to help every student thrive.

Program planning and delivery analysis. In addition to performance in the classroom, teachers demonstrate professional growth and expertise in planning and presenting sessions for others. For example, a team of teachers planned a professional development day for their colleagues. Another teacher coordinated the planning of a math, science, and technology exhibition. These "performances" can provide a basis for observation and dialogue about promising practices that promote student learning.

Reflective journals. Time for reflection fosters analysis. Writing about thoughts and perceptions after experiences causes one to think about behaviors and consequences. For example, when a teacher or principal thinks about instructional and curricular planning in relation to student learning, this activity promotes an analysis that adds to his or her own knowledge base about what promotes learning. The ability to think critically about one's professional performance is a cultivated skill that enables one to grow. This also entails exposing one's inadequacies and reaching out to other sources of knowledge (if journals are shared) within and outside of the school to solve instructional dilemmas. Journal formats may include a variety of forms: free writing, mapping, interactive journals, reaction, contemplation, elaboration, or cause-and-effect. Once journal writing becomes a regular professional practice, reflection will become habit. Looking through past writings, one is often able to note growth and insights that become cause for celebration!

Portfolios. The portfolio approach is designed to promote reflection and analysis as well as demonstrate professional growth. Portfolios are generally a collection of artifacts that represent growth in thinking, planning, delivering, and assessing teaching. The goal of these endeavors is to promote student learning. They might also demonstrate growth in a particular area (e.g., integrating technology, interdisciplinary planning). Portfolios should not simply be scrapbooks of lesson plans and student work, but rather they should demonstrate progress.

Many teachers who use this approach elect to designate a portfolio focus such as literacy. Typical contents of a portfolio may be audio or video, student work, lesson plans, samples of tasks, and snapshots. Sometimes student or parent letters or graduate work related to the portfolio theme are included.

Peer coaching. Peer coaching occurs when a two or three colleagues with similar role status join together to preconference, observe, and postconference with one another. Often, the cognitive coaching model is employed. It is critical that the inviting teacher, who requests feedback, steer the focus of the observation and determine the parameters of the discussion. The content of peer coaching activities should be confidential—shared only between the colleagues engaged in the process. Many schools hire math and literacy coaches who serve as experts within a school setting and add to teachers' repertoires. Models vary, but typically coaches, who may be full- or part-time, instruct and conduct demonstration lessons.

Problem solving. Sessions are designed to encourage staff to share problems and collaboratively problem solve in a way that fosters learning. A variety of problem-solving approaches may be used. Not only do staff members learn as a result of this process, but they also use the problem-solving tools in their classrooms and meetings.

Action Research. Staff members who elect to participate in Action Research select an area of focus, develop a research question, identify a data collection plan, and create a data analysis plan. They identify who will assist in data collection and analysis as well as how findings will be posted and used. Data are collected and analyzed. Findings are described, summarized, and reported.

Study groups. This structure provides staff with the opportunity to select a topic or theme and identify ways that they will study it. For example, one study group identified the theme of working with at-risk youth. Their mechanisms for studying included discussions of current practice, analysis of case studies, selected journal readings, a field trip to a local prison and dialogue with prisoners, and readings from books. Members of the group kept journals about insights and experiences. As they learned and applied ideas and practices in the classroom, they frequently met to share experiences. Some teachers and administrators decided to begin student study groups as a result of their experiences as adult learners.

Lesson study. Lesson study engages teachers in codeveloping lessons. After a lesson has been taught, professional colleagues reflect on teaching practices that foster student learning. Catherine Lewis (2002), writing about lesson study conducted in Japanese classrooms, describes five characteristics of this process. "They are lessons:

- observed by other teachers
- planned collaboratively
- designed to bring to life in a lesson a particular goal or vision of education
- recorded
- discussed with co-teachers or planners and sometimes an outside educator or researcher" (pp. 59–60)

Teachers report that this ongoing process is meaningful, helps them see their teaching, and fosters learning.

Professional book talks. These talks center on a particular book or article series in which staff members voluntarily indicate interest. At one school, for example, a weekly book talk was organized using Jane Healy's (1990) *Endangered Minds: Why Children Don't Think and What We Can Do About It* as a focus for discussion. At another school, a book talk was organized around Marzano,

Pickering, and Pollock's (2001) *Classroom Instruction That Works.* At another, Pat Wolfe's (2001) *Brain Matters* was the focus of the book talk. What is essential when implementing book talks is that there are specific plans to use the content of the sessions in the classroom. This is often missing in the implementation process.

Individual professional growth plans. This growth option accommodates the individual who prefers to pursue independent study. For example, one teacher wanted to increase his instructional repertoire. He chose to read *Models of Teaching,* by Bruce Joyce and Marsha Weil (1972). He visited classrooms where *Models of Teaching* was being used. He rented, watched, and analyzed videotapes of *Models of Teaching.* With this background, he began writing lesson plans to employ these models in his daily teaching. He kept samples of his plans and student work associated with these lessons in a portfolio.

E-learning, webinars, podcasts. These professional development activities engage individuals in taking online courses offered by a number of professional organizations and universities or educational consultants. E-learning and webinars are interactive and should require follow-through. They foster networking among other professionals with similar interests. A cautionary note: although the promise of electronic networking and other technologies is enticing, designers are still grappling with how to replicate the value of face-to-face interaction. How do you replicate the spontaneous laughter that bursts out in a session? Or that moment in time when the presenter looks out at an audience and observes they are visibly moved by an experience?

■ SELF-ASSESSMENT: ESTABLISHING BENCHMARKS OF PROGRESS

In addition to developing professional growth goals and identifying which approaches will be used to address them, it is important that each staff member who participates in a differentiated professional growth options program identifies benchmarks of progress with projected dates of completion. For example, an early portfolio benchmark might be the decision about where artifacts are to be stored. Another might be the creation of a portfolio theme or goal. In addition to benchmarks, resources needed—human and material—should be noted. The benchmark target dates should be reviewed quarterly and progress celebrated. The final benchmark, no matter which approach is taken, needs to be evidence that teacher learning is impacting student learning.

■ INDIVIDUAL REFLECTION AND INSTITUTIONAL RENEWAL

It has been said that an event does not become an experience until one has time to reflect. Reflection is a precious resource in settings where most activities are characterized as fast paced, involving a constant stream of decision making. The tools for differentiated professional growth options are many. They provide choice for different types of adult learners who have a variety of interests and are at a variety of stages in their careers. What they have in common is the capacity to foster reflection and, potentially, an enduring desire to learn more about educational craft. Ultimately, the result of these activities should be an increased capacity to serve students and foster high levels of learning.

Implementing a system of professional growth options provides recognition of the need to nourish the professional growth of every individual in the school and to stimulate a collaborative effort to pursue learning about learning. Through this process, the entire institution becomes a richer knowledge source with increased capacity to serve its adult and student learners.

REFLECTIONS

This space provides a place for you to write down ideas that have been generated by this chapter, things you want to try, or adaptations of ideas presented here.

1. How does the concept of differentiated professional growth options fit with your philosophy regarding professional growth?

2. What might be some advantages and disadvantages of differentiated professional growth options?

3. What professional growth options do you prefer? Would you add any?

4. How might differentiated professional growth options support teachers in their efforts to help students address challenging state and national standards?

5. What insights or new questions do you have as a result of reflecting on the ideas presented in this chapter?

11

Building a
Collaborative School

*The Power of Teacher Leadership
and Community*

What does ethical leadership mean? For me as a practitioner it means promoting democratic values and beliefs within the school community through collegiality and shared decision making. It also means showing respect for teachers and students, and recognizing that teachers are experts in curriculum and instruction. In the classroom, ethical leadership means encouraging respect for each student and helping students to do their best, share ideas, and take risks as they learn and work individually and cooperatively.

—A principal's voice

PORTRAIT OF A COLLABORATIVE SCHOOL: ■
A PROFESSIONAL LEARNING COMMUNITY

Imagine a school where teachers work on teams to design curriculum, plan instruction, develop authentic assessment tasks based on specific standards, analyze data and plan instructional interventions, problem solve, counsel students, support each other, and teach. They collaborate to design and participate in professional growth activities. As part of this effort, they peer coach with one another. Their focus is learning about learning. When one walks into the faculty room, the dialogue is about teaching and learning. There is a parent-teacher-student organization that meets regularly. Their work focuses on collaboration to support learning. When one visits classrooms, often cooperative learning is observed. At the classroom level, the students experience the same type of collaboration and respect that adults model at the building level. Teachers work with students on the student council. Support staff, including bus drivers, cafeteria workers, instructional and library aides, office personnel, and playground supervisors, frequently meet to receive training and to discuss how they can facilitate and enhance the learning process.

Administrators and instructional staff meet frequently and share decision making to promote better and lasting decisions about the quality of the workplace and learning. There is open communication at all levels. Trust exists. People are committed to values, beliefs, and activities that focus on learning.

This school or collaborative center for learning extends its activities to include partnerships with the community and local businesses. There is two-way dialogue about what skills students need to be successful in both school and life. Students develop important life skills as a result of service projects they do in the community. Community members attend school activities, and school community members take part in local civic activities. Business leaders and school staff attend shared professional development activities. There are learning fairs where all who contribute to learning are recognized and celebrated for their efforts.

■ AN IMAGE OF REALITY

The above scenario is far from reality in many schools. The history of the teaching profession is rooted in norms of isolation, stemming from the original "school"—an isolated one-room schoolhouse. Thus professional isolation is a condition familiar to many teachers. In many of today's schools, this one-room schoolhouse structure is repeated every few yards down the corridor. In fact, Maeroff (1993) concluded that teachers go about their jobs as if each classroom were a separate building. Although classroom endeavors are largely communal—one teacher interacting with several students simultaneously—professional interactions within schools often tend to be one on one. A principal meets with a teacher in a supervisory visit or communicates about a particular student. A teacher inquires of another about a particular curricular issue. Teaching, in the main, tends to be a solitary, private act with regard to adult interaction. Whole-faculty gatherings for professional interaction offer one potential forum for articulation and communication about learning. Yet, in many cases, there are collective bargaining agreements that limit faculty meetings to one a month or, in some schools, one a semester!

Sometimes perceived as an intrusion on planning time—or, as a result of past experiences, not worthwhile—time for professional collaboration among colleagues is limited within many workplaces. In many schools, the schedule would need to be altered to create common planning time for professional colleagues to articulate curriculum and plan meaningful learning experiences.

Many recognition traditions tend to be individualistic as well, such as "Teacher of the Year" or "Staff Member of the Month." Success is defined as making it alone. As a result of these conditions and traditions in some schools, teachers seldom have the opportunity to experience the benefits of collaborative work and, as a consequence, lack the values and beliefs necessary to sustain collaboration. It seems ironic that the very individuals who are being asked to foster cooperative learning experiences for the students in their classrooms are sometimes not encouraged to engage in similar experiences with their professional colleagues. This lack of personal experience, in some instances, limits one's awareness of the subtleties that influence collaboration as well as the feelings and opportunities it brings. Some school staffs, however, have committed to challenge traditional isolation and have created cultures of learning-focused colleagues. They operate as Professional Learning Communities.

■ THE CASE FOR COLLABORATION

What is the difference between schools that learn and make progress and those that don't? Jan O'Neill and Ann Conzemius (2002), in "Four Keys to a Smooth Flight," report that "schools showing continuous improvement in student results are those whose cultures are permeated by: shared focus; reflective practices; collaboration and partnerships; and an ever increasing leadership capacity" (p. 15) characterized by "individuals who focus on student learning, reflect on student assessments, and learn as a collaborative team" (p. 17). Ann Lewis, quoted in an article by Mike Schmoker (2004), notes that schools that function as Professional Learning Communities are four times more likely to be improving academically than those which operate in isolation.

In addition to the research, teachers report that their work is becoming increasingly more complex. Many report that students today have different needs and problems than those who occupied classrooms during the teachers' preservice and initial years of practice. A large number of teachers speak of increasing classroom demands and a discontented public. These difficult times point to the need for colleagues to join together in addressing them to ease the individual burden they pose.

Research and experience tell us that collaboration makes a difference. Roland Barth, former director of the Principal's Center at Harvard University, once shared with a convocation of principals, "Four years of public school teaching—and 10 years as a principal—convince me that the nature of relationships among adults who inhabit a school has more to do with a school's quality and character, the accomplishments of its pupils, and the professionalism of its teachers than any other factor."

Judith Warren Little (1982), in a keynote address to mentor teachers in Napa, California, observed that in collaborative settings, such as the teachers' room, when the dialogue focused on teaching and learning, the school typically was improving. This was not the case when the teachers' talk focused on griping about students, administration, or one another.

Similarly, the late Susan Rosenholtz (1989) studied 78 schools and characterized them as "stuck," "in-between," or "moving." The moving schools were found to be learning enriched. Their environments were characterized by shared purpose and direction, teacher collaboration, teacher on-the-job learning, and teacher certainty (efficacy). In these settings, there was evidence of teacher commitment and student learning. Rosenholtz noted,

> In the choreography of collaborative schools, norms of self-reliance appeared to be selfish infractions against the school community. With teaching defined as inherently difficult, many minds tended to work better than a few. Here requests for and offers of advice and assistance seemed like moral imperatives and colleagues seldom acted without foresight and deliberate calculation. Teacher leaders . . . reached out to others with encouragement, technical knowledge to solve classroom problems, and enthusiasm for learning new things. (p. 208)

In the learning-enriched settings, Rosenholtz (1989) found that principals played a critical role in contributing to "an abundant spirit of continuous improvement" where no one ever stopped learning. They did this through "frequent and useful evaluations which seemed also a powerful mechanism for delivery on the promise of school improvement as they also served as guides for future work." In addition to evaluation, these principals often orchestrated collaborative relations between more and less successful teachers. Teachers came to realize that these relationships helped contribute to classroom success. Having experienced the power of these alliances with other professionals, teachers desired to continue such relationships. Collaborative principals were found who "uniquely rewove schools that had come altogether unraveled" (Rosenholtz, 1989, p. 208). In contrast, principals who seemed

> unsure of their technical knowledge and concerned with their own self-esteem, did teachers and students an enormous disservice. In protecting their turf, even the smallest attempts by teachers to solve school or classroom problems were met by distance, intimidation, or defeat. Most often, it was here teachers learned the unassailable lesson that

they must shoulder classroom burdens by themselves. . . . [N]o teacher could impose upon another. (p. 207)

In an article titled "How Our Schools Could Be," Deborah Meier (1995) emphasized

When schools see themselves as membership communities, not service organizations, parents and teachers discuss ideas, argue about purposes and exercise judgment, because taking responsibility for making important decisions is at the heart of what it means to be well educated. Students can't learn unless the adults who must show them the way practice what they preach. (pp. 369–370)

Indeed, William Cunningham and Donn Gresso (1993) in *Cultural Leadership* state that "collegiality is the most important element in the success of and commitment to school improvement." Robert Eaker and Janel Keating (2008) note

Never before has there been such widespread agreement among researchers and practitioners regarding the most promising approach (Professional Learning Communities) to significantly improve schools. . . . [However] the concept will have little impact on schools unless professional learning community practices become embedded into day to day culture. . . . [C]ollaboratively developed shared values and commitments can be a powerful tool for shaping school culture. (p. 15)

Three cultural shifts are critical for Professional Learning Communities to be sustained, Eaker and Keating (2008) explain. First,

a shift in fundamental purpose from teaching to learning. This shift is seismic. . . . Second, a shift in the work of teachers. . . . [T]eachers organize into high performing, collaborative teams. . . . [T]hird, a shift in focus. Their focus shifts from inputs to outcomes and from intentions to results. (p. 15)

Thus proponents of the research on collaboration and those experienced in it report "together, we are better than alone." Yet achieving the goal of collaboration is a distant target in many schools. Therefore, the movement toward it must be gradual. Gradual change allows for the provision of experiences so that individuals have the opportunity to participate in collective activities that will build the necessary values, beliefs, commitments, and desire for continued collaboration.

■ MOVING TOWARD COLLABORATION

Because the collaborative experience tends to be an uncommon one, the initial activities designed to foster the development of values and desires for collaborative work and, eventually, the creation of norms for collaborative practice need to be introduced, facilitated, and structured by someone or some group outside or within the organization. Expect resistance. Staff members do not always perceive the need for this type of experience. Collaboration may be a foreign activity. People may not see a purpose for collaboration and view it as an invasion of privacy. Furthermore, adults have a lot to lose—especially their professional image and self-esteem. It is important that a staff's initial experiences with collaboration do not require them to put their professional selves on the line. Rather, the experiences should be designed to be "low risk," that is, activities that do not require participants to expose professional knowledge, skills, or talent. Examples of this might be reading and analyzing articles from professional journals, suggesting implications for practice, or discussing curriculum.

As individuals become more comfortable with one another, they will be more willing to expose their professional selves. As they benefit from this type of collegial activity, they may come to value and seek additional opportunities for collaboration with colleagues. As individual values and beliefs within organizations begin to change, the organizations change. And as individual values that celebrate collective action develop, new traditions and collaborative practices will emerge. An example of this comes from Central Park East Secondary School in New York City:

Another priority for us was creating a setting in which all members of the community were expected to engage in the discussion of ideas and in "the having of their wonderful ideas," as Eleanor Duckworth (from Harvard University) has put it. "One of our most prominently stated, up-front aims was the cultivation of what we came to call 'Habits of Mind'—habits that apply to all academic and nonacademic subject matter and to all thoughtful human activities." The five we came up with are not exhaustive, but they suggest the kinds of questions that we believed a well-educated person raises about his or her world.

- How do we know what we think we know? What's our evidence? How credible is it?
- Whose viewpoint are we hearing, reading, seeing? What other viewpoints might there be if we changed our position—our perspective?
- How is one thing connected to another? Is there a pattern here?
- How else might it have been? What if? Supposing that?
- What difference does it make? Who cares?

In order to carry out our basic mission of teaching students to use their minds well and preparing them to live productive, socially useful and personally satisfying lives, we approach curriculum with these habits as a backdrop and specific "essential questions" at the core. (Meier, 1995, p. 371)

Judith Warren Little offers a cautionary note about

when people are brought together to do work that is defined by others . . . data analysis, looking at evidence, mapping out standards, aligning curriculum and assessment. All of that may be really valuable work. The question is who owns it? So the leadership task becomes both organizing the school . . . to support that kind of ambitious work and creating conditions where people really endorse and claim it as central parts of what it means to be professional. If working as a community doesn't carry value added over what teachers are able to accomplish independently, then it won't be worth the transactional costs, the investment of time and the competition with what teachers feel that they have to do individually. (quoted in Crow, 2008, p. 54)

NECESSARY CONDITIONS FOR A COLLABORATIVE SCHOOL ■

In a collaborative school, all staff members engage in the study of learning and those practices that facilitate the learning process. In a sense, the school becomes a Professional Learning Community with a focus on continuous improvement. Although no specific recipe exists to make this a reality, Rebecca and Rick DuFour described some key ingredients at the 2002 Association for Supervision and Curriculum Development conference. These included "shared vision, mission, values, goals, collaborative teams, collective inquiry, action orientation, commitment to continuous improvement, and results orientation." As Roland Barth and others have said, for profound learning to occur—whether by students or adults—an individual must

- acknowledge areas in need of improvement
- pose the problems
- take risks
- use humor
- collaborate with other learners
- demonstrate compassion
- model learning
- maintain a focus on learning
- communicate well with colleagues

Yet, in some schools, individuals might not feel safe to demonstrate these behaviors. In schools where cultures of isolation exist, the path to collaboration requires that staff members change the way they think and relate to one another. One principal commented, "You want people to feel 'Hey, I'm part of this,' but it's hard to do when what is modeled is 'dog eat dog.'"

Additionally, time for collaboration, training in strategies and guidelines for collaborative work, trust among all involved in the collective enterprise, and tangible support (in word and deed) must be provided for norms of collaboration to develop and thrive. "Teachers are more likely to cooperate when barriers to common action are removed and they feel their problems are shared" (Bird & Little, 1984). When this is the case, teachers, inspired by a common purpose, may be able to bring about change at both the classroom and school levels.

Critical to the development of a collaborative school is the notion that collaboration cannot be forced. Therefore, groups of colleagues who desire joint work should be supported with resources to pursue it. Others, who have not yet developed values for collaboration, may be exposed to opportunities for collective action. Wells Junior High School, in Wells, Maine, developed a norm asserting "Everyone has the right to participate. No one must. If you choose not to, however, you must go along with decisions of the collective group. If you choose to disagree verbally, we will take time with you to work out the disagreement."

The focus of collaborative work must be its ultimate impact on students. To that end, colleagues must engage in work that ultimately leads to a heightened awareness of the conditions necessary for learning to occur. Maeroff (1993) asserts that a faculty can be renewed intellectually if it views change as a team or collaborative endeavor. Moreover, as staff members gain comfort with the process of change, the actual process can become as natural as the desire to improve one's teaching and students' learning.

In a collaborative workplace focused on learning, all staff would assume some responsibility for the professional welfare and growth of both students and colleagues. For this to occur, however, requires—for many schools—a fundamental change in the school's culture. In a collaborative culture, the core values, which are reflected in the practices, reward structures, rules, sanctions, and traditions of the school, must be characterized by a spirit of curiosity about teaching and learning and a belief in joint work. When such a culture exists, staff members join together to share the responsibility of integrating the curriculum, developing and executing plans to address the specific needs of at-risk students, problem solving classroom frustrations, developing students' reflective and analytical skills, and creating meaningful academic tasks. They also celebrate one another's accomplishments and share the learning implicit in these feats. This recognition serves as an intrinsic motivator, creates synergy, and perpetuates the belief that "together we are better than alone." Cooperative goal structures are, as a consequence, reinforced and advanced.

Each school differs in how it evolves to have a culture of collaboration. Leadership; the history of professional development; experiences of the staff; and existing norms, values, and beliefs will influence the development of a collaborative workplace. However, there are some specific activities that tend to take place in a developmental way. Collaboration tends to emerge as staff members move from relationships characterized by congeniality, to cooperation, and then to collegiality. How much time is spent in each of these stages will be a function of the existing characteristics of an individual school.

The collegiality that exists when staff members collaborate is not created overnight. In fact, the building blocks for collegiality go beyond work and take considerable time. Thus, when a school principal visits a teacher or other staff member who has experienced a family crisis or is recovering from a serious operation or accident, he or she often finds that sharing the moment of crisis is invaluable in building trust. At times, several activities—some congenial, some cooperative, some collegial—might take place simultaneously.

A teacher and a principal, reflecting on how their staff grew to become a collaborative one noted, "We had come to know each other as human beings . . . sharing about our families, interests, and sports. This was essential to build the trust so you can bare your soul with your colleagues and say, 'Here's the problem.' To be intellectually honest requires a foundation of trust." They described a continuum:

Congeniality   Cooperation   Collaboration

As a staff moves from left to right on the continuum, trust increases among colleagues. This continuum is significant in that it reminds one that if a basic respect for one another as human beings does not exist, people will experience a more difficult time collaborating.

Hargreaves and Dawe (1989) provide a useful typology for considering the impact of school culture on the development of a collaborative workplace. They suggest that there are four types of cultures:

- *Fragmented individualism*—the traditional form of teacher isolation
- *Balkanization*—subgroups and cliques operating as separate subentities
- *Contrived collegiality*—leading to a proliferation of unwanted contacts among teachers that consume already scarce time with little to show for it
- *True collaborative cultures*—"deep personal enduring cultures central to teachers' daily work" (p. 14)

Thinking about these cultures, one could assume that if the nature of relationships among adults in a school is characterized by individualism or balkanization, it is very probable that individuals will not take much of a risk when revealing their professional selves in working with others. Therefore, when planning activities to foster the development of a collaborative workplace, low-risk activities in which individuals' professional knowledge is not at stake would be more likely to engage staff members than high-risk activities in which individuals might be asked to display their knowledge publicly. Cultures in which contrived collegiality exists might be transformed by inviting staff members to come together and share activities that have personal meaning for each of them. Here, the matter of creating choice of collaborative tasks versus delivering top-down mandated initiatives is essential.

Although congenial activities build rapport and community, it is critical to move swiftly into collegial work. However, congenial activities may continue to be interspersed. The following portrays a range of activities and examples as well as illustrates the difference between congenial tasks and collegial tasks.

Congenial activities. These are designed to create a sense of comfort with one another as human beings. The experiences typically are not professionally focused. Examples might include potluck lunches, volleyball games, swap meets to exchange educational resources, or Friday afternoon gatherings.

Collegial, professionally focused experiences. These develop interest, respect, and cooperation among and between individuals as professional colleagues. The focus of collegial interactions tends to be curriculum, instructional practice, assessment, and data analysis. Ultimately, the results of these activities must be an enhanced capacity to serve students and a staff commitment to help every student succeed. These are represented by a broad range of activities.

Low-risk activities do not require participants to expose their professional knowledge and skills. Rather, these activities are designed to raise awareness of the value of multiple perspectives and a realization of the resources that may exist beyond one's classroom door in neighboring classrooms. These tend to create a desire for collaborative work. Examples might include a cooperative learning activity in which a small group of teachers read different journal articles and then meet to discuss them.

- Group process and communication skills sessions are conducted, during which staff members build their own ground rules regarding how they will treat one another while working collaboratively, learn about how to facilitate collegial work, and learn about the subtleties of communication. These sessions would also include information about group development, conflict resolution, consensus building, fierce conversations, and problem-solving models.

Medium-risk activities require professionals to expose some of their professional knowledge and skills. These activities generally occur outside of one's classroom and may include such tasks as professional sharing of successful practices; problem solving; or curriculum mapping, articulation, or integration. These tend to build a desire for more knowledge about content areas or teaching practices.

- Professional development sessions should provide information about either content areas or instructional practices and their consequences. Examples of these might include workshops about teaching reading or writing across the content areas, working with English Language Learners using technology in the curriculum, learning about research on the brain, or using specific instructional strategies that are associated with fostering student achievement.

High-risk activities require professionals to expose their professional knowledge and skills. These might include the rigorous examination of teaching, curricular, or assessment practices and their consequences. Training to prepare staff members for this type of collegial work might include sessions on conferencing skills, classroom observations, and data collection. Examples of high-risk activities might include peer coaching, mentoring, conversations about student work, or lesson study.

- Study groups focus on interests that address student data to ensure the ongoing nature of collegial work and develop increased capacity to address difficult cases and promote student learning.

- Collaborative action research projects provide opportunities for professional colleagues to formulate research questions, develop a plan to collect and analyze data, collect data, analyze data, summarize and publicize their findings, and identify new questions that may have emerged.

Because there is an intrinsic similarity between the goals of the activities discussed in the previous list and the goals of supervision—the development of knowledge and practices regarding staff and student learning—in some schools that have actualized true collaborative cultures, these activities have become a way of addressing the professional growth goals of individual teachers identified during the initial supervisory conference (this concept is discussed at length in Chapter 10).

Differentiating professional growth experiences for staff increases staff members' understanding of the value of providing differentiated learning experiences for students. Collectively, this fuels the school's capacity to serve students.

A SPECTRUM OF ACTIVITIES   ■

The descriptions that follow provide more detailed examples of low-, medium-, and high-risk activities designed to build the values necessary for a collaborative school. Principals, teachers, and support personnel have used these activities during faculty meetings, team or department meetings, job-embedded learning experiences, and professional development days. The broad goal of their use is to provide experiences to develop values for collaboration that will lead to joint work among professionals and ultimately enhance the resources the collective staff possess to ensure every student thrives.

Listening posts. In listening posts, staff members are asked to generate professional topics about which they would like to chat. For example, some may wish to talk about common assessments, whereas others might want to converse about brain research, differentiated instruction, or grading, to name a few. Each topic is assigned to a specific area or "post" in the room by the facilitator. Staff members gather by the topic area of their choice and have a discussion for 15 to 30 minutes. At the end of this time, the individuals who have discussed each topic develop a 1- to 2-minute summary of their discussions and report back to the larger group. In this way, the entire group benefits from hearing about the separate topic area discussions. In fact, seeds of interest across topic areas are often planted as a consequence of such sharing.

Article sharing. Another out-of-classroom activity that brings teachers together for dialogue, sharing, and learning is a collaborative learning strategy in which articles are selected to be read. These articles usually reflect a common theme. Suppose there are five articles to read about closing the achievement gap. Staff members form groups of five. Each person in the group numbers off, one through five, and each reads a different article. Then people who have read the same article across groups (e.g., all the "ones") meet to discuss what they have read, decide on the critical points, and plan how they will share their articles with colleagues who have read different articles. Colleagues then gather in their original groups, and each teaches about his or her article. Hence, through this activity, staff members realize that a richness exists when colleagues work together—which is not possible when individuals work alone. Further, colleagues discuss how ideas and strategies gleaned from the articles might be integrated into their classroom practices.

Carousel brainstorming. As trust begins to develop and values for collaborative work are created, staff members become more comfortable sharing professional knowledge. Carousel brainstorming promotes this type of sharing within a relatively safe context. In carousel brainstorming, four to six sheets of butcher paper are posted around the room. Topics are assigned and written on each sheet. For example, one sheet might be titled "Motivation Techniques That Work." Staff members are then divided into groups and position themselves in front of one of the sheets. They brainstorm for three minutes, writing their brainstormed ideas on the sheets. They then rotate to the next sheet, taking with them the colored marker that has been assigned to their group. The process continues until each group has brainstormed at every chart. At this point, the group members walk around the entire room, reading the completed charts. Frequently, when this activity is conducted there are requests to have the charts typed and distributed.

Helping trios. As staff members feel increasingly comfortable and trust one another, they are willing to let their rough edges show, resulting in greater adeptness in joint problem solving. Helping trios lend a structure to the problem-solving process. Peers form groups of three and designate one person as A, another as B, and the third as C. During Round 1, which lasts five minutes, A shares a problem while B and C listen. During the next five minutes, B and C ask clarifying questions about the problem. Finally, during the last five minutes, B and C offer solution ideas to A, who writes them down. The process is repeated so that B and C have a chance to discuss their problems as well.

Pinwheel activity. Another problem-solving strategy that engages larger numbers of faculty is the pinwheel activity. Groups of six are formed and stand in a pinwheel configuration. That is, three people stand in the center, each facing a person in an outer circle. The three individuals in the center each pose a professional problem or dilemma they are experiencing to the person facing them. The people they face generate possible ideas about how to address the specific problem posed. After they brainstorm solution ideas for three minutes, the people on the outside rotate. In this way, the individuals in the center are able to gain additional ideas about how to address their problems or challenges. The process continues until each person in the center has three different sets of ideas from the three outside "consultants." Then the pinwheel is turned inside out, and the outside people who had brainstormed solution ideas previously have a chance to share their problems and garner ideas from professional colleagues. This process makes the staff aware that other people share similar problems or challenges and that a tremendous amount of expertise exists among faculty members that begs to be tapped.

What's your bag? Teachers post questions about curriculum, instruction, special needs students, resources, or assessment on the outside of a brown lunch bag (one question per bag). The bags are stapled to a bulletin board in the staff room (leaving an opening on the top). Blank 3" x 5" index cards and a pen are also put in a container on the bulletin board. Staff members are invited to respond to the bag questions using the index cards. They write ideas on the cards and drop them into the bags. Question owners read the ideas in the bag and redeposit the cards in the bag so others may read them as well.

Once a foundation of trust, comfort, and risk taking is created, the opportunities for peers to support one another through collaborative exchanges are limitless. Some additional activities might include coplanning lessons, developing curriculum materials to address standards, creating cross-age learning opportunities for students, developing interdisciplinary units, sharing lesson plans, creating differentiated units of instruction, examining artifacts of student work, developing authentic assessment tasks, participating in study groups, portfolio sharing, and engaging in collaborative Action Research around teacher-generated questions.

As joint work among colleagues continues, norms of collaboration evolve. Working together becomes "the way we do business around here," as one staff member put it. Eventually, governance structures may reflect collaboration as well. For instance, one school designed a structure called the Principal's Advisory Committee (PAC). The PAC was made up of three teachers elected by the staff and the principal. Together they met and planned faculty meetings. The PAC members rotated responsibility for conducting the meetings as well. The teachers on the PAC provided a bridge for communication with faculty members at large. In the process of serving on the PAC, they received training in meeting management, problem solving, decision making, conflict resolution, effective staff development, and communication skills. Hence, in addition to serving their colleagues, they developed critical leadership skills.

TEACHER LEADERSHIP AND THE ■ COLLABORATIVE SCHOOL

Douglas B. Reeves (2008), reporting on a study of the effects of teacher leadership in Clark County, Las Vegas, Nevada, stated, "Teachers not only exert significant influence on the performance of students, they also influence the performance of other teachers and school leaders" (p. 2); "the quality and practice of leadership at every level have a demonstrable impact on organizational health in general and on student achievement in particular" (p. 10).

Cindy Harrison and Joellen Killion (2007) describe a wide range of roles teacher leaders play that impact school and student success:

- *Resource Provider*—"sharing instructional resources"
- *Instructional Specialist*—helping "colleagues implement effective teaching strategies"
- *Curriculum Specialist*—using "the curriculum in planning instruction and assessment"
- *Classroom Supporter*—working "inside classrooms to help teachers implement new ideas, often by demonstrating a lesson, co-teaching, or observing and giving feedback"
- *Learning Facilitator*—"facilitating professional learning opportunities among staff"
- *Mentor*—"serving as a mentor for novice teachers"
- *School Leader*—"serving on committees . . . acting as a grade level or department chair . . . representing the school on community or district task forces"
- *Data Coach*—leading "conversations that engage their peers in analyzing and using information to strengthen instruction"
- *Catalyst for Change*—as visionaries, posing "questions to generate analysis of student learning"
- *Learner*—modeling "continual improvement, demonstrat[ing] lifelong learning, and us[ing] what they learn to help all students achieve" (pp. 74–76)

Expanding the leadership role to include teacher leaders can enhance efforts to build community and contribute rich resources to the repertoire of skills staff members have available to them to help every student succeed.

THE PRINCIPAL AND COLLABORATION   ■

As noted earlier, a key factor in the development of a collaborative school is the principal's role. The principal must truly believe in and value professional collaboration for this type of work to be sustained over time. This must be reflected not only in what is said but also in the actions of the principal. For instance, if opportunities for professional collaboration are provided, do they occur during prime time, or are they placed at the end of a meeting's agenda? Does the principal collaborate as well? Is there a budget item to support this type of endeavor? For many principals who have not experienced collaborative efforts heretofore, such activities may be uncomfortable. Some principals, for example, have indicated a discomfort with shared governance because they felt, from the district's perspective, the principal still has accountability for decisions. In these cases, many principals solve the problem by requesting staff input but reserving the right to make the final decision. So that the staff did not feel "sold out" by this, one principal first facilitated a session in which the faculty brainstormed all the decisions to be made, which were recorded on butcher paper. The principal and the staff then labeled who would have primary responsibility for input for each decision.

In other instances, although the principal sensed a degree of discomfort, it was simply acknowledged, and the principal expressed the belief that this was part of the collaborative learning process that everyone, at one time or another, experiences. Staff support for this new role was requested. In other settings the principal shares leadership responsibilities for creating a learning community with teachers. Jo and Joseph Blase spoke about this at the 2002 National Association of Secondary School Principals Conference: "It's time to craft a new kind of educational leader, whether principal or teacher. This new leader is capable of building a constructivist, data driven, dialogic, inclusive learning community in which the development and achievement of all is pre-eminent."

■ SOME FINAL THOUGHTS ON COLLABORATION

Creating a collaborative culture has been described as "the single most important factor" (Newmann & Wehlage, 1995) for successful school improvement initiatives. Regardless of how a collaborative organization develops, schools that are able to reach such a state report a sense of synergy, creativity, and a capacity for innovation and learning uncommon to those that function in isolation. Moreover, in true collaborative cultures, joint work among teachers has developed as a daily norm for operating. It is reflected in daily work habits; meetings; and ongoing, planned, job-embedded professional growth experiences. In these cultures, staff members are willing to put their professional knowledge and practices on the line to be scrutinized by their colleagues. They view one another as sources for learning.

Time is a precious resource in schools. Therefore it is essential that collaborative time in schools is focused on capacity building to ensure high levels of quality student learning. There should be strong links between core beliefs, vision and mission, data analysis, goal setting, and site-level collaborative work. Planning in this way enables the realization of excellence.

REFLECTIONS

This space provides for you a place to write in ideas that have been generated by this chapter, things you want to try, or adaptations of ideas presented herein.

1. What do you believe are the obstacles and opportunities afforded by Professional Learning Communities?

2. Thinking about the goal of enhancing student learning, what additional collaborative activities would you add to those offered in this chapter?

3. Thinking about the staff of which you are a part, how would you characterize their capacity to engage in risk-taking behavior (low, medium, or high risk)? What activities might you share?

4. What types of teacher leadership currently exist in your school? What new roles might you incorporate?

5. What insights or new questions do you have as a result of reflecting on the ideas presented in this chapter?

12

Fueling the Learning Organization Through Professional Development

It takes a whole village to educate one child.

—African proverb

WHY PROFESSIONAL DEVELOPMENT? ■

Educating a child begins with a village of elders who themselves model and find their lives enriched by the quest for lifelong learning. Students learn as a result of what they see modeled within the school. Building-based professional development, by design, provides opportunities for members of the school community to grow professionally in ways that will ultimately benefit both teacher and student. In the process, the entire system improves because of its increased capacity to influence productivity. Echoing this notion, Margaret Arbuckle, from the Western Maine Partnership, addressing a group of principals, stated, "Schools that support the continuous learning and development of students also support the continuous development of the educators for them. Schools must be places of learning for both students and educators. You can't have one without the other. Building a culture of professional learning in schools is a necessary condition for sustained learning and particularly critical if we are to link professional development with reformed concepts of teaching, learning, and schooling."

PROFESSIONAL DEVELOPMENT DEFINED ■

Professional development consists of any activity that directly affects the attitudes, collaboration, knowledge levels, skills, and practices of individuals that will assist them in performing their roles—present or future. Ideally, such development will not only make the individual a visible learner and responsive teacher but also ultimately affect the student as learner. Research and experience suggest that the principal plays a vital role in collaborating with staff members to create and maintain a climate conducive to professional development, in ensuring that professional development activities address specific needs and that activities are assessed for impact. Creating attitudes among the staff of "good but growing" is a critical first step. This is important because some staff members feel that when they are invited to attend professional development, there is an implicit message that they need it because of an inadequacy related to their performance. Professional development delivery should emphasize building relationships among professional colleagues that culminate in increased staff collaboration to serve all students.

■ CREATING AN ATMOSPHERE FOR PROFESSIONAL DEVELOPMENT TO THRIVE: SOME GUIDELINES

Creating an atmosphere for successful professional development involves attending to the following guidelines:

Provide opportunities to create a sense of purpose for professional development. This purpose should reflect the school's vision, organizational members' professional growth needs, and student needs, as evidenced by performance data. For example, the staff can share professional growth goals and discuss student performance in relation to desired levels of achievement. Then, relevant professional development activities can be identified to address these need areas.

Encourage and promote collaboration and mutual respect among all in the school community. This can be a critical source of support and will contribute to the implementation and institutionalization of professional development practices. Keeping all individuals informed, inviting people to participate in follow-up activities after training, and recognizing and celebrating collaborative efforts are essential events.

Focus on continuous improvement in quality. When precision training is developed that matches both staff and student growth needs, individual and organizational performance is enhanced. Time should be taken to discuss and analyze needs according to responsibilities associated with roles. Student performance data and desired skills should be examined. Training should specifically address the needs identified in this process.

Conduct readiness-building activities and plan collaboratively prior to training and implementation. Include maintenance activities to ensure institutionalization of professional development. Wood, Thompson, and Russell (1981) suggest five stages for a professional development program: readiness, planning, training, implementation, and maintenance.

When training is designed, attention should be paid to five key components (Joyce & Showers, 1981): presentation of material, demonstration of skills, practice, feedback, and coaching in the correct use of the new skill. There should be a focus on providing frequent opportunities for staff members to revisit professional development content, share successes, problem solve, and refine skills. This ensures opportunities for staff members to adapt new behaviors and learnings to their own situations. It ensures that training can be designed to address teacher concerns (mentioned in Chapter 7) that initially focus on how the professional development will affect them personally; then, how they will manage a new program's implementation; and later, it may develop into how the programs will affect students (Hall & Loucks, 1978).

Design training for a variety of skill levels. Training may be delivered to provide awareness, knowledge, skill development or application opportunities, or to foster internalization of concepts. Choose the appropriate focus given staff needs. Also, training should be spaced over time to promote the integration of new ideas, approaches, and behaviors into the classroom or workplace.

Design training that addresses learner needs and context variables. The late Susan Loucks-Horsley, in an interview with Dennis Sparks (1999), executive director of the National Staff Development Council, reflected, "We recognize that young people learn in different ways, but often don't acknowledge that this applies to teachers as well when we plan learning experiences for them." Loucks-Horsley, describing contextual learning strategies for teachers, emphasized the following:

> Selecting strategies is really the process of designing staff development. It is a dynamic process similar to one teachers go through in designing lessons for their students. Staff development leaders have to ask themselves which strategies make sense to use at that particular time with that particular set of teachers for a particular set of outcomes. Context variables are important in making these decisions. What are the district or school standards and goals for student learning? What do teachers already know and what do they need to know? What current policies and practices influence student learning? What is the school culture? What is the nature of the student population? Teachers' levels of content understandings are also very important, especially at the elementary level where teachers may not have a deep understanding of content, as is often the case with science and mathematics. A lot of different aspects of the context come into play when selecting the right combination of strategies.

Training activities need to reflect and model those attributes of good teaching that we want to promote in classrooms: active learning, a brain-compatible approach, time for reflection, and tasks that respond to multiple intelligences. To illustrate:

1. Active learning opportunities can include cooperative learning tasks, small-group work, role-playing, simulation, direct instruction, reciprocal teaching, videotape analysis, discussion, e-learning, and case studies. Emphasis should be on teaching that engages the whole class. For example, questioning strategies should be modeled to increase participants' awareness of the power of questions to engage the entire class and give all students the opportunity to respond to a variety of thinking and skill levels. These would include the skills of convergent and divergent thinking and the use of wait time to enhance the quality of student responses.

2. The brain-compatible approach recognizes the need for active involvement of the learner with the learning task and with fellow participants. It also highlights the need for participants to rehearse new learnings. It underscores the importance of not teaching too much too fast and linking new learning to previous experiences when applicable. Finally, it acknowledges the need to develop schemata or frameworks into which new information or knowledge fits.

3. Time for reflection allows the mind time for rehearsal and analysis. Reflection fosters the development of new neural connections. Insights can be gleaned as a result of providing time for thinking. Reflections may be recorded in logs or journals. They may be shared or remain confidential.

4. Multiple intelligences theory (Gardner, 2006) suggests there are at least nine *ways of knowing*. These include verbal-linguistic, logical-mathematical, visual-spatial, bodily-kinesthetic, musical, interpersonal, naturalist, intrapersonal, and existential. Designing staff development tasks with these in mind lends credence to the importance of highlighting the multiple ways we perceive and respond to the world.

Effective professional development programs use what is known about adult learning. Adults are more likely to be motivated when there is a relationship between professional development and their on-the-job responsibilities. Adults come to any learning experience with a rich background that begs to be tapped. Also, adult learning is ego involved. Learning a new skill may promote a positive or negative view of self. There is sometimes a fear of external judgments that we adults are less than adequate, which produces anxiety during new learning situations. Adult learners need to see the results of their efforts and have accurate feedback about progress toward their goals.

Staff development programs should involve choice. Respecting staff members as professionals and treating them accordingly means providing each individual with the right to set meaningful professional development goals and allowing them the freedom to choose how they will meet those goals. These goals should be related to building a staff member's capacity to serve students in areas identified by assessment data and other qualitative data. Expect that not all staff members will embrace wholeheartedly the notion of professional development. Often, however, when key individuals seek such experiences, peer examples and peer pressure are more powerful influences than mandates. Influence, pressure, and support will play important roles in generating participation among those staff members who do not jump on board immediately. Providing a variety of learning experiences that address common goals from which professional staff can choose is a way of modeling differentiation

When training is a "required opportunity" associated with implementing a new program or using new materials or equipment, provide the staff with choices regarding when training might be scheduled, the format, or the time frame. When professional development is designed for new staff members or beginning teachers, it is helpful to consult staff members who joined the previous year. They can lend valuable suggestions regarding their first-year needs that will contribute to planning responsive professional development.

Involve the staff in planning for professional development. One way to increase participation or buy-in is to create a forum where teachers, support staff, administration, and classified staff can talk about the tasks associated with their roles and define areas that training would enhance. In addition, desired student outcomes could be examined in relation to current levels of performance. Training topics and approaches might then be identified that would provide all staff members with the knowledge, skills, and strategies to support students in reaching their potential.

Provide opportunities for the staff to learn about classical pedagogical knowledge and current practice. It is important to provide staff members with information about current trends and developments in education, such as powerful teaching strategies, new approaches to writing, technology resources, interdisciplinary curriculum approaches, critical thinking skills, and authentic assessment. Equipped with knowledge, understanding, application opportunities, and the chance to analyze and evaluate how these developments affect or fit with one's work, the practitioner then has the background to distinguish between fleeting fads and sound practice when confronted with professional development choices.

When professional development occurs away from the school site, encourage school teams to attend. This provides a building-based system of support when colleagues return from training sessions and begin to implement new practices.

Demonstrate administrative support for professional development. Strategies include attending training with the staff, using the techniques or approaches, and allocating time for planning and implementing new learnings. Discussion time should be allocated to provide opportunities to problem solve and share examples of practice. As the principal conducts Leading and Learning by Wandering Around visits, taking time to write a note regarding a teacher's implementation of a strategy learned in professional development is a great way to celebrate learning. It also fosters the development of schoolwide norms of practice.

Use professional development as a public relations tool. With limited time, energy, and financial resources, using professional development as a public relations tool while it is being used to develop the individual and the organization provides the chance to get the most out of the investment. In some settings, the public relations venture might be an awareness session for parents about a new instructional, curricular, or assessment trend such as cooperative learning, differentiated instruction, emotional intelligence, or student portfolios. Providing information in this way also takes the mystery out of what the school is doing. In other schools, the public relations effort might be an invitation to businesses or key individuals from the community to attend training along with faculty members. One district typically shares training with the local college, university, and industry personnel, for example.

Avoid jargon. One way to diminish the possibility that professional development will become threatening is to eliminate the use of jargon and acronyms as substitutes for phrases or structures. A principal recently commented, "It's like alphabet soup around here . . . 'the SST will meet to develop IEPs in accordance with IDEA 2004.' Why can't they just say, 'The student study team will meet to develop the individual educational plans for students in accordance with IDEA 2004'?" Using language that a person on the street can understand helps make the professional development activity user friendly.

Build local school capacity. Once a staff has received training in a specific area and applied it in classrooms, that often represents the end of the particular professional development effort. One way to continue the development of individuals while creating a local resource is to provide opportunities for staff members to participate in training for trainers. This fosters the development of presentation skills and helps a school build site-level support. Ultimately, this enhances the prospects that professional development activities will become institutionalized. It also affords the school on-site trainers who can provide professional development to newcomers to the building. The entire staff benefits from having a "common language" and experiences.

Assess the context in which professional development is to occur. The questions that follow can serve as guidelines for program development.

- Does the venture have relevance for the staff? Is it related to student needs?
- How much is already going on?
- With what will the intended professional development activity compete?
- What will be the financial and emotional cost associated with the effort?
- How many cohorts of people will it affect (students, teachers, administrators, parents, substitutes)?
- How complex will the implementation be?
- Has the staff been involved in the decision to consider the staff development activity?
- In what ways will follow-up support be provided?

The following example demonstrates how these guidelines can be combined to plan a school-level program.

■ PLANNING A PEER-COACHING PROGRAM

To implement a peer-coaching program or any other professional development program, the context must be assessed and the approach matched to key variables in this assessment. The following steps will help you create awareness, develop readiness, build commitment, plan, and implement a peer-coaching program in your school (Robbins, 1991b):

1. Set up a planning group to learn about peer coaching, assess your school environment and support for coaching, develop a program plan, and organize activities.

2. Assess the school environment to identify the factors working for and against a successful peer-coaching program.

3. Provide information about peer coaching, including the rationale, what peer coaching is and is not, the various forms that coaching can take, and so on.

4. Provide opportunities for teachers to raise questions and concerns and get answers to them.

5. Solicit input from teachers on what they want the peer-coaching program to be like. Discuss how coaching activities will positively impact student learning.

6. Analyze the types and levels of support and resources available.

7. Examine other demands on teachers' time and energy.

8. Develop a plan for and provide training in peer coaching for teachers who volunteer to participate.

9. Examine the issue of time (for training, practice, follow-up, and networking).

10. Develop a plan for and provide follow-up with frequent review and refinement sessions.

11. Develop a plan for bringing new teachers into the program.

12. Go slowly but steadily. Keep peer coaching in the forefront of organizational members' minds.

The National Staff Development Council (2001) has published the *NSDC Standards for Staff Development*, which addresses key context, process, and content standards that are requisites for professional development success. These provide helpful tools when planning, implementing, evaluating, or maintaining staff development initiatives. They are available online (www.nsdc.org/bookstore.html) or by calling 800-727-7288.

■ FACILITATING THE INDIVIDUAL'S PROFESSIONAL DEVELOPMENT EXPERIENCE

In working with thousands of individuals over several years, the authors have noted that participants welcome specific aspects of professional development experiences. Principals need to keep these tips in mind when facilitating professional development opportunities:

Choose trainers who do their homework to learn about participants with whom they will be working and federal, state, and local mandates affecting the training and the trainees. This information can then be used during a session to increase its relevance for participants.

Begin with time for participants to share their expectations about what they hope to get out of the session. Eliciting expectations enhances the consultant's ability to tailor examples, comments, and activities to participant needs. In this way, as adults, participants feel they have control, or at least influence, over what happens to them during a session.

Focus on ways to build meaning into a session. Stories or video clips, followed by time for discussion of personal experiences and time to reflect, contribute to meaning. When a session has personal meaning for participants, they are more likely to buy into activities and use them in their own context.

Relate the session content to formal and informal data about students. Emphasizing how the professional learning experience will build staff capacity to address student needs is a critical strategy for creating commitment and implementation.

Invite participants to take responsibility for the pace of the workshop by providing "working" and "ready" cards. As a table group works together on a task, the working card is displayed. When the task is completed, the ready card is put up. This allows the consultant to pace the session according to participant needs. It also conveys the message that the workshop's success depends on both participant involvement and trainer planning and delivery. Encourage the trainer to model monitoring to ensure on-task behavior.

Use participants' names. This makes individuals feel as if the consultant cares enough to personalize their experiences. Moreover, it indicates that the consultant has taken a personal interest in each individual from the first moment of contact. It models that the relationship is important and communication is key.

Provide participants with handouts that are hard copies of Microsoft PowerPoint presentations, document camera copies, or transparencies. This allows participants to focus on what is being said, rather than on copying what is on the screen. Because the mind can only pay conscious attention to one thing at a time, this enhances the participants' experiences. Research suggests that 68 percent of the population learns best visually. Providing visual support also models effective practice and increases the possibility that teachers will provide this for students.

Provide Post-it notes. Many participants do not want to write on their handouts. Providing Post-it notes so that comments can be written on them and then placed on the handouts takes care of this problem. Some participants even use the Post-it notes to mark sections in their handout packets or make comments about which pages they wish to use immediately.

Deliver training content in a user-friendly way. Participants welcome overviews, agendas, and outcomes for a session. Instruction should reflect a healthy balance of research and practice. Frequent opportunities for movement should be provided, such as the "TalkWalk" (discussed in more detail in Chapter 13). There should be a variety of tasks that address the multiple intelligences and the needs of the auditory, visual, and tactile-kinesthetic learner in the session. Refreshments are always appreciated!

Search for and use humor. Cartoons, jokes, and sometimes seizing the moment add a special touch of warmth to a session. Consultants should be able to laugh at themselves. Humor often relaxes people. When the brain is in a more relaxed state, it is able to retain more.

Arrange furniture to reflect desired participant interactions. For example, consider positioning tables to facilitate participant discussion and table-group tasks as well as access to the presenter's direct instruction. Invite participants to sit with a variety of people. People should be invited to sit where they wish. Assigning seats takes control away from adults. Create opportunities for participants to interact with other table group colleagues during activities throughout the training.

Establish norms regarding risk taking, participation, and accountability. Consultants should model risk taking and accountability, for example, by asking participants at the end of a session to review the expectations they generated, reflect on the session's content, and offer feedback. In the beginning of the session, the trainer lets participants know that feedback will be solicited at the end of the session; hence the request for expectations is not an idle gesture. In this way, the person who conducts the workshop demonstrates a commitment to continual growth. The participants should be invited to set goals for themselves, take risks, participate as they feel comfortable, and assess their learnings. Many times participants are asked to brainstorm responses to questions such as "What have you learned?" and "What new questions do you have?" This data is used for program evaluation and future program planning. The adult participants recognize, in this way, that input can influence a program. This contributes to a growing sense of efficacy. Modeling accountability in training also reinforces the importance of teachers focusing on the results that their instruction produces in the classroom.

■ THE BIG PICTURE

Principals play the key role in creating a context or culture in which adult learning flourishes (Champion, 2002). Validating this notion, Rick DuFour (2001) wrote, "I have come to understand the most significant contribution a principal can make to developing others is creating an appropriate context for adult learning. It is context—the programs, procedures, beliefs, expectations and habits that constitute the norm for a given school—that plays the biggest role in determining whether staff development efforts will have an impact on that school" (p. 14).

Principals who use the information in this chapter will increase the probability that the professional development program at a school will be responsive to both individual and organizational needs, will model effective practice, and will provide a variety of learning activities for the adults in the building who serve students. Student success will be a consequence. It is essential that the program be ongoing and provide for continuous improvement. Implicit in this orientation is the need to constantly assess how well the professional development program is meeting the goals for which it was ultimately intended: student and staff growth as well as increased learning-focused collaboration among staff. As Roland Barth (personal communication, 2007) once said to a group of principals, "I've yet to see a school where the learning curves of students are upward and the learning curves of adults are downward. Learning goes hand in hand, or not at all."

REFLECTIONS

This space provides for you a place to write in ideas that have been generated by this chapter, things you want to try, or adaptations of ideas presented herein.

1. Which of the guidelines for creating an atmosphere for positive professional development are most meaningful to you?

2. Create a plan for professional development with attention to the five stages (readiness, planning, training, implementation, and maintenance) related to student and staff data. Emphasize how staff learning will impact student learning in your plan.

3. Reflect on a professional development activity with which you have been involved. Evaluate it using your learnings from this chapter.

4. What insights or new questions do you have as a result of reflecting on the ideas presented in this chapter?

13

Faculty Meetings

A Tool for Capacity Building

Faculty meetings: 30-minute opportunities or obstacles.

—A principal's voice

Faculty meetings present opportunities to talk about curriculum, instruction, and assessment; increase our understanding of student development; strengthen staff collaboration; and build faculty morale and school culture. Although meetings have the potential to be used for these ends, too often they are not. As a result, they are sometimes perceived as a waste of time. A faculty member might be overheard saying after such a meeting, "We could have received the same information in an e-mail." In schools where faculty meetings have been transformed into learning opportunities, staff members look forward to these sessions. They know they can count on getting strategies and information they can use immediately with students. As you read this chapter, you might also reflect on how these same ideas might apply to team or department meetings.

FACULTY MEETINGS AS ■
LEARNING OPPORTUNITIES

Faculty meetings should always be viewed as learning opportunities. A principal should consider the meeting a success if teaching and learning are the central themes. Faculty members should walk out of these meetings feeling like they have actively participated in the meeting, had involvement in developing the agenda, and, most important, learned something. In a sense, these meetings represent a celebration, a gathering of teachers to reduce the isolation of the classroom, in which teachers share ideas about what works and what does not work. Meetings also create opportunities to build a more collaborative learning-focused culture.

Faculty meetings should not be used for "administrivia." Letting the staff know that you will not cover information during the meeting that could be communicated in an e-mail or memo can be comforting and helps build positive attitudes and perceptions about meetings. The trade-off is that teachers should read the written communication. Many times, to encourage this, gimmicks have been built into the text of the e-mail or memo. For example, a message might be written within the text regarding entering a drawing. The staff might need to estimate the number of reams of paper used by the school. Prizes might be gifts donated by local businesses. Keeping creature comforts in mind (e.g., location of the meeting, how much sitting is involved, availability of refreshments) enhances the affective appeal of the meeting.

At one school, staff members routinely ask themselves at the end of the meeting, "What have we done for students today?" Asking this question keeps the mission of the school in the forefront of everyone's minds.

The suggestions that follow represent practices many principals have used successfully. Many principals also use meetings as opportunities to highlight teacher leadership by engaging teacher leaders in designing faculty, team, or department meetings.

■ THE SCHOOL MISSION AND FACULTY MEETINGS

The principal and teacher leaders should view meetings as opportunities to emphasize the school mission. Certainly, in the beginning of the year and with new faculty, this is especially important. By coming back to the mission periodically, the message is going out that the mission is not just an idea that looks good in the handbook or on the school Web site. Examples of classroom activities that are taking place to support the mission further reinforce the interrelationship between daily classroom activities, schoolwide goals, and the mission statement. Reviewing the mission statement and the corresponding goals periodically provides the staff with opportunities to tailor the guiding principles and documents of the school to current needs.

The following activity represents a mission-building strategy. It can also be used to refine a mission statement. Individual staff members are asked to reflect on the following:

- Describe the place you would like to go to work each day.
- Describe the place you would like to send your children to school.

Staff members are then asked to fuse these visions into one. Following this, individuals are asked to share at table groups and to develop a composite vision. Table groups then share these composites and ultimately create one that represents the collective vision. When this is recorded, it can become the basis of a school mission. Many schools have included parents and students in the mission-building process.

An alternative activity can help teachers focus on a vision of the future. Principals can encourage teachers to think about the world students will face in the future. The activity would begin with the principal briefly reviewing four or five trends that futurists have predicted. These might include the movement toward the global village, the aging population, the increasing mosaic of America, more leisure time, global warming, the widening gap between rich and poor, the technology explosion, or single parenting. The staff would also be encouraged to suggest a couple of trends. A discussion would then take place focusing on the following questions:

- What do I personally think/feel about these trends?
- Are we teaching to address these trends?
- Should we be considering alternative teaching, curriculum, and assessment strategies to address these trends?

- How are our nation's democratic principles affected by these trends?
- What are we doing on a schoolwide basis to address these trends?

The discussion can help raise consciousness about the general outcomes of education as opposed to the microview of teaching objectives on which we so easily become focused during day-to-day classroom activities.

INCREASING TEACHERS' ROLES ■ IN FACULTY MEETINGS

As we work to foster greater teacher decision making in schools, faculty meetings become an important arena for teacher leadership and teacher involvement. Teachers can collaborate in setting the agendas, coplanning the meetings, and presenting or facilitating (with or without the principal). Often, a teacher may desire to facilitate a meeting but would prefer to work with the principal or with another colleague. Presenting in front of the staff may not seem like a major occasion for a principal, but for a teacher who has not done so before, it can be both very stressful and rewarding. In many schools, the staff select members to serve on a faculty advisory committee (FAC). The FAC works with the principal to develop the agenda and to plan, implement, and evaluate meeting effectiveness. The meeting agenda should be made public in advance by sending out a memo. This meeting memo can invite faculty members to submit additional agenda items in a designated space on the memo. Their feedback, if appropriate, is incorporated into the final agenda for the meeting. Meeting minutes can be recorded on butcher paper by faculty members so that staff members can provide immediate feedback on the accuracy of the record of meeting proceedings. The recorder and facilitator roles can rotate on an ongoing basis. This level of involvement increases staff ownership and commitment to the school's activities.

Teachers and support staff may also play a major role in determining the focus of presentations during a given meeting. For example, the jigsaw activity mentioned in Chapter 3 could be used to share articles on integrating technology, working with English Language Learners, or an innovative teaching strategy. At one school, when interest in a new piece of software grew, the teachers set up a series of presentations by colleagues who were using the software successfully in their classrooms. Displays of student work and how the teachers implemented some of their ideas made for an engaging and successful meeting, helped build staff pride, and made teachers aware of resources just beyond the doors of their classrooms.

Time should be allocated for teachers to discuss specific teaching or assessment strategies, fine-tune questioning skills, or diagnose problematic areas of math, for example. Often, teachers can select DVD or video presentations, teaching and learning Web sites, guest speakers, or written materials that can be part of the faculty meeting. At some schools, teachers host monthly faculty meetings in their classrooms. This increases awareness of what is going on in individual classrooms across the school. Still other schools use faculty meetings to study and analyze data or to articulate the curriculum.

SOME SUCCESSFUL FACULTY ■ MEETING STRATEGIES

Success Stories

The following activity has been successfully used during faculty meetings and takes 20–30 minutes, depending on the size of the group. It is a good idea to do this activity across grade levels or subject areas. Generally, a note to faculty is sent out in advance so that teachers and support staff can plan what they want to share:

> What works? Often we read about research studies that draw broad conclusions regarding how we should teach. These studies are very helpful. However, they frequently miss the day-to-day successes that teachers experience in our particular school. Please share with your colleagues a success story from your class that you have experienced recently. Why were you satisfied with this experience? Can the experience apply beyond the context of a particular student or class? If the success story involves instructional resources or student work, please bring these items to the meeting.

A variation on this activity is to bring a frustration or problem to a meeting. Asking colleagues how to approach a difficult problem or dilemma can be extremely rewarding. However, the staff must be supportive and willing to take risks to implement this activity. If this activity is used, be sure not to end on a frustrating note. Here is where humor comes in handy! For example, at one meeting, the FAC playfully handed out chocolate to support teacher efforts to problem solve. On a more serious note, the support of individual classroom teachers was the critical element for problem solving. Sharing success stories is a routine practice in Professional Learning Communities. These stories also build more collaborative, learning-focused cultures.

"Great Teachers" Visualization Exercise

This strategy is a powerful way to begin or continue a conversation about effective teaching practices.

Instructions:

Reflect for the next few minutes on the *one* teacher who made a positive difference in your life. Visualize the teacher's face, the entire person, the teacher with you and your classmates, and the classroom. As you picture this teacher and the surroundings, record on an index card the qualities this teacher possessed and the practices this teacher implemented that made him or her most impactful in your life.

Meet with a colleague to compare your reflections. Then brainstorm a list of common or unique qualities and practices. Post these on a sheet of butcher paper.

Questions for Group Reflections: On Great Teachers

1. The list you developed can be sorted using the categories "personal qualities" and "instructional practices." What other categories could be used to sort the list? Which list is longer?

2. Are there teacher characteristics (e.g., qualities, practices) that represent a difference between what a novice teacher does and what an experienced teacher does? Please explain.

3. Are some qualities and practices innate and others "coachable"? Which fall into each category?

4. Can an average teacher become a great teacher? Why or why not?

5. Are there fundamental qualities and practices that one must have in order to embrace the potential to become a great teacher? If so, what are they?

6. Should we strive for greatness?

7. Are there some qualities and practices that are more important to students? Teachers? Parents? Administrators?

8. What additional questions should be asked?

Using Humor

Humor is a great tool for faculty meetings. Goleman, Boyatzis, & McKee (2002) note "Research on humor at work reveals a well-timed joke or playful laughter can stimulate creativity, open lines of communication, enhance a sense of connection and trust, and, of course, make work more fun. . . . Small wonder that playfulness holds a prominent place in the tool kit of emotionally intelligent leaders" (p. 14). In one school, a teacher approached a principal on the morning of a faculty meeting and mentioned that she would probably have to leave during the meeting for emergency root canal work. She was sorry that she would miss part of the meeting. To open the faculty meeting that day, the principal mentioned that one of the teachers had to decide which was worse, the faculty meeting or having to get a root canal. The teacher was such a masochist, the principal said, that she chose to accept a little of both! That opening got the meeting off to a good start. When necessary, such remarks also can come in handy at the end of a meeting. Often, an anecdote about a student can fit the occasion and emphasize an important theme. One teacher shared such a story by telling about a second-grade student who, while completing a math paper, counted on her fingers, recorded the answer, and then blew a kiss for every problem. When questioned about this technique, the student explained that her first-grade teacher told her, "When you get to second grade and do math, you can just kiss your fingers good-bye!" The story added humor to the meeting and reminded everyone about the importance of meaning in our actions.

Spreading the Word About Effective In-School Practices

The principal and teacher leaders can use faculty meetings to review some of the effective practices that are being implemented in the school. Citing specific examples of effective classroom practices spreads the word about instructional and curricular approaches that work and serves as a source of recognition for those teachers whose practices have been noticed. If you are Leading and Learning by Wandering Around, share highlights of your visits with an emphasis on effective practices at these meetings. This is an excellent way to remind teachers of the goals emphasized for the year or about the risk-taking behaviors being modeled by the staff. Let the staff know about positive comments made by parents and students about the school. Again, faculty meetings are great opportunities to build staff morale, celebrate staff expertise, build collegiality and keep the mission alive.

Book or Article Talks

This strategy engages faculty members in reading books or articles and having professional dialogue about the content. The faculty also reflect on strategies and techniques they might consider implementing in classrooms. For example, one faculty committed to reading *Classroom Instruction That Works* (Marzano, Pickering, & Pollock, 2001). This book identifies nine instructional strategies that have a "high probability of enhancing student achievement for all students in all subject areas at all grade levels" (p. 6). Following the reading of each chapter, teachers tried specific strategies in their classrooms and reported back to their colleagues about the effects of that strategy on student learning. Eventually the teachers began coplanning units of study, addressing key standards that employed the use of a variety of these strategies. Another faculty read *True North* (George, 2007) and discussed key ideas. Still another read *How People Learn* (Bransford, Brown, & Cocking, 2000).

Supporting Vertical Articulation and Interdisciplinary Curriculum and Instructional Practices

Faculty meetings are great opportunities for teachers in elementary, middle, or high schools to meet across grade levels and within departments. Traditionally, the social studies, science, and foreign language departments meet separately following a faculty meeting or on a different day. However, the principal can allocate time to facilitate departments meeting across disciplines to explore the possibilities for interdisciplinary curriculum work and to promote the sharing of effective teaching practices across disciplines and grade levels. Interestingly, when we discuss the interdisciplinary curriculum, we usually overlook the interdisciplinary instructional practices that should be considered. For example, if only one teacher is using cooperative learning, performance assessment, or reflective writing in a classroom, students may not see the practice as valuable throughout their other classes. The faculty meeting provides a special forum to foster the development of interdisciplinary planning for curriculum, instruction, and assessment. Approaches to differentiating learning experiences for students may also be shared. Interdisciplinary department meetings also give the staff opportunities to pursue consistent strategies and activities to meet the school mission. Some teachers have had students submit one product for two different classes, emphasizing the importance of integrating disciplines.

In the elementary school, faculty meetings offer wonderful opportunities to break up into small groups across grade levels or departments. For example, teachers across grade levels can meet to share successful instructional strategies they have used with English Language Learners. In another school, groups of second- and third-grade teachers met together to reflect on the following questions: What are you finding out about the students we sent to you last year? What are their strengths and weaknesses? Standardized test results can also be reviewed in this way. What are the students' strengths and weaknesses based on the test results? How can we work together across grade levels and disciplines to meet our school or district goals to help all students succeed? In one high school, all departments and grade levels examine how they can promote writing across the curriculum.

The following faculty meeting guides have been used to pursue some of the goals mentioned previously while promoting articulation across grade levels.

Discussion Guide: Vertical Articulation of the Curriculum

Grade Levels _____ (two or more)

The following questions are intended to stimulate discussion across grade levels. Please add to these as you see fit.

1. When your students leave your grade, what do you expect them to know? To do (key concepts, content, and skills)?

2. What would you like the incoming students to know? To do (key concepts, content, and skills)?

3. What are the congruencies and discrepancies in your view regarding the expectations?

4. What are your conclusions?

5. What next steps do you plan to take?

At certain times during the year, staff members have found it helpful to meet to discuss standardized test results. The following guide has been used as a conversation starter.

Analyzing Standardized Achievement Tests Results

Grade Level _____ Subject Area _____

1. What response patterns emerged as important for your grade level/subject area?

   Strengths:

   Weaknesses:

2. How can the results be helpful for the remainder of this year?

3. Do you have any recommendations for the previous grade level or the next grade level?

4. What are some of the major similarities and differences between the objectives of the standardized tests and our school curriculum? Differences between standardized tests and how assessment occurs in classrooms?

5. What are some of the major goals of our curriculum that cannot be assessed through standardized tests? How should we assess these goals?

6. What are your conclusions?

7. Examining data from subgroups, what inferences can we make about student learning? What do we need to keep doing, stop doing, and start doing?

8. What next steps should we take?

With software programs available to disaggregate data, many principals and teachers have found this information useful in schoolwide conversations about student learning and student needs.

The Standing Faculty Meeting for Short, Informative Sessions

Often when you have promised the staff that a short faculty meeting will take place to report on an immediate or emergency issue, the meeting tends to drag on. If you ask the staff to stand during the last 10 minutes of the meeting, you are symbolically illustrating that you are serious about holding a brief meeting. The staff member who wants to hold up the group with his or her own agenda will be very reluctant to do so when colleagues are standing and ready to go. Also, you can ask staff members to stand near the end of a regular meeting and promise them the meeting will end in 5 minutes. You will have to keep your promise! Furthermore, the staff will enjoy the opportunity to stretch!

TalkWalk for Energy, Exercise, and Dialogue

Teachers often come to meetings exhausted after a hard day's work. Imagine their surprise at an invitation to take a walk with one or two colleagues for 10–15 minutes! The TalkWalk (Caro & Robbins, 1991) engages the staff in professional dialogue while providing exercise, energy, a change of environment, and the opportunity to share expertise. Staff members tend to return from the walk in a more relaxed, reflective mood. They then articulate key points from their TalkWalk dialogue. (This promotes accountability.)

Encouraging Participation in Professional Growth Activities for Responsiveness and Meaning

The faculty meeting can also be used to share ideas about professional growth activities. Is there a new university program in the area? Is there a new e-learning opportunity? Is a well-known consultant presenting in the district or school within the next few weeks? Is grant money available for summer study? Are there professional growth experiences that teachers would like to see take place on site? Are teachers willing to share their professional growth experiences with other staff members? Does the English Language Learners or Special Education Department desire to share strategies for the mainstream classrooms? The possibilities for professional development are endless. These possibilities can be highlighted on a professional development bulletin board kept in a prominent place. By making this an issue during faculty meetings, the principal and staff are taking an important symbolic stand in supporting professional growth.

Video-Stimulated Discussions for Fun, Reflection, and Dialogue

Many staffs have begun a practice of bringing in a popular DVD or video and playing a portion of it to stimulate discussion. Examples range from *Robin Hood*, to begin a discussion on developing teams and, eventually, a collaborative workplace; to *Rain Man*, as a beginning for conversations about inclusion; to *Freedom Writers*, to stimulate a dialogue about working with at-risk students. Staff members rotate responsibility for bringing in videos. A variation of this approach is to use stories (literature for either adults or children) as a springboard for conversation.

Swap Meets for Clean Rooms and Effective Use of Resources

To build a positive climate and to facilitate sharing, some faculty meetings periodically include a swap meet. Swap meets provide the opportunity for teachers to exchange instructional or curricular resources. To illustrate, for the swap meet, teachers bring items they no longer use to exchange for items that other teachers bring. Sometimes these meets are preceded by classified ads in which teachers identify needs for resources in a "want ad" format. Requests range from coupons to books, plastic jars to magazines, and ideas—either written or recorded—to Internet resources.

■ A FINAL THOUGHT

It is important to reiterate that the faculty meeting is an opportunity for professional growth and the celebration of teaching as professionals gather together to share and learn. We often hear that teaching is the second most private act. The faculty meeting is the perfect forum for teachers to interact, build community, and break down the traditional barriers that serve as obstacles to discussing what goes on in our classrooms. Faculty meetings also provide the context to model those teaching behaviors that educators wish to see implemented in the classroom with students. Further, it is a powerful stage for building culture and schoolwide norms of practice.

REFLECTIONS

This space provides for you a place to write in ideas that have been generated by this chapter, things you want to try, or adaptations of ideas presented herein.

1. What are the level and type of staff involvement in your faculty meetings? Explain. What are some strategies to increase staff involvement?

2. Which idea from this chapter might you implement during the next faculty meeting?

3. What are some ways teacher leaders might take a greater role in faculty, team, or department meetings?

4. What is an initiative your school is currently implementing? How might faculty meeting activities support this?

5. What insights or new questions do you have as a result of reflecting on the ideas presented in this chapter?

14

Asking the Right Questions About Curriculum, Instruction, and Assessment

Getting to Know the C.I.A.

Are we testing student knowledge of the curriculum or how to successfully take a test?

—A principal's voice

■ KEEPING THE CURRICULUM RELEVANT

The notion of teachers closing the classroom door and deciding for themselves what should be included in the curriculum is no longer acceptable. Previously, research and experience indicated that many teachers taught what they were comfortable with and what was expedient. A middle school principal described it this way: "Today, teachers have to focus more on curriculum. They have to adopt texts that meet standards and focus on competencies and skills. I used to love to do my 'moon unit.' Today I could not do it. It does not meet the state standards."

Administrators and teachers feel the pressure to address state standards and experience anxiety about meeting federal and state high-stakes testing expectations. It is not pleasant to be labeled "in need of improvement," the No Child Left Behind (NCLB) euphemism for a failing school. Ironically, local schools are expected to implement the democratic ideals of site-based management and yet embrace federal and state expectations related to curriculum and high-stakes testing. Principals must ensure that the pressure and anxiety that some teachers might be feeling do not overflow into the classroom. For example, most teachers are uncomfortable with "teaching to the test" if the test does not meet curriculum expectations and the unique needs of the students in their classes. In fact, although most administrators and teachers welcome standards, the enthusiasm for standards has been partially clouded by NCLB testing issues that are fairly or unfairly linked to standards.

Zemelman, Daniels, and Hyde (2005) maintain, "Most states had linked their newly created curriculum frameworks to testing systems that deeply contradicted the national curriculum standards. Across the country, state tests . . . predominantly favored multiple-choice, factual-recall formats that pushed teachers right back toward a superficial curriculum of coverage and time-eating test-prep" (p. ix). This cannot be stated too strongly because a teacher's attitude and enthusiasm regarding curriculum standards and high-stakes testing send a subtle but strong message to students about the importance of learning. The attitudes that we convey (e.g., regarding the hidden curriculum) and the processes or strategies that we use teach children and adults how we feel about learning and how we learn. If lifelong learning is the vision, then what is taught and how it is taught must be considered in tandem. Generating the momentum toward accomplishing this vision is perhaps one of the greatest challenges for the principalship. To help address this challenge, this chapter will examine curriculum, instruction, and assessment issues by raising significant questions.

ASKING THE RIGHT QUESTIONS ■

Principals, because of their daily interaction with students, teachers, and parents, may be in the best position to reflect on how the curriculum is affecting the total school community. From this vantage point, principals must consider and facilitate discussion concerning the following questions and issues as curriculum, instructional, and assessment decisions are made. By promoting these questions and encouraging dialogue among the staff, principals can do a great deal to facilitate teacher thinking about curriculum, their students, and ways of teaching.

How Should Curriculum Be Defined?

There is no one definition of curriculum that is universally accepted. For example, curriculum can mean a sequenced plan to educate students or a broad field of study (e.g., examining various curriculum models). Yet defining curriculum is a very difficult and important task. The definition says much about the scope of school experiences that one believes has a direct impact on student learning. For example, a narrow definition of a curriculum plan usually focuses on specific classroom content and skills that can be objectively tested, whereas a broader definition moves beyond specific classroom content and skills and involves activities that have long-range implications and sometimes are not easily tested. Additionally, a broader definition implies that almost all of the actions of a classroom teacher and activities within a school may have far-reaching curriculum implications for students. Although a narrow definition of curriculum is easier to grapple with, especially when considering the testing implications, reality tells us that the social and cultural forces influencing curriculum favor a broader definition.

Thus, based on the comments and connections made in this book about a school's overall mission as a learning community for continued adult and student growth, a broad definition of curriculum is appropriate. Hence, curriculum is defined as planned and unplanned concepts, content, skills, work habits, means of assessment, attitudes, instructional strategies taught in the classroom, and the variety of school activities in and out of class that influence students' present and future academic, social, emotional, and physical growth.

What Are Some Important Shifts Related to Curriculum, Instruction, Assessment, and Learning That Influence the Practices of Principals and Others in Supervisory Positions?

To gain a clear understanding of the shifts, it is important to consider five conceptual themes that illuminate logical categories of division among these shifts.

First, there is the conceptual theme of supervision and evaluation being distinctly different from one another in focus, but nonetheless interrelated. This relationship is both problematic and, paradoxically, useful. Supervision is, by its nature, a growth-oriented process, not a punishing one. Its intent is to foster teacher growth and deeper conceptual understanding of the interplay between instruction, curriculum, and assessment practices that promote student learning. Evaluation, in contrast, is a process (usually district or state mandates) focused on examining areas of teacher competence. The paradoxical part is that although the intent of evaluation is to ensure teaching practices that promote student learning are recognized and those that do not are remediated, rarely does the evaluation instrument state explicitly the connection between the competence being assessed and its impact on student learning. The following are shifts related to this theme:

- The clinical supervision process, traditionally focused on observing teacher behavior, is now refocused on student behavior and work. Consequently, pre- and postobservation conferences are targeting data; teacher decision making with regard to curriculum, instruction, and assessment; student work samples; teacher strategies; curricular expectations; differentiated instruction; data-driven decisions related to student learning; and traditional and alternative assessments.
- Differentiated supervision is customized for novice, experienced, and at-risk teachers needing intensive assistance.

The second conceptual theme of shifts is that of supervisory practices that have an inherent focus on learning. Some of these practices focus on student learning, some on staff learning, and some on enhanced understanding of curriculum, instruction, and assessment. The following are shifts related to this theme:

- There is a shift toward observing quality, meaningful, and engaging student work; previously, supervisors concentrated primarily on the teacher delivery system.
- Supervisors and teachers are addressing the notion that quality, meaningful, and engaging work must be offered to each student—with success for each student in the school as the goal.
- Decisions related to student diversity and exceptionality are being addressed through instructional, curricular, and assessment differentiation.
- Continuous teacher growth, in contrast to mastery, is a more suitable approach for addressing the complexities of teaching, learning, and assessment.
- Individual principals are serving as culture-building instructional leaders by shaping faculty meetings as learning opportunities, increasing their classroom visibility to celebrate student and teacher work and success, using technology and the Internet to facilitate data analysis and sharing, involving parents, and fostering nonhierarchical Professional Learning Communities.

The third theme of shifts addresses professional development as an extension of the supervisory process and, at the same time, an embedded part of it. The explicit goal is to build the capacity of staff members to address a wide spectrum of student needs and ultimately foster student learning. Capacity building is accomplished in a variety of forums and led by both administrators and teacher leaders. The following are shifts related to this theme:

- Districts and schools are addressing the best and promising practices research on instructional strategies, curriculum standards, assessment, student learning, and leadership behaviors.

- Recognizing the holistic interrelationship of instructional, curricular, assessment, and professional development work, educators are systematically and intentionally aligning decisions among these four areas.
- Teacher Leaders are initiating and directing contextualized collaborative professional development practices such as individual and group coaching and mentoring, peer-coaching teams, book study groups, critical friends, lesson study groups, teacher curricular and instructional breakfasts, and Action Research projects. These practices have inspired teachers to shift from isolated to collaborative work.
- Supervisors are supporting Teacher Leaders engaged in collaborative professional development, individual reflection, self-evaluation, and professional goal setting. Supervisors recognize that sharing and distributing leadership is essential as supervisory expectations and accountability responsibilities expand.
- Building-level teacher leadership is expanding regarding instructional, curricular, assessment, and professional development decisions.

The fourth theme of shifts embraces supervisory actions in response to and reflective of site-level data. Here the goal is to examine those promising practices that appear to be contextually relevant. An example of this might be a supervisor identifying specific teachers who, according to school-level data, have narrowed or closed the achievement gap. Supervisory visits would focus on promising practices that are particularly influential when embedded in the local context. The results of these visits would inform both professional development efforts and supervisory visits to other, less successful teachers who might benefit from the knowledge gleaned from visits to exemplary staff members. The following are shifts related to this theme:

- Data-driven assessment decisions, especially decisions related to closing the achievement gap, are influencing supervision and evaluation strategies. Proactive early intervention programs to assist all students and detracking policies to maximize opportunities for all students are being instituted.
- Traditional summative assessments (e.g., state and national tests) and alternative formative assessments (e.g., portfolios, performances, exhibitions) are increasingly valued by educators and the general public.
- Summative and formative assessments are addressing expectations related to the world of work and global citizenship responsibilities.

The fifth theme is simple, rare, and powerful: feedback on feedback. The intent of practices that relate to this shift engage the supervisor in asking staff members for feedback about strategies employed during conferences and observations. The supervisor might ask a teacher in a postobservation setting, "What strategies did I employ that facilitated your thinking and learning? What other approaches or techniques might I have used? Is there anything I did that impeded your learning? If we were to replay this experience and do it differently, what would you change? What would you keep the same?" These questions and related actions would have a leveling influence on interactions between teacher and supervisor, build trust, communicate that the supervisor will work just as hard in the supervisory role as the teacher does in the teaching role, emphasize a focus on learning about learning, and portray supervisory actions that focus on the core work of schools. The following are shifts related to this theme:

- Recognizing that personal professional growth is imperative in today's complex world, supervisors are embracing George's (2007) notion that "to be an effective leader, *you must take responsibility for your own development*" (p. xxxiii).

- Expert supervisors and teachers must not be overlooked as recipients of feedback. They have earned the right to receive feedback on their work. As Jim Collins (2005) has stated, "Greatness is an inherently dynamic process, not an endpoint. The moment you think of yourself as great, your slide toward mediocrity will have already begun" (p. 9).

What Kind of Authentic Student Work and Assessment Results Are Essential to Prepare Students for Successful Living in a Democratic Society?

It is important to consider student work and related outcomes and assessments that go beyond traditional school-related tasks and expectations. Each proposed outcome should answer satisfactorily the question: Will this learning help students when they are not in school, as citizens and in the workplace? According to many educators and business leaders, we must identify the skills that will be needed in the future and how to best teach those skills. For example, if we accept Drucker's (1992) view that to work successfully in an organization one must have "the ability to present ideas orally and in writing; the ability to work with people; [and] the ability to shape and direct one's own work, contribution and career" (p. 5), then we must teach the appropriate content and skills to foster these competencies.

Thus a multicultural curriculum, cooperative learning activities, independent and challenging thinking activities, and multidisciplinary and interdisciplinary activities (that include oral, written, and cross-subject analyses) become important, not because they are fashionable but because they provide essential skills that can be transferred to the workplace. Moreover, when deciding on key student learnings, it is essential that one asks: What are the specific instructional techniques and activities (e.g., cooperative learning, drafting several versions of a report, debating) that best teach specific curricular expectations and foster applications of these learnings in the workplace? To illustrate further, in elementary, middle, and high school community service programs and in middle and high school courses, workplace experiences become essential links to support and highlight the connections between school and real-life experiences.

To develop relevant curriculum expectations, a structured approach that covers essential questions is very helpful. The classic Tyler Rationale still provides us with four essential questions that should be addressed by individuals and committees when developing curriculum. These questions are as follows: "(a) What educational purposes should the school seek to attain? (b) What educational experiences can be provided that are likely to attain these purposes? (c) How can these educational experiences be effectively organized? (d) How can we determine whether these purposes are being attained?" (Hyman, 1974, p. 40). Add to this model what we now know from research on the human brain and developments in teaching methodology, and we have the key elements to engage in a meaningful dialogue on curriculum, instruction, assessment, and learning within a school setting. An approach close to Tyler, but subtly different, is expressed by Wiggins and McTighe (1998) as they effectively tackle curriculum "backward" with a design strategy that initially may appear counterintuitive:

This backward approach to curriculum design also departs from another common practice: thinking about assessment as something we do at the end, once teaching is completed. Rather than creating assessments near the conclusion of a unit of study (or relying on the tests provided by textbook publishers, which may not completely or appropriately assess our standards), backward design calls for us to operationalize our goals or standards in terms of assessment evidence as we *begin* to plan a unit or course. It reminds us to begin with the question, What would we accept as evidence that students have attained the desired understandings and proficiencies—before proceeding to plan teaching and learning experiences? (p. 8)

In addition to recognizing the type of learning needed to succeed in the future, and how curriculum and assessments should be aligned, schools need to ask: Are the assessments democratic? Are the assessments addressing the needs of all students? Assessment expert Rick Stiggins (2005) laments that, traditionally, educators competitively ranked students and seemed gratified with that broad distribution of tests scores that labeled a large segment of the student population as failures. These students either dropped out of school or failed to develop needed basic skills because ongoing feedback and skill development were not part of the assessment equation. According to Stiggins,

> The driving emotional force cannot merely be competition for an artificial scarcity of success. . . . The student must believe that, "I will succeed at learning if I keep trying." Students must have continuous access to believe evidence of credible academic success, leading to the new role for assessment in school improvement: We use it to help students see and understand the achievement targets from the beginning of the learning, and we use it to help them watch themselves grow and succeed. (pp. 73–74)

Stiggins (2005) calls this process *assessment FOR learning* in which students have the opportunity to work on and improve performance in a supportive environment. He contrasts this with *assessment OF learning,* the traditional summative process, that lets students know if learning occurred following the instruction. According to Stiggins, "assessments OF learning ask if students are meeting standards . . . [and] assessments FOR learning ask if our students are making progress toward meeting those standards. One is for accountability, while the other is intended to support learning" (p. 75). Bransford, Brown, and Cocking (2000), using the more popular term *formative assessment,* note that this type of assessment is "ongoing," "make[s] student thinking visible," and "help[s] both teacher and students monitor progress" (p. 24).

What Instructional Considerations Effectively Communicate the Curriculum to Students?

One of the keys to ensuring that the curriculum content is communicated well is sound instructional approaches. Caine and Caine (1991) present a very strong argument for basing instructional considerations on recent discoveries in research on the human brain. Central to their thesis is that the brain is constantly making connections; thus curriculum and teaching models and methodologies should emphasize learning based on an integrated curriculum, thematic teaching, thematic orchestration, and cooperative learning (pp. 118–122). Furthermore, Caine and Caine stress that because the human brain is both an emotional and a cognitive organ, it responds to motivating stimuli that immerse the learner in a variety of engaging experiences such as reading, listening, and talking (p. 6).

The Best Practice research by Zemelman et al. (2005) echoes the work of Caine and Caine (1991). Their comprehensive review of almost every major curriculum standards document, beginning with the National Council of Teachers of Mathematics (NCTM) pioneering work on standards, has led the researchers to conclude that "all the authoritative voices and documents in every teaching field are calling for schools that are more student-centered, active, experiential, authentic, democratic, collaborative, rigorous, and challenging" (Zemelman et al., 2005, p. vii). Zemelman et al.'s Best Practice analysis leads them to surmise that, when considering instructional strategies, teachers should engage in LESS "whole class, teacher-directed instruction . . . one-way transmission of information from teacher to student . . . student time spent reading textbooks . . . attempts by teachers to thinly 'cover' large amounts of material . . . emphasis on competition and grades . . . tracking or leveling . . . [and] reliance on standardized tests" and MORE "experiential, inductive, hands-on learning . . . talking and collaborating . . . higher order thinking; learning a field's key concepts and principles . . . deep study of a smaller number of topics . . . whole books, primary sources, and nonfiction material . . . choice for students . . . attention to affective needs . . . [and] heterogeneous classrooms" (pp. 8–9).

How Can Data-Driven Curricular, Instructional, and Assessment Decisions Help Educators Foster Student Academic Growth?

Background

In the past, when student test scores on national norm-referenced tests were shared with faculty or parents, few changes were made based on the testing results. The tests may have given us some insight into how a particular child, school, or district was performing, but there was little concern about teacher or student accountability. Today the situation has changed. The standards movement in most states is accompanied by assessment systems that align the standards with high-stakes tests in specific disciplines.

The Purpose of Data-Driven Decision Making

Quite simply, data-driven decision making takes an analytical and hard look at the question: How are the students doing? This question is grounded in state and national expectations for student achievement (i.e., standards) that hold administrators and teachers accountable in each school. These standards target areas in which students and schools are expected to show progress over time. Both quantitative and qualitative trends and patterns of student progress are monitored and interpreted, often related to the standards deemed essential within a particular state. As Manobianco (2002) notes, "Interpreting data in isolation is useless without linking the data to what we want students to know and be able to do as well as looking at our instructional strategies" (p. 17).

In addition, effective data-driven decision making implies that teachers will use multiple sources of data to fine-tune their teaching in order to meet various student needs. Scherer (2001) refers to this important assessment responsibility as the examination of "multiple data waves" (p. 15) in which teachers might use data collected from portfolios, reading records, classroom observations, and audio recordings in addition to norm- or criterion-referenced tests and standardized tests.

Creating a Culture That Supports Data-Driven Decision Making

It is not easy to create a school culture that embraces the examination of testing. Yet it is one of the most important trends occurring in schools today. Often these schools include principals who are "effective school leaders [and] are hunters, gatherers and consumers of education" (National Association of Elementary School Principals [NAESP], 2001). Schools are willingly examining curricular, instructional, and assessment practices that account for strengths, weaknesses, and puzzling student scores without blaming or pointing fingers because of testing outcomes. Instead, teachers comfortably ask: How can we use the data to target difficulties and improve teaching and learning? This reflects a climate in which accountability is balanced with honest analysis in a nonthreatening manner. Lachat, Williams, and Smith (2006) suggest using a team approach to examining data: "A data team expands the control of data beyond a handful of administrators and allows a group of staff members to develop and model data analysis skills" (p. 19). Lachat et al. also suggest that schools should develop essential questions relevant to the specific site to organize the data and use a data coach to facilitate the process until the school team has a greater understanding of how to maximize the use of data. It is important that schools are deliberate about the steps of collecting, organizing, and analyzing data because thoughtful action should be the culminating activity (Parsley, Dean, & Miller, 2006).

Leaders can set a positive tone in schools by promoting a dialogue about assessment. To illustrate, principals can encourage data analysis during faculty meetings, pre- and postobservation conferences, classroom teaching, grade-level meetings, and other professional development activities. One middle school assistant principal stated, "The most exciting activity that we encountered as a faculty concerned data-driven decision making related to sharing writing samples across the curriculum during a faculty meeting. During the meeting we established rubrics aligned with state standards as we scored student work together. This activity made all of us aware of the writing expectations that students should be held accountable for within each discipline." Also, faculty meetings can provide forums for inviting representatives from other schools, with demographic profiles similar to your own school, to share information about progress and concerns with their curricular standards and assessment measures. Principals can help with purposeful scheduling to provide time for teachers to diagnose data in teams to more effectively plan teaching and learning.

Recently, a retired teacher shared the following observation: "When I was teaching I did not worry about standardized tests because the tests were not given until the following year. Today, with standards and the increased testing and accountability, teachers cannot ignore how the progress in their class might affect testing the following year." Consequently, opportunities must be provided that allow teachers to compare notes with grade-level or department colleagues to review standards and benchmarks and discuss effective instructional strategies. During these meetings teachers can remind one another to concentrate on essential curriculum elements, pinpoint areas that need greater emphasis, identify strengths, and explore grade-level or subject area trends (e.g., "How are our students doing on word problems in math? The data indicate that we are accomplishing our goals in this area. Let's continue to use these curricula and instructional practices—and use some of these practices in other areas, too").

This horizontal articulation must be complemented by vertical articulation with grade-level or subject area colleagues above and below a particular grade to reduce curriculum repetition and share successful teaching strategies. These horizontal and vertical grade-level meetings provide opportunities for critical friends and Action Research activities to occur, linking state standards and state assessment with actual classroom performance.

Pre- and postobservation conferences and class observations should also be used to promote data-driven decision making. During preobservation conferences, principals need to ask teachers about targeting standards, benchmarks, and assessment data with student work in particular classes.

Data-driven decision making also uses feedback generated from student, parent, or community surveys. For example, data revealing how present high school students or recent graduates are succeeding in the job market can help schools with curricular and instructional decisions.

Types of Data

The risk of using scores on one high-stakes test to make important decisions about a student has encouraged educators to examine various ways to measure success. Thus, both qualitative and quantitative assessment measures, also referred to as *soft* and *hard data,* are being explored to make better curricular and instructional decisions about student needs and teaching strategies (NAESP, 2001).

Hard data. Hard data sources include norm- and criterion-referenced tests, which are usually externally developed and graded. Often, these tests are given once a year or once every few years. Traditionally, these tests have not been aligned with state goals and objectives. Today, however, criterion-referenced tests measure student success based on state expectations. Disaggregating testing data helps schools examine trends and diagnose specific strengths and needs.

Soft data. Soft data sources include a variety of alternative assessment measures and teacher-generated tests. These forms of data are usually internal (i.e., developed at the school site or in the classroom) and often carry greater meaning for teachers, students, and parents. Common forms of alternative assessment include portfolios, senior projects, exhibitions, performances, digital video and audio recordings of student progress, group presentations, lab experiments, and teacher observations.

A portfolio, as a record of student growth over time, is especially promising as a rich source of student data. When a teacher, parent, or community member can look at a specific student's work, generated during a year or over several years, one can see progress right before one's eyes. Hard-copy evidence of student work as artifacts of progress is very powerful. Hearing and/or seeing a brief audio or video recording, taped over several months, of a first grader learning to read is equally powerful. The popularity of student-led conferences showcasing student work attests to the power of these sources of data. Paperless electronic portfolios are also very popular and enable students to display a variety of work samples in a digital format that can include artifacts that range from a math exam, to video of a field trip, to an interactive dialogue with British students debating the causes of the revolutionary war.

Disaggregating Data

Data-driven decision making seeks "to look deeper into the surface data" to help schools identify why some students are doing better than others (NAESP, 2001, p. 64). Because of the electronic data resources available to schools, disaggregating information is much less difficult today than even 10 years ago. Principals can lead this effort, along with guidance counselors, school psychologists, technology teachers, and central office assessment specialists.

Multiple demographic variables can be examined by disaggregating data. Examples of demographic variables include gender, attendance patterns, ethnicity, race, student mobility, teacher mobility, teacher tenure, free or reduced lunch eligibility, tardiness, behavioral referrals, and second-language learners. It is critical to engage in a dialogue when disaggregating data to examine trends or patterns that emerge as variables are considered.

One cannot exaggerate the importance of analyzing data demographically. For example, a majority of students in a particular school may have achieved outstanding results on the state's math assessment test. However, disaggregated data may reveal that 75 percent of the students in the school who are eligible for free or reduced lunch scored below the minimum expectation on the test. Clearly the school needs to target this population to help these students improve their test scores.

Finally, a cautionary note. Disaggregating data helps principals, teachers, and parents examine whether schools are succeeding with their various populations. However, whenever we separate groups and highlight differences, there is a risk that data might be misinterpreted or misused—leading to stereotypical remarks and possibly racist or prejudicial generalizations. Unfortunately, the history of standardized testing, going back to the 1920s and the original intelligence testing movement, is filled with prejudicial use and abuse of data results that led to limiting school and career opportunities for both indigenous and immigrant American populations (*Education Week*, 2000). School leaders must guard against this abuse of data. This sentiment is supported by the American Educational Research Association's position statement on high-stakes testing. That statement includes two key recommendations: "The intended and unintended effects of the testing program must be continuously evaluated and disclosed" and "the negative side-effects of a high-stakes assessment program must be fully disclosed to policy makers" (Amrein-Beardsley, 2008, pp. 72–73).

What Is the Best Way to Determine Whether Students Have Grasped the Key Curriculum Goals?

This question presents one of the most difficult and controversial issues in education: finding the best way to judge what students know and are able to do. Unless educators and other stakeholders are satisfied with the ways of assessing students, curriculum accountability will always be questioned. Standardized tests give us some insight into how students in each school "rate" when compared to each other and to students in other schools. State assessments, based on curricula standards, serve as a crucial and very public source of information for comparison and accountability purposes. This is especially true when high-stakes tests are used to make decisions for promotion and graduation. However, we need to go further if each teacher's expertise about his or her class is to count—and if we are to identify the diverse strengths and needs of each student. The nature of assessments may need to vary in each class. Thus a major part of a school's discussion on curriculum must be related to the learning tasks at each grade level that indicate whether students have grasped the essentials of the curriculum. Clearly, assessment is not separate from curriculum and instruction.

Probably one of the richest activities for a teaching staff is to develop acceptable performance standards and performance tasks to be assessed. To illustrate, let us assume that an 11th-grade American history class has just studied the governmental system of checks and balances. Instead of giving a traditional essay exam to assess their knowledge of the system, why not try a simulation activity in which groups of students represent the three branches of government (executive, legislative, judicial) and debate over which branch or branches should be responsible for handling scenarios presented by the teacher? Before beginning the activity, a teacher should have a strong sense of which concepts are critical for understanding. The activity should be structured so students have an opportunity to display and reinforce their understanding of the concepts (e.g., When does a police action by our military become a war? What role does each branch of government play if America is fighting a war?). This will give students an opportunity to really wrestle with issues, debate, think on their feet, and see the different interpretations that are possible. This type of performance task adds some credibility to those trying to address the following concern: developing student tasks that can give us insight into how students in five years may apply what they have learned today. Such a task also presents opportunities for students to practice critical thinking, decision making, public speaking, and listening skills in addition to demonstrating knowledge about the branches of government.

The positive response of so many teachers to alternative assessment strategies probably indicates a realization that the search for ways to authenticate learning has brought greater meaning to both teachers and students. Principals would be wise to encourage these explorations if teachers are taking ownership of the various strategies to pursue meaningful curriculum goals. Portfolio assessment, for example, has enabled teachers to see significant growth over time and has encouraged students to take greater ownership and reflect more on their work (Tierney, Carter, & Desai, 1991).

Howard Gardner's (2006) multiple intelligences theory has increased interest in various assessment strategies to give students an opportunity to display their talents. To illustrate, Thomas Armstrong (1994) has cited anecdotal records, work samples, audiocassettes, videotapes, photography, student journals, sociograms, informal tests, and student interviews as suitable ways to demonstrate understanding through a multiple intelligences approach (pp. 116–123). Finally, having students write their own homework or test questions or use learning logs, webbing, and semantic mapping are all indicators that teachers continue to search in creative ways to help determine how best to find out whether students have grasped the curriculum goals.

How Can a Principal Help Keep a Conversation on Curriculum Active?

Principals can promote this process by providing a forum through monthly grade-level or department meetings devoted at least partially to answering questions already raised in this chapter and others, such as the following: Are the state and district curriculum standards being addressed in our school? Is our curriculum relevant? Are we accomplishing our primary curriculum objectives? Are we behind? Are we ahead? What can we leave out without hurting the program? What are we doing about addressing the needs of students who are not reaching standard? The idea is not just to "cover" the curriculum but to address the essential components of the curriculum necessary for students to succeed in present and future grades—and, more important, in life. We hear often that less is more. If we accept this notion, then selecting key learning objectives and focusing on those objectives should be a much greater concern than touching on each chapter recommended in a textbook.

The principal needs to facilitate the development of a forum so teachers interact across grade levels to align and articulate the curriculum. First-grade teachers must meet with second-grade teachers to ask about expectations and how they can meet student needs across grade levels. In middle school and high school, subject area specialists should do the same so important content skills and concepts are not overlooked and subject area fragmentation is minimized. Discussions of this kind across the curriculum can facilitate interdisciplinary planning and highlight key concepts that individual teachers can emphasize to reinforce students' prior experiences with the same concepts. At one school, the principal allocated time so that teachers could identify key themes that they taught. For example, one teacher taught the Civil War; another, the War on Poverty; still another, the Vietnam War. The key theme was the concept that all oppression brings resistance and conflict. By teaching this concept, teachers helped students make connections across classes and enhance understanding regarding the connectedness of knowledge. The discussion also increased the amount of future dialogue about curriculum among professionals at this school.

The development of statewide curriculum documents that describe important student learnings is of paramount importance. To help guide teachers and enhance the conversation on curriculum, teachers should work with principals, curriculum specialists, or grade-level leaders to develop locally relevant and brief curriculum guides based on state expectations that may include key concepts and skills, essential questions, and assessment components. Curriculum maps and pacing charts with general timelines to meet unit or thematic goals can also be helpful.

The written curriculum should be a living document frequently reviewed and discussed by teachers. What good is a curriculum that remains in a desk drawer gathering dust? By having teachers involved in refining the state-, district-, or school-developed curriculum to meet the needs of particular students, the principal can help facilitate and maintain a dialogue on curriculum and teaching.

How Much Should Curriculum Change?

Before addressing the issue of curriculum change, it is important to consider a school's overall belief on whether curriculum is dynamic or unchanging. Without getting into a major discussion of various curriculum philosophies, let us remember that a classical education is very different from John Dewey's notion of curriculum as process and experimentation in a democratic society—adjusting to changing world needs. The classical ideal maintains that there are essential skills and classical works that are enduring regardless of how the world changes.

If one accepts the notion that curriculum is dynamic, then there is always something new to add to the curriculum. Changing societal needs, technological innovations, national security concerns, and political realities all mean curricular changes. For those who accept the changing curriculum, these are the crucial questions:

- What do we need to do to prepare students for the future?
- What should be added to the curriculum?
- What should be removed from the curriculum?

It is not easy to differentiate the latest fad from a meaningful curriculum innovation. Which new curriculum ideas should be adopted? Which traditional ideas should be discarded or revived? Again, staff dialogue is a key. How can the school principal help the staff determine which ideas are worth examining? Which state standards and benchmarks should receive greater or less emphasis based on the local setting? Encouraging teachers to read professional journals, using time during faculty meetings to discuss innovations, sponsoring brown-bag or study groups, and encouraging professional growth experiences beyond the school (e.g., conferences, workshops, courses) are all ways that principals can help the staff examine the changes that are taking place. Ideally, the principal should empower the teachers to take the lead regarding an innovation. When necessary, principals can productively contribute to innovative projects by sharing research with the staff and revisiting the school vision and mission. Principals can then provide the support to encourage an innovative or pilot program in a class, grade level, or throughout the school.

States, school districts, or individual schools with institutionalized curriculum review cycles (usually three to six years) go a long way in making sure that systematic decisions are made when innovations come down the pike. (In larger districts, schools should try to have representation on the district committees to ensure that curriculum decisions are relevant to site-based needs.) The review cycle, which provides for an examination of different subject areas in a systematic way each year, can bring productive change, thoughtful decision making, and exciting curriculum discussions to a district office or school. Furthermore, the process "puts the skids" on those who try to pressure a change without a comprehensive review. The most refreshing aspect of a review cycle may very well be that the process institutionalizes change within the structure of the organization. The very nature of the cycle encourages renewal because teachers examine the recent research in the curriculum area and other curricular and innovative instructional methods. This is essential in keeping an organization on the cutting edge.

An excellent project for a school to stay abreast of curricular innovations is to collect articles on various curricular or teaching trends and conduct a jigsaw activity at a faculty meeting to discuss the ideas. Various topics might include the following:

- Assisting special needs students
- Is the curriculum a help or hindrance to closing the achievement gap?
- Are data-driven curriculum decisions inhibiting creativity?
- Alternative assessment
- Integrated curriculum
- The revised NCTM standards
- Are the state tests aligned with standards?
- Multicultural education
- Using technology
- Developing rubrics for student work samples

A variation of this activity might be to revisit the ideas of curriculum innovators such as John Dewey or Robert Hutchins or possibly to discuss the ideas of more current theorists such as Howard Gardner on multiple intelligences or James Banks on multicultural education. This activity might encourage staff members to review what these educators propose and then reflect on whether the ideas are right for the school.

To pilot a curricular idea, a school might decide to tackle a topic such as integrated curriculum as an innovative project. For example, an integrated environmental education activity could result from this curriculum project. Students could write poems about the environment, conduct scientific experiments examining the environment, use rainfall percentages in math, and discuss the social implications of Earth's changing environment. These activities could culminate in a schoolwide Earth Day activity.

What Can We Learn From the Differences Between Elementary and High School Curriculum Expectations That Can Help Us Develop Effective Interdisciplinary Practices?

Relating this question to an interdisciplinary curriculum approach can help shed light on how we can do a better job teaching across disciplines. A high school principal, observing an elementary school classroom, is immediately struck by the variety of subjects that elementary teachers are expected to teach within their classes. High school teachers face a considerable challenge because of the number of courses they teach in a major discipline and the depth of knowledge they are expected to master for each course. On the other hand, the elementary school teacher and often the middle school teacher must maintain broad knowledge in a variety of disciplines. An elementary school teacher cannot be an expert in every discipline; the principal must accept this reality yet work with the teacher to ensure that each core subject is addressed competently in the elementary classroom. The various expectations of high school, middle school, and elementary school teachers can be discussed at grade-level meetings, during conferences with teachers from different schools, on inservice days, or as a focus of peer-coaching activities. Some schools regularly schedule vertical articulation days.

It is important to note that the traditional high school master schedule dictates how subjects are taught and the time frame of a class period. Until we take a hard look at the schedule and exchange and pilot ideas—as many schools are now doing—it will be difficult to try interdisciplinary strategies. In recent years, hundreds of high schools have rejected the traditional schedule and have moved to instructional blocks of approximately 80 minutes, with many block schedule variations. These new designs have enabled many high school teachers to experiment and succeed with interdisciplinary activities either alone or with colleagues. These interdisciplinary strategies rely heavily on planning time as well as class time.

Interestingly, elementary teachers may have a clear advantage in making curriculum connections because one teacher is assigned to instruct students in a variety of core subjects. Thus elementary school teachers can capitalize on the common subject area concepts and the interests of students across the curriculum. This can be a powerful motivator and, of course, sets the stage for understanding that the various disciplines should be integrated, not fragmented. We must recognize relationships and connections among the academic disciplines. Focusing on key interdisciplinary concepts is one way of doing this. If one teacher teaches about the circulatory system and another about the solar system, the key concept is *system*. If the concept of what a system is is taught well, then other teachers can capitalize on adding to this existing student understanding. Elementary school principals have a distinct opportunity to promote this important educational principle with the teaching staff. They also need to allocate time for planning across classrooms and grade levels and for teachers to share their interdisciplinary approaches.

A major challenge for high school principals is working with the staff to develop more integration among the various disciplines. Approaches can range from paralleling a couple of courses, to teaching common themes when possible, to complete integration of two or more courses through team teaching and the synthesis of a variety of subject or thematic areas. In addition, providing a forum for secondary teachers to discuss what they teach and when they teach it can enable them to reinforce one another's subject area themes. For instance, in one high school, teachers of history and English were teaching World War II topics. By discussing the curriculum and how and when it was being delivered, they were able to emphasize and parallel key themes across their two classes for students. In another high school, dialogue led to the discovery that the English teacher was teaching *The Diary of Anne Frank* in November and the history teacher was addressing the Holocaust in March. By coordinating the time frames in which these were taught, the teachers enhanced the student experience. At another school, staff members selected the theme of the Baroque period and used this as a backdrop for their particular areas of specialty.

CONTINUING THE CURRICULUM DISCUSSION ■

A principal's most important responsibilities regarding curriculum may be in providing the forum or setting to facilitate teacher curriculum discussions and ensuring that state and district curriculum standards are thoughtfully implemented in the local school setting. This must occur in a school setting that is able to balance the need to cover the curriculum due to the pressure of high-stakes testing with the need to ensure that teachable and relationship-building moments are not lost. As one teacher summarized, "We should be aiming to help children become caring adults, builders of communities, sharers of learning, lovers of the printed word, citizens of the world, and nurturers of nature" (Teeter, 1995).

REFLECTIONS

This space provides for you a place to write in ideas that have been generated by this chapter, things you want to try, or adaptations of ideas presented herein.

1. Do you agree or disagree with the definition of curriculum provided in this chapter? Discuss your ideas with a colleague.

2. Are the shifts related to curriculum, instruction, and assessment relevant to your setting? What would you add to the list?

3. What are the most important curriculum issues that currently need to be addressed in your school? Why are these issues important? How can you begin energizing the staff to address these issues?

4. Speculate on some societal trends that could affect the curriculum. Are schools addressing the curricular areas necessary to cope with these trends?

5. Should the curriculum reflect current societal trends or ideal societal possibilities?

6. What steps would you include in directing a curriculum review cycle?

7. How might staff interest in curriculum review, development, or implementation be enhanced?

8. What are the pros and cons of the federal and state initiatives related to high-stakes testing and curriculum standards?

9. What insights or new questions do you have as a result of reflecting on the ideas presented in this chapter?

PART V

Starting Effectively and Staying the Course

15

First Days of School

A time for renewal.

—A principal's voice

The first days of every school year are always both exciting and nervous times for students, parents, new principals, seasoned administrators, and teachers. Regardless of how many years one has spent in the profession, the new year is always a time of renewal and uncertainty. This is a time of renewal because it is a chance to try a fresh approach with new and returning students and teachers. It is a time of uncertainty because, whether one is a newcomer or a veteran, there are always questions: Will I succeed this year? What will be the new challenges? Which state and federal mandates need to receive particular attention this year? Often, principals try to speculate about what the challenges and issues will be for a new year. The best approach to take may simply be, "I don't know what challenges or issues will come our way, but I'll try to be ready!"

The beginning of the year also has special significance because the brain remembers beginnings and endings. The first impression that a principal makes with the staff will be a lasting impression. Additionally, in the beginning of the year our senses are heightened, and the opportunity exists to face new and old challenges with a fresh perspective. On the other hand, too much change in the beginning of the year can be unnerving—especially if the changes come as a surprise to the staff. A blend of tradition and change may be the best approach if one has the chance to influence the beginning of the year.

■ LOGISTICAL CONCERNS

Distributing a schedule of beginning-of-the-year activities to teachers with a "Welcome Back" letter a couple of weeks before school begins is a good way to let teachers know that all is moving along smoothly. The letter can help encourage the staff to begin thinking about the new year and plan activities and actions that need to be taken care of before initial school meetings begin. In a year-round school, this will be necessary for each track. The letter also models valuing preparedness.

During the first days of the new school year, the principal needs to be very concerned about logistics, yet ensure that human needs and curricular, instructional, and assessment goals are not overlooked. The following "Beginning of the Year Checklist" addresses many of these concerns:

- Review district and school mission, curriculum goals, and school and grade-level testing data—alone, and then with key personnel.
- Consider which district, state, and federal mandates will need special attention this year.
- Review Individuals with Disabilities Education Act regulations, and consider whether any particular compliance issues will need special attention. Discuss these issues with district and school special education experts.
- Prepare the "Welcome Back" letter to staff, noting goals for the year, which will likely be based on the School Improvement Plan.
- Carefully review previous beginning-of-the-year memos and newsletters to staff, students, parents, and the community.
- Examine faculty assignments and last-minute hiring issues.
- Review master schedule, enrollment trends, and class lists with counselors and administrators.
- Review the budgetary expectations for the year—alone and with the district.
- Meet with assistant principals, department chairs, and grade-level leaders concerning goals for the year and beginning-of-the-year logistical issues.
- Review with secretaries the beginning-of-the-year tickler file (see Chapter 16).
- Review orientation for new students with counselors and appropriate staff.
- Review orientation for new teachers with key veteran faculty or coaches.
- Meet with special services team, including counselors and teachers.
- Remind secretaries of their role as ambassadors for the school.
- Walk through the school with the head custodian to make sure rooms have sufficient furniture for students and staff and that outlets, lights, windows, ceilings, walls, halls, and playgrounds are all meeting cleanliness and safety standards.
- Ensure that restrooms have necessary supplies and are absolutely clean.
- Review security, health and safety procedures, and critical phone numbers for fire, ambulance, police, and poison control.
- Make sure procedures are in place for preventing intruders.
- Meet with transportation and food service personnel.
- Review the year's activities with athletic/activities director.
- Review disciplinary procedures, especially new mandates, with assistant principals.
- Carefully examine and test relevant computer hardware and software upgrades with technology personnel to minimize first day glitches.
- Invite student government representatives to lunch.
- Make sure substitute teacher policies are in place.
- Carefully organize beginning-of-the-year faculty meetings, combining staff development and logistical concerns. Seek input from faculty and other administrators. Consider reviewing the School Improvement Plan during the faculty meeting.
- Meet with Parent Teacher Association representatives.
- Make sure orientation signs for "first days" of school are completed. Include a banner in the front of the school with a slogan that students are familiar with from television, such as "Good Things Are Happening" ("Good Morning America," ABC News, June 17, 2002). If appropriate, post the first day signs in various languages to meet student and parent needs.
- Schedule your time to be especially visible during the first few days of school.
- Walk through the school on your own, "visioning" a typical day.

One principal thought he was ready on the first day, except for one problem: the automated school bells had not been calibrated for the year. The custodian had forgotten about the bells, and the principal did not know how to set them. The principal quickly learned. What a way to start! Although operating the school bells should never be confused with educational leadership, the ability to calibrate bells in this case contributed to things running smoothly.

Before classes begin, teachers want to make sure they have resources and time to work in their classrooms. Scheduling a workshop in lieu of providing time to set up classrooms could be a "kiss of death" to the feeling tone in the school. There should be a balance between how time is organized and used prior to classes and a sensitivity to teacher and classroom needs. Regarding instructional resources, each teacher should receive, without asking, essential classroom supplies and instructional resources. These items should include:

Computer hardware and software	Crisis planning handbook
Curriculum guides	Teacher editions
Grade books	Planning book
Activities calendar	Copy of school's student planner
List of recent media acquisitions	Class lists and attendance forms
Whiteboard markers	Pens, pencils, a flash drive, and erasers
Paper, tape, and a stapler	Media request forms
Bulletin board material	Garbage cans

Having these items in classrooms when teachers arrive tells them that you care. If you have not used this procedure, develop a beginning-of-the-year supply list with three or four veteran teachers and a secretary. Also check with the library media center personnel and technology area personnel to make sure they have necessary resources and are ready for the first day of school. Teachers welcome lists of new library, technology, and media acquisitions.

Another logistical concern should be school maintenance. The principal should review the summer maintenance requests with the custodian and walk through the school several days before the year begins to make sure that the repairs have been completed and that the school is clean and safe. In elementary schools, the playground areas should be carefully checked for hazards. In middle and high schools, checking locker conditions and common gathering areas is a must.

To remain on top of logistical concerns from year to year, keep a beginning-of-the-year folder as part of your "tickler file" (see Chapter 16). Although the monthly tickler file will include important activities covered during each month, the beginning-of-the-year file is especially important to help you begin successfully. Remember to update the file a few days after the school year starts. Soliciting staff input can be helpful in enhancing beginning-of-the-year activities. The file is especially valuable to a principal who will be taking over a new school. Typical items that may be in the file include letters to parents, the previous year's teaching schedules, programs from various school productions, minutes or agendas of faculty meetings, and reflections on how to improve Back to School Night.

■ BEGINNING-OF-THE-YEAR FACULTY MEETINGS SET A TONE

Faculty meetings are extremely important in the beginning of the year as colleagues, old and new, gather together, work collaboratively, and, it is hoped, grow professionally. These meetings present special opportunities for principals to strengthen staff cohesion and morale. Your first obligation during the meetings should be to remind staff members that you are there to serve them.

Consider a specific theme to set the tone for the year. For instance, if the theme is "The School as a Community of Learners," activities need to be structured to reflect that. One such activity is to remind teachers of the wealth of knowledge that exists among the staff. During a faculty meeting, teachers might be asked to add up their collective years of teaching at a table group and share. The table group members with the greatest number of years might be awarded a prize. Such activities remind one of the rich resources that exist just beyond one's classroom door. By seeking advice from colleagues, staff members are able to tap the wisdom of practice that exists in a school. Without doing so, one runs the risk of repeating an initial year of teaching several years in a row.

Professional development should always be a significant part of faculty meetings. The beginning of the year is the perfect time to make this point. A principal should consider activities that help teachers think about the year and possibly create a vision of the kind of year they can have with their students and colleagues. Before beginning this visioning activity, review the school's philosophy and mission with the staff. Ask whether they believe it needs revisiting or revising. Here is a variation on a "reverse visioning" activity from *If It Ain't Broke . . . Break It!* (Kriegel, 1991) that has been used successfully in the beginning of the year:

Reverse Visioning—A Variation

You are 85 years old . . .

1. What did you do with your life?

2. What were the significant milestones at 30, 40, . . . 80?

3. What qualities did you exhibit?

4. How do other people describe your life?

5. Do you have any regrets? If so, what are they?

6. What would you have done differently?

7. As you are sitting in your rocking chair, a former student comes to visit you on your 85th birthday. The student states that he or she remembers you very well. Ideally, what would you hope that the student would say about you?

8. Pair up with a new teacher or someone who is not on your grade level or specialist area and discuss your ideas.

After the exercise, teachers were asked to write on a small poster what they wanted the students to say about them. Teachers were given markers and poster paper to complete the activity.

These faculty meetings should be used also as a link with previous years. Review the school's traditions, successes, and what characterizes the culture of the school. This is not a time to review every topic in the faculty handbook. Certainly, new or very significant school changes should be mentioned, but teachers should read the handbook on their own. This is the time, however, to remind staff members of the noble purpose of their profession and their years of dedication to students. Remember, what you pay attention to communicates what you value.

If yearly goals are developed, then a review of last year's recommendations and the refinement of that document need to begin (see Chapter 8). These goals are important for teachers and students. The common goals can send a signal to students while they are in a class that the teachers are working together. For example, if fostering critical thinking is a school goal, emphasizing the goal in each discipline can be especially powerful in high schools as students move from class to class and realize that teachers are encouraging the same behaviors. This lets students know that teachers are communicating and working together.

Team-building activities should also be part of a school's opening. For example, the following activity helped the staff in one school become better acquainted and proved to be a pleasant icebreaker:

1. Teachers were divided into groups of four.

2. Each group member listed four statements about him- or herself—one statement was false.

3. Each person then read his or her list, and the other group members guessed which statement was false.

4. After all guessed, each person revealed which of the statements was false.

5. Points were awarded for accurate guessing and for "stumping" the group.

Another staff had a back-to-school breakfast. Following the meal, a scavenger hunt was scheduled so staff members could find additional resources. The winning team received gift certificates to a local teaching supply store.

■ DEPARTMENTAL AND GRADE-LEVEL MEETINGS

These meetings should be prescheduled because the time for small groups to get together to plan the year is critical. Grade-level and departmental meetings should be held for reviewing and refining curricular, instructional, and assessment goals and estimating timelines for completing work. This should include a review of the successes as well as hurdles of the previous year. The emphasis should not be to cover everything but to discuss key outcomes that should be stressed for the year. Also, this time should be used to review some of the major activities that are held during the year (e.g., Thanksgiving program, Spirit Weeks, Martin Luther King commemoration, state testing dates, Earth Day activities) to adjust time accordingly. Ensuring that all members of the grade-level and department teams have sufficient supplies should also be a goal of these meetings. During this time seasoned teachers should discuss the instructional resources available and share their materials with new teachers.

Reviewing the vertical articulation of the curriculum and aligning the curriculum with assessment expectations should be an objective of these meetings (see Chapter 13). For example, sequential grades (e.g., Grades 3 and 4) can meet to review the expectations for the present and following year. Too often, we forget to consider the next year and micromanage the curriculum for the next day. To facilitate a more far-reaching view of the curriculum, the third-grade teachers, for example, should ask the fourth-grade teachers: What do you expect fourth graders to be able to do when the year begins? This helps the staff project for the next year, not the next day, and can have important implications for how one teaches. In middle and high schools, departmental members should be asking similar articulation and alignment questions of one another to project for the future. Ideally, the teachers in exit grades in each school should talk about their expectations to all of the teachers in grades below them as well as to receiving teachers in the grades above them. State standards, benchmarks, and frameworks are helpful tools to guide these discussions.

Discussing interdisciplinary curriculum and instructional strategies should, in addition, be considered at this time. Often Professional Learning Communities schedule dates several months at a time for various departments to meet and discuss possibilities for a parallel curriculum (e.g., teaching related topics at similar times), developing common assessments, or actual interdisciplinary teaching (e.g., teaching common themes and concepts, developing interdisciplinary essential questions, working on projects and activities together, team teaching). In elementary settings, grade-level meetings can also be devoted to these possibilities.

ORIENTING TEACHERS WHO ■ ARE NEW TO THE SCHOOL

Separate orientation sessions for new teachers and teachers who are new to the school should be set up. Usually one or two days before veteran school staff members return is sufficient time to hold the meetings. Whether a teacher is new to the profession or simply new to the school, this is an anxious time. A veteran teacher who may have been very successful in previous schools can find this time especially taxing because he or she will be experiencing some of the same frustrations as the total newcomer: Exactly how does that copier work? What are the rules for duplicating material? What is the schedule? Where are resources housed? How difficult will it be to go from a Mac to a PC (or vice versa)? Will I develop strong professional relationships?

As with the general faculty meetings, the principal should view this time as an opportunity to set an example with the new staff by not only responding to their immediate needs but also emphasizing the school mission and the possibilities that exist for students when teachers are committed, have energy and enthusiasm, and care about children. The principal should talk about the school culture and celebrate teaching. Also, the principal can use this time to stress that the school is a learning community and that the principal, too, is learning along with the teachers.

- Devote very little time during the meetings to the faculty handbook—emphasize only those procedures that are new or essential. Send the message that you know the teachers are professionals and can read the manual on their own. Welcome questions about the handbook for the next meeting. Because they will be anxious about curriculum material, make sure the material is available on the first meeting day with curriculum guides, teacher editions, and supplementary resources. A tour of the school and available instructional resources (both basic and enrichment) should be a priority. For the beginning teacher, stress the importance of structuring the classroom early in the year.
- Suggest resources to create a positive class climate.
- Provide a variety of models for room arrangement.
- Encourage teachers to review basic school and classroom routines with their classes during the first few days of school. (This should help save time and reduce possible student problems as the year progresses.)
- Offer time for teachers to check out resource materials.

Asking new and veteran teachers about the needs and questions they considered during their first year of service can be useful in determining elements for an orientation session. The following guidelines for assisting new teachers were developed by a combined group of new and veteran teachers in the school supervision graduate class at Eastern Washington University:

- Develop a new teacher packet with school philosophy and mission, schedules, staff data, routines, crisis plan, holiday policy, copier directions, hardware and software instruction, and community information.
- Purposefully use a mentor/coaching program through the district and school, and initially assist with curriculum, instruction, assessment, time management, and social issues.
- Assign equitable course loads and grade-level responsibilities.

- Share strategies for working with parents.
- Schedule luncheons with the principal every few weeks during the first year. Include one session devoted to explaining the school's jargon.
- Visit classrooms, observing veteran colleagues, possibly with help of coaches or other teacher leaders.
- Minimize extracurricular commitments during the first year.
- Provide funding for professional development workshops related to the school's curriculum, instructional, and assessment initiatives.
- Allocate sufficient instructional resources and office supplies (e.g., curriculum guides, teacher editions, manipulates).
- Plan social events.
- Encourage team planning with department, grade-level, and/or special service faculty.
- Schedule a welcoming coffee with parent and community representatives.

Many school districts have new teacher induction programs that systematically help newcomers during their first and second years. If your district does not have a formal program, instituting a buddy or coaching system for new teachers is a wonderful way to ease their transition into the school. Research suggests that induction programs can have a positive impact on the newcomers and minimize the number of new teachers who quit during their early years usually because they feel isolated and unsupported. Encouraging the veteran staff to show newcomers around and take them out to dinner or breakfast, at the school's expense, can go a long way in helping newcomers feel like part of the group. By simply answering the various questions that newcomers have—and are reluctant to ask the principal—the buddies can give teachers a sense of security and help them get off to a successful start.

■ TEACHER TIME IN THE CLASSROOM

Besides receiving their instructional supplies, teachers want to spend time in their classrooms. Teachers should have ample opportunity to do so. If you have several days scheduled of pre-school-year meetings with teachers (this varies from district to district), try to make a symbolic statement by having one day, or the greater part of a day, without any meetings to show staff members that you respect their need to get into the classroom. Certainly, classroom time should be built in to every day before school. Moreover, many teachers will want to work in their classrooms the weekend before school opens. Make it easy for them. If building security is a problem, facilitate the process to keep classrooms open so teachers know you are serving them; the bureaucracy should not become an obstacle during this critical period. Besides, you will be at school the weekend before classes begins!

■ WELCOMING STUDENTS AND PARENTS

If possible, hold an open house for new students and their parents the Friday afternoon before school opens. For middle schools, alternative schools, and high schools, ask selected veteran students attending the school to come to the open house to give the newcomers a tour of the school. Many middle, alternative, and high schools have peer support groups supervised by counselors, activities directors, teachers, or administrators to organize social activities and/or academic strategy sessions for new students. Many programs extend throughout the school year, especially to help high school freshmen make the transition. An open house is a good time to introduce assistant principals, teachers, counselors, secretaries, support staff, paraprofessionals, and custodians to the students and parents. This should be a light function, a social gathering, with refreshments. It should be scheduled for about an hour. The gathering can include ice cream for students. A few students from the upper elementary school, middle school, or high school, depending on the setting, can serve as guides.

Ask the parent association to assist on the first day, orienting new parents, serving coffee, and so on. Encourage the association to have a welcome table for parents. Try to have parent volunteers, including several parents who can serve as translators, to assist new families for whom English is a second language.

■ BE VISIBLE ON THE FIRST DAYS OF SCHOOL

Finally, on the first day of school, plan on being visible to teachers, students, and parents throughout the day. One principal wears a funny hat on the first day so people will gravitate toward him with any logistical questions. Again, the time needs to be built into your schedule well in advance. Circulate on the campus, in the hallways, and in the cafeteria. Also try to visit as many classes as possible during the first couple of days to personally welcome students and wish them a successful year. Some principals have classes visit their office to emphasize school rules, review activities, answer questions, and generally get acquainted.

Often, assemblies are held to go over school goals and rules. During the assembly, emphasize the school's commitment and personal concern for all students and the importance of community. Introduce the new teachers, and honor veteran staff. Remind students that academic success and caring about each other are mutually important school goals that both faculty and classified staff are committed to achieving with students. If possible, consider holding the assemblies on the second day so teachers and students can start smoothly and begin their classroom routines.

Most important, by being out there (e.g., in the cafeteria and corridor, on the field, by the buses) on the first days of school, the principal reaffirms that important events in the school happen in the classroom and on the campus, not in the administrative offices. In doing this, the principal can proactively troubleshoot logistical problems to see that the school year gets off to a smooth start.

REFLECTIONS

This space provides for you a place to write in ideas that have been generated by this chapter, things you want to try, or adaptations of ideas presented herein.

1. Make a list of 5–10 priorities that a principal should act on before the school year begins.

2. Develop a two-day orientation schedule for faculty.

3. Create an agenda for the first faculty meeting. Consider collaborating with staff members to plan it.

4. Share one or two fun activities that could be included during the faculty orientation period.

5. What were two or three particularly difficult situations for you as a first-year teacher? How could the effect of those situations been minimized?

6. What insights or new questions do you have as a result of reflecting on the ideas presented in this chapter?

16

Tips

Ideas That Work and Align With the School's Mission

Let's not reinvent the wheel.

—A veteran teacher, now a principal

We are often advised to work smarter, not harder. This chapter will help you follow this advice. There are many suggestions that we have made throughout the book that are really tricks of the trade, so we are bringing some of these ideas together in this chapter for you as a quick read. We add new ideas that can help enhance your performance and tackle new problems. In addition to the tricks of the trade, we include suggestions that can firm up the core values important to your school. Each idea has gone through a kind of litmus test. That is, the idea is included because it has been used successfully.

■ ORGANIZING YOUR TIME

Using a Tickler File

Probably one of the best organizing tools a principal can use is a "tickler file" that includes all of the important events, critical activities, memos, e-mails, and time deadlines (e.g., end of semester or quarter, testing, grading periods, open house, parent conferences) for each month; you "tickle" the file monthly. Thus, when November is about a month away, the principal and secretary meet, review a list prepared by the secretary of items in the November file, and examine each previous November memo or important activity description. It is helpful to have separate "beginning of the year" and "end of the year" files in addition to the August/September and May/June files. A useful addition to the file is a monthly section that includes your reflections on the events so errors are not repeated, successes are noted, and ideas for next year can be immediately added to the file. A tickler file is invaluable to a principal new to a school.

Blocking Your Personal Schedule

We know that if principals are not careful about monitoring their time—and often interruptions are unavoidable—they will have little control over their schedule. A very helpful tip is to block in time well in advance if you want to be in certain places and engage in particular activities, such as exercise! We are not only talking about scheduled assemblies or formal observations. Principals should also block in morning walk-throughs to classrooms and short periods to greet or say good-bye to students during the day if these activities are important. Principals must ask themselves, "What message(s) do I need to send to the staff, students, and parents through my behavior? What are my priorities? Am I spending time on these priorities?" As Kent Peterson, noted author and professor of educational administration at the University of Wisconsin–Madison, said, "What you pay attention to communicates what you value." It is especially vital that the school secretaries know the principal's priorities because secretaries can have tremendous influence on the schedule. Finally, principals often feel conflicted because they want to be available, but know that the question "Do you have a minute?" usually means a half hour. One principal responded this way: "I have a minute if you can walk and talk with me on my way to my next appointment." This allows the principal to be responsive and to save precious time.

MAKING RECORD KEEPING EASIER ■

Pocket Planner

Record keeping is a difficult job, given the fragmentation and variety that characterize the principal's role. To help keep things together, a pocket planner can be used. A pocket planner is a 3" × 5" index card system that one carries in the pocket. You can do this with your personal digital assistant (PDA). It can be used to keep track of things accomplished that address goals or supervision data. For goals, for instance, one writes the goal at the top of the card like this:

Goal: To implement reading, writing, and thinking across the curriculum	
Accomplishments:	**Date of Completion:**
Distributed article to staff	9–10–09
Faculty meeting discussion	9–18–09
Leading and Learning by Wandering Around (LLBWA) visits	(ongoing)

Every time something is accomplished that addresses this goal, record it. Then when reports are due, the data are all on the card. Similarly, the school vision can be noted, and indicators of that vision becoming reality can be noted and celebrated with the staff.

For supervision, write teacher names down the left side of the card. Across the top write the months. Then every time a visit is made, jot down a note on your card (for an example, see the sample card at the top of page 164).

By keeping this record, you can make sure that your visits are distributed evenly among staff members. This also can help if you need documentation when working with a marginal teacher or other member of the staff. The walk-through technique, often an aspect of LLBWA, can be used to learn how the first and last 10 minutes of classes are used and whether or not valued instructional, curricular, and assessment approaches are being practiced. Many principals use this time to interview students to learn of their perceptions of classroom experiences and to examine the quality of student assignments. Principals who use the pocket planner approach say that it is simple, convenient, efficient, and effective.

Sample Card

Names	Sept.	Oct.	Nov.
Alvarez	9/13 walk-through		
Bond			
Cathay	9/15 left a note		
Denny			
Elton			
Foster			
Gage	9/16 visit w/ kids		
Hunt			

■ ADDITIONAL HELPFUL IDEAS TO STAY ON TASK

Reflection Log

Keep a log of your reflections. This provides an avenue for a "professional time-out" and increases your capacity to be reflective and analytical. The art and practice of reflection allows one to view a situation from a different perspective because time has elapsed between the occurrence of an event and when one creates the time to think about it. Often fresh insights emerge, or one resolves to handle future, similar situations in a different way.

The Look Book

An excellent way to communicate daily morning announcements is to use a "Look Book" for all teachers to quickly read. It works equally well in elementary, middle, or high schools. The book can be placed in strategic spots to help save paper and reduce loudspeaker interruptions. Today, in many schools, the idea of a Look Book has vanished. E-mail is predominantly used to relay messages. However, one must ask: Does e-mail promote isolation at the expense of building community? School leaders must decide, given the local context, what is the best communication strategy.

In a Look Book, the teachers view important information for that day. For example:

1. The report card comments were thoughtful, objective, and informative. Your hard work is much appreciated.

2. Assembly at 10:10 instead of 10:15 because we are recognizing five students for their environmental work.

3. Building Leadership Team meeting at 12:05.

4. Math Department meeting during 8th period.

5. Reminder: Student Council representatives will be visiting seventh-grade classes during homeroom to generate interest in the charity drive.

6. Today is Mr. Abram's birthday; we can't give his exact birth year because records were not kept in those days!

The book keeps everyone informed, enhances the idea of community, and, when humor is added, can create a friendly and positive tone to begin the day. The principal should write in the Look Book before leaving on the previous afternoon. The Look Book has a couple of extra benefits: It serves as a record of highlights regarding what took place each day at school, and it breaks down the isolation that sometimes occurs in schools by bringing everyone to a central area to read the daily comments. It really works!

A variation of the Look Book is used at P.S./I.S. 123 in the Bronx, New York. Virginia Connelly, the principal, uses a large flip chart on which to post daily announcements, recognitions, and communications. The flip chart is placed in the office where staff members check in daily.

TIPS ON USING TECHNOLOGY TO ENHANCE A PRINCIPAL'S PERFORMANCE ■

By Dr. Kevin Pyatt

We have gone from being hunter-gatherers of information to being filter-feeders.

—Seth Lloyd

Tip 1: Stay Current

- Use Real Simple Syndication (RSS) to keep up to date with critical information and to remain on the cutting edge of teaching and learning, professional development, and school leadership.
- With RSS technology, users create syndication feeds from a variety of information sources and within a given set of information resources.
- RSS allows for the delivery of essential information to your desktop.
- Receive updates from online resources without having to visit each site to see new material.
- Subscribe to online resources that are consulted regularly (e.g., Web sites, weblogs [blogs], wikis, podcasts) and feed new information to your desktop.
- These feeds are then accessed from the user's customized browser.
- Examples of feeds:
  - U.S. Department of Education (http://www.ed.gov/rss/ edgov. xml)
  - National Science Foundation's Education Discoveries (http://www.nsf.gov/discoveries/index.jsp?prio_area=7)

How

Step 1. Download client software (e.g., Feedview, Feedreader, BottomFeeder, others listed at http://en.wikipedia.org/wiki/List_of_feed_aggregators).

Step 2. Find feeds (e.g., Web sites that have the feed icon or an icon with "RSS" embedded).

Step 3. Subscribe to and syndicate (feed) yourself the information your care most about.

Tip 2: Reduce E-mail

- Use blog technology to minimize email exchanges and maximize communication.
- Blogs can be used as school/class Web sites that have discussion forums.
- Forums are used as platforms to elicit feedback, share information, and/or respond to questions surrounding important topics.
- The moderator decides how strict or open the feedback and discussion boards are, along with who is a member of the space.
- Members can subscribe to RSS feeds originating from the blog.
- Examples of educators' blogs:
  - PrincipalsPage.com (http://principalspage.com/)
  - 2¢ Worth (http://davidwarlick.com/2cents/)
  - Bud the Teacher (http://budtheteacher.com/blog/)

How

Step 1. Download client software (e.g., Blogger, Edublogs, Drupal, Class Blogmeister, others listed at http://en.wikipedia.org/wiki/Blog).

Step 2. Select or design an appropriate template.

Step 3. Develop a page.

Step 4. Post information and set up RSS feeds for members to subscribe to.

Tip 3: Share Information Resources

- Use social bookmarking technology to share relevant information sources.
- Social bookmarking allows users to tag Web sites, online resources, documents, and materials.
- The tagged sites can then be organized, shared, and accessed by others in the organization.
- Network, subscribe, link, and/or post your bookmarks or others' bookmarks that are relevant to your interests and information needs.
- Examples of online educational leadership sites commonly bookmarked:
  - techLEARNING (http://www.techlearning.com/)
  - ASCD For the Success of Each Learner (http://www.ascd.org/)

How

Step 1. Download client software (e.g., Simpy, Furl, Delicious, BlinkList, Backflip, BottomFeeder, others listed at http://en.wikipedia.org/wiki/Social_bookmarking).

Step 2. Find significant sites and resources.

Step 3. Tag these sites, archive, organize, and share using client software.

Tip 4: Make Important Information Available and Accessible

- Use podcast technology to make important information available and accessible.
- Podcasts of significant or essential presentations, meetings, and forums can be made available to the school community.

- Podcasts can be downloaded and accessed at any time.
- Important meetings, conferences, training, and the like can be accessed by those who may have missed them.
- They can also be set up to be accessed via RSS feeds.
- Examples of podcasts:
  - ○ The Practical Principals (http://practicalprincipals.net/)
  - ○ The Podcasting Principal (http://principalmiller.podomatic. com/)

How

Step 1. Obtain audio recording device (preferably digital), and make audio recording.

Step 2. Edit audio, and save to preferred format (e.g., .mp3, .wav, .ogg).

Step 3. Upload audio file to online platform (e.g., school Web site, blog) and/or to online libraries that warehouse audio and make it available to the masses (via, e.g., indiepodder, iTunes).

Tip 5: Make Cost-Effective Technology Decisions

- Open-Source (Free) Software
  - ○ Consider obtaining open-source software rather than purchasing licenses for similar products.
  - ○ Dollars saved on nonessential licensing costs can be directed to promote purchasing of computers for classrooms (Solomon & Schrum, 2007).
  - ○ Many emerging Web 2.0 software tools (e.g., social bookmarking, WebStart pages, blogging, wikis, assessment tools) are open source and highly usable. High usability minimizes training needs.
  - ○ For a list of open-source software see http://www.opensourceconsortium.org/.

- Free Online Resources
  - ○ Consider supporting the use of free online resources for classroom use to supplement and/or replace antiquated texts and curricula.
  - ○ Many federal- and state-funded curriculum projects are highly accessible and available online (e.g., U.S. Department of Education, National Science Foundation, PBS)

- Wireless Connectivity
  - ○ For areas of your building where Internet connectivity is limited, consider installing wireless networks, or Wi-Fi zones, for Internet access.
  - ○ Although this is fairly obvious, wireless networks do not require the infrastructure of hardwired networks.

Tip 6: Close the Digital Divide (Technology and Equity)

- Computers and their associated applications can serve as a "least restrictive medium" for learners of all ages and abilities.
- Computers can be used as an assistive technology for all students, including nonnative language learners and students with special needs.
- Assistive technologies, such as screen readers, are used to improve reading fluency and comprehension.
- These technologies are also used to promote universal accessibility for all learners. Technologies such as Skype can be used for promoting inclusion (see a classroom example at http://share.skype.com/sites/en/2007/04/inclusion_helping_a_classmate.html).

Tip 7: Use Technology to Support Learning

- School leaders should expect new technologies to be coupled with well-accepted and -described teaching methods and implementations.
- Technologies that become widely adopted and persist over time are those that positively impact instruction, have well-grounded teaching methods and examples, and have high usability.

Tip 8: Evaluate Performance

- Consider utilizing online evaluation tools to measure performance within the organization.
- Online evaluations are advantageous because they (1) allow anytime access, (2) ensure ease of delivery, (3) eliminate data entry, and (4) have useful data analysis tools.

Tip 9: Use Task Management and Scheduling Systems

- Consider utilizing online scheduling systems for coordinating meetings.
- These systems allow users to see everyone's schedule and availability and minimize the time delay that might otherwise occur when scheduling via e-mail or voicemail.

Tip 10: Know What to Look for in 21st-Century Classrooms

- These classrooms are places rich in information access, networking, and collaboration (Jukes & McCain, 2007a).
- The tools of these environments are networked computers (e.g., desktop computer, laptop computer, PDAs, handheld devices).
- In such environments, students and teachers engage in research activities that incorporate a variety of information sources into their teaching and learning experiences.
- Learning in these environments requires access to networked computers that allow learners to go "off campus" online.
- Classrooms should utilize an acceptable framework for evaluating media that allows learners to do the following (Jukes & McCain, 2007b):

  1. Demonstrate initiative by critically assessing problems and implementing creative solutions
  2. Read for information and application
  3. Locate and manage resources for problem solving

- Classrooms should incorporate safe collaborative spaces for children through blogs and/or wikis.
- Classrooms should incorporate simulations and serious games that involve role-play, networking, and collaboration and center on solving and/or explaining complex phenomena. Examples:
  o Sid Meier's Civilization III (http://www.civ3.com/)—serious game on the dynamics of civilization
  o ElectroCity (http://www.electrocity.co.nz/)—simulation on the dynamics of building and managing a sustainable city.

Tip 11: Make Good Hiring and Training Decisions

- Hire and/or train school leaders who embrace and welcome new ideas surrounding the methods that describe how technology supports learning.

Tip 12: Learn About Web 2.0

Web 2.0 is not a technology in and of itself, but rather a description of the way in which the Internet is being accessed and used. Web 2.0 is really Web 1.0 operating at faster information-exchange rates, utilizing technologies that allow for more dynamic and collaborative interaction, and wireless access. The technology has made way for video and audio data exchanges at speeds never seen before, which can be accessed using wireless devices. Web 2.0 has been popularized because with its emergence has come new client software. This software bridges former applications with new applications that center on real-time interaction, collaboration, and wireless access (e.g., blogs, wikis, social bookmarking). In the context of educational organizations, the implications of Web 2.0 are great. Its technologies have the potential to change the way in which we access information, where we access it, and how we share it.

A Story About Technology Adoption and Schools

Fifteen years ago an educational technology expert answered a survey on technology and its associated implications on teaching and learning. One of the questions asked: "What has been the greatest technological achievement since the printing press?" One of the options to choose from was "the computer," which is what the expert picked. Several years later, the expert answered a similar survey. One of the questions was: "What has been the greatest technological achievement since the printing press?" This time the expert selected a new option—"the Internet." Based on these experiences the expert reflected, "While I am sure there will be similar surveys in the near future, I wonder what the options will be. Perhaps the next survey will have new options to select from: something like *wearable electronics, wireless energy,* and *ubiquitous computing.* Whichever the new option might be is not critical. What is critical is that we recognize that technologies have life spans. These life spans are governed by the following principles: The technology's (1) relative usability, (2) ability to do what other technologies have not, (3) ability to perform better than the technology it is replacing, (4) inability to do what others have promised it would do. These principles will dictate a technology's ability to persist within the organization."

A Final Reflection on Technology

Do not assume that technology will solve all of your time management and communication problems. But if you use technology properly, you will likely be more creative and effective on the job. As software companies have become more familiar with schools and their needs, the programs for scheduling, attendance, student records (including discipline), disaggregating data, supervising teachers, and report cards have significantly improved. However, it is a school's responsibility to examine the programs carefully and to encourage the software companies to work closely with schools to work out program glitches. It is also important to avoid a situation in which only one technology "guru" knows how a system works. If that is the case, the software program is not suited for the school. A cautionary note: Principals spend time with people. Because technology is fascinating and powerful, one can easily spend a lot of time in his or her office working with it. A fancy word-processed memo is no substitute for personal interaction.

■ PROVIDING EXPERIENCES TO CELEBRATE THE SCHOOL'S CULTURE

The following activities, events, projects, strategies, and professional development recommendations have all been successfully implemented. A few of the ideas may be right for your school or, we hope, may spark an idea that will strengthen the values essential to your school.

See Them Teach Before They Leave

When teachers are permanently leaving a school, especially the retiring veterans, ask the departing teachers if it would be okay for other teachers to watch them teach during the final month of the school year. Use the slogan "See them teach before they leave" (e.g., in the Look Book) for a couple of days to encourage teacher visits. The principal should offer to cover some of the classes while staff members visit their departing colleagues. This type of project could become a catalyst for increasing classroom visits among teachers during the school year. At one school that observed this tradition, the departing teacher was presented with a plaque with the doorknob from her classroom mounted on it. Under the knob were the words, "Thank you for opening your door and sharing well-kept secrets. You saved the library of knowledge from burning."

Principal for a Day

A contest can be held in which individual students send the principal letters stating why they should be chosen from among their classmates to "take over for a day." The principal would become the student when the exchange takes place. To get several students involved, the position can change each hour or class period. Principals have also exchanged jobs with business leaders for a day as a community project.

Phoning the Good News

How often do principals call parents to communicate good news? Unfortunately, the reflex goes like this: Billy has messed up again; is it time to call his parents? It is rarely: Johnny was very helpful with that new student; should I call his parents? Principals need to call home and send letters home when good news takes place. In some schools, students call from the principal's office to give the good news themselves. Principals use cell phones while Leading and Learning by Wandering Around and call parents about positive student behaviors with the student present. This has served to favorably influence parental attitudes toward the school.

The Principal as Reader and Teacher

Students at all grade levels enjoy having the principal visit class to read a story or a poem. The holiday season is a perfect time for this type of activity. The school librarian can be very helpful in selecting a variety of stories for each grade level to be read by the principal. About 15–20 minutes of time in each class works. Two or three classes a day for several weeks will do the trick. One principal who is a Vietnam veteran teaches when secondary students are studying this part of the curriculum. It is very important for students to see the principal in a role other than the traditional one—the disciplinarian or person "in the office."

The Principal's Scrapbook

School principals receive notes, pictures, artwork, poems, photographs, and so on from students throughout the year. Posting these items as a principal's scrapbook is a rewarding exercise. Students are drawn to this interesting three-dimensional scrapbook as it "grows out" on a bulletin board near the principal's office. It becomes a folk history of the principal's school year.

Building Traditions to Celebrate Important Values

October 24, United Nations Day, is an excellent opportunity for any school to unify around themes such as respecting all humanity, global unity, strength in diversity, exploring other cultures, or the work of the United Nations. A school should celebrate and commemorate the importance of respecting one another regardless of race, ethnicity, religion, or gender. Having the faculty working together on an activity such as United Nations Day reminds everyone of one of the most important reasons for schools: learning to get along with one another. There are, of course, other special days that can equally serve this type of theme, such as Earth Day or Martin Luther King Jr. Day. These days also give a school opportunities to celebrate a theme that should go to the heart of schooling. A variety of activities stressing particular themes should occur throughout the day, or possibly week, of the special occasion. Student projects, films, and outside speakers should all be involved in the activities. School principals should do whatever they can to support faculty committees organizing these special events. Faculty, students, and parents all take an interest in the important values that are brought forth on these days and, one hopes, throughout the school year.

Student Tutors and Peer Counseling

High school students enjoy tutoring younger students, and elementary school students welcome help offered by older students. A relationship between a high school and middle or elementary school to develop a student-tutoring program is an extremely worthwhile activity. It is especially helpful for elementary school students who need special attention and for high school students who can use a boost with their self-confidence. For all involved, this process builds important social and emotional skills. Often, these programs can be set up following the regular school day. Many secondary schools offer course credit for this type of work. In one high school, seniors in the French Club tutor first graders one day a week.

Peer counseling is also a very worthwhile activity for middle and high schools when organized by school guidance counselors who can provide meaningful orientation sessions and monitor the peer counseling during the year. The peer counselors work with fellow classmates who may need someone to talk with because of a personal difficulty or just someone who can help them get into gear regarding their studies. Peer counselors have even worked with upper elementary school students, especially in conflict resolution on the playground. School principals should view these student-to-student programs as important opportunities to assist students in their social and emotional growth. Some high schools have peers operate a mock court system. Such judicial systems have greatly reduced a variety of crimes at the school site and in the immediate community. They have fostered the development and understanding of important principles as well.

School Recognition Assemblies

These assemblies should be scheduled every six to eight weeks to recognize students for positive accomplishments. Teachers submit student names for recognition by the principal for a variety of accomplishments: attendance, citizenship, improved academic performance, service, persistence, and so on. The assembly gives the principal an opportunity to emphasize important themes (behavioral, social, emotional, or academic), wish happy birthday to students and staff, and welcome newcomers or say good-bye to students leaving the school. A student musical interlude or class play may be a part of the assembly program.

■ TIPS ON OPENING A NEW SCHOOL

By Dr. Becky Cooke

The following tips are offered for school leaders who have been designated as "Planning Principals" charged with opening a new school. The tips are offered in two parts: Bricks and Mortar pertains to building the actual building, and Creating a High-Performance School Culture pertains to planning a start-up school that has not yet existed.

Bricks and Mortar

As with all aspects of leadership, process is important. How you go about the process of planning a school is a reflection of your values and vision.

Use participatory teams that include global thinkers and detail people. The detail people are those who know that the ideal storage space in a closet is a "Xerox box plus four inches"—so that the size of boxes found commonly in schools can fit neatly in the spaces created (true story!).

Visit other sites and staffs who have gone through the process recently. Learn from their victories, challenges, and defeats.

There are various stages commonly known to the construction industry but are a little more mysterious to educators. They are educational specifications, schematic design, design development, construction document development, construction, and final punch lists. The educational specifications are the key to the entire process. What the architect hears from the team as the priorities and the vision will be reflected in the design and referenced as a rudder to guide decision making. Be very deliberate and careful in this process.

The construction documents development is the other vital step. These documents are extremely detailed plans that all the trades use in the construction of the school. As soon as they are ready, sit down with the architect, your facilities manager, or someone in the field to go over them with a fine-toothed comb because they become essentially unchangeable. The interpretation of the educational specifications by the design professionals is sometimes very different than how the users (educators) would want them interpreted. This is the time to clarify your ideas so changes can be made. There really is no realistic and affordable going back after the construction documents are firm.

Planning for a school building with an indefinite life span, compared with planning for technology that is out of date the moment it is purchased, provides for an interesting contrast. Remember all of the users of technology in the planning of the building. Consider computer projectors, document cameras, laptop or desktop computers, and sound amplification systems as a start. Many of these need power sources and cabling, so again ensure that they may be used however the room is configured and for any number of users. Again, "maximum flexibility" is the mantra.

Building a new school will test your mettle. Know when to be firm on things that will significantly impact the use of the facility for the education of students and when to give on more subtle issues. Keep your integrity, and build relationships. When the building is completed and the process is done—the relationships remain. Give credit to the many members of your district staff who were participants in the process in addition to the design team.

Celebrate with the voters and community. It is their school. Ensure that you have a ground-breaking ceremony, a dedication ceremony, and an open house. The district began way before your arrival and will continue on past your departure. Honor all of the participants. Build connections.

Some keys to an educationally efficient facility:

- *Storage, storage, storage:* If materials are individually managed and in classrooms rather than storage rooms, no one has to go clean out the storage room periodically.
- *Maximum flexibility:* Try to ensure that rooms are similar in size and detail. You never know if that kindergarten classroom will end up serving sixth graders in future years.
- *Furniture:* Try out the furniture options in classrooms with students. They will quickly let you know about quality and usability.
- *Lighting:* Natural light is a bonus in the learning environment, but remember potential afternoon glare on screens and whiteboards.
- *Displays:* Consider how to best display student work in hallways and common areas. Some well-placed chair railings can help set off displays and make them look more intentional.
- *Traffic flow and supervision needs:* Dark corners and congested areas result in potential safety and disciplinary concerns.

Creating a High-Performance School Culture

Begin with a planning grid that includes significant activities dealing with the construction and with the development of a positive school culture. The construction process can easily overtake time spent on planning to shape a positive culture if you are not extremely intentional about attending to both.

Understand the nonnegotiables from your district and state. Keep district leaders informed all along the way.

Be thoughtful about your vision from the outset. Although it will certainly be influenced by the team that you build, teachers and other staff want a picture of what they are signing on to before they decide whether to join your staff. Your vision, leadership, and who you are as a person are perhaps under the most scrutiny of your career at this stage—so be sure you communicate about these aspects every chance you get.

Work with your human resources department and your educational association to agree on hiring practices that will result in creating a "best-fit" staff rather than staffing solely on seniority. For instance, one high school principal, advertising for teaching positions in a new school, created a brochure that highlighted the vision and core values they were looking for in candidates. After the list of core values was a simple, but powerful line: "Those who do not embrace these student-focused values need not apply."

Remember to involve parents from the beginning, not only on the building of the facility but in the creation of the culture. They are full partners in creating the vision and mission of the school.

Create your parent organization a year in advance, and meet periodically. Under your leadership, they can create by-laws, establish 501(c)3 tax status, and elect officers. You can then hand over the reigns of the group to the officers and participate as you normally would. With careful planning, this group can be your biggest asset in quickly establishing celebrations and traditions with the student body and the parent community.

Carefully design a participatory decision-making process and norms for working together. If you go slowly at this stage, you can eventually go quickly through the plethora of decisions that need to be made, while developing trust and relationships along the way. This process, pertaining to adults, may be applied to building trust and relationships among the student body as well.

After you have the foundational work completed, work on the way you will do business for the future. As a team, read the research and the works of leaders in the field, partner with higher educational institutions in your area, set specific and measurable goals, conduct job-embedded professional development based on those goals, conduct Action Research, ensure that you design vertical and horizontal teams, and model curiosity.

This is a once-in-a-career opportunity, so use it to inspire all of the participants to be their best. This may be some of the most generative work you will ever do—dream big.

Remember the words of Robert Jarvik: "Leaders are visionaries with a poorly developed sense of fear and no concept of the odds against them. They make the impossible happen."

■ PRACTICAL GUIDELINES FOR PREPARING PRINTED MATERIALS FOR INTERNAL AND EXTERNAL SCHOOL COMMUNITY MEMBERS*

The following guidelines are offered for developing weekly or monthly parent and staff newsletters, posters, letters, electronic or hard-copy memos, daily announcements, handbooks, planning documents, reports, policy manuals, school profiles, yearbooks, student newspapers, calendars, brochures, and menus. Guidelines include the following:

- Decide on a clear purpose or objective for the document, always considering the mission of the school. Ask yourself: What does this memo/article have to do with student learning and quality teaching?
- Use school letterhead and logo on appropriate documents to reinforce the mission.
- Keep the document concise and to the point.
- Target a specific audience.
- Consider issues of appearance related to format, graphics, font, white space, headings, and balance. Decide whether the document is attractive and eye-catching.
- Use clear, understandable, comfortable, and familiar language. Avoid jargon!
- Consider how each newsletter article is organized, and think about sequencing, placement of articles, and graphics.
- Make sure the document is timely and up to date.
- Weigh budgetary issues relating to quality of paper, number of copies made, quality of print, method of distribution, and color copying.
- Keep articles unbiased, and avoid language that might be interpreted as sexist, racist, or otherwise insensitive.
- Ensure the material reaches the targeted audience.
- Consider other stakeholders who should receive the printed material in addition to the targeted audience.
- Keep the information relevant to your school/community.
- Use newsletters and other documents to intentionally display student work and celebrate student successes.
- Consider the 30-second, 3-minute, and 30-minute "rule" when publishing a newsletter: Audiences that have 30 seconds, 3 minutes, or 30 minutes must all feel the newsletter is worthwhile. Thus headings and subheadings are critical.

*These guidelines were developed by school leadership graduate students in a School-Community Relations course at Eastern Washington University, following an examination of several hundred documents distributed by their public and private schools.

- Seek feedback to evaluate the success of the document. Consider how to obtain reliable and helpful feedback concerning the document. If two-way communication is a goal, how is it being reached?
- Keep newsletters up to date on a school's Web page if a decision is made to post digital copies.
- Print a hard copy proof to review document. Do not depend on finalizing a proof that has only been examined on a computer screen.
- Proofread, proofread, and proofread.
- Remember that all documents that emerge from the school are a reflection of the administration and the school.

USING TIPS IN YOUR SETTING ■

The ideas in this chapter are all tried-and-true strategies used by principals and other school personnel to improve their effectiveness or positively influence the culture of the school. Although only some of the ideas may work in your school, all of the ideas are intended to identify themes or strategies that might lead principals and their professional colleagues to come up with successful activities for their schools. Perhaps one of the most powerful ways to continue this tradition is by organizing support groups of principals (no larger than 10 members) to meet regularly, problem solve, and share successful practices.

NOTE

More tips: We encourage our readers to send their tips for us to use in subsequent editions of this book. Send tips to Pam Robbins, 21 North Newport Drive, Napa, CA 94559, or Harvey Alvy, Department of Education, Williamson Hall, Eastern Washington University, Cheney, WA 99004.

REFLECTIONS

This space provides for you a place to write in ideas that have been generated by this chapter, things you want to try, or adaptations of ideas presented herein.

1. What are some tips that you can offer to your colleagues?

2. What kind of events, activities, or strategies might be added to those mentioned in the chapter to positively affect the values of a school?

3. What insights or new questions do you have as a result of reflecting on the ideas presented in this chapter?

PART VI

Understanding Your Constituencies

17

Working With Parents and Partnering With the Greater Community

When it comes to schools, everyone is an expert!

—A principal's voice

■ EFFECTIVELY COMMUNICATING WITH PARENTS

A strong parent-school partnership is a valuable resource. This chapter examines facets of this relationship and relationships with the greater community and offers several tools to enhance these relationships. It is clearly the responsibility of all school personnel and especially principals to communicate effectively with parents. Thus schools need to take the initiative in this area, engaging in two-way communication and seeking to initiate partnerships with various organizations and businesses. In the past, school leaders and teachers were reactive with parents or viewed the relationship as a back-burner priority. This should not be the case. As one assistant principal noted, "Principals must be PR persons today. You have to welcome parents and be much more accommodating to a very demanding public. Parents need to be courted. Also, they want their kids to come to school with green hair!"

Principals and faculty members need to be proactive when communicating with parents regarding all school issues, from a new program to an individual child's progress report. For example, unsatisfactory grades on a report card should not come as a surprise to parents. Parents should be notified if their child is having difficulty well before the report card is distributed. School principals need to build this idea into the system and communicate ways this can be done. Moreover, the benefit of partnering with families goes beyond improving communication: "Studies confirm that when families are involved, more students earn higher grades in English and math, improve their reading and writing skills, complete more course credit, set higher aspirations, have better attendance, come to class more prepared to learn, and have fewer behavior problems" (Epstein, 2007).

When schools have good news to report, parents should hear about it. There is no better public relations effort than reporting good news. For example, an elementary school principal may hold recognition assemblies about every six to eight weeks to positively reinforce students for a variety of accomplishments. These may include helping a new child in school, a first-rate math test score, having a painting sent to a museum, intervening appropriately when a classmate was bullied, or improved behavior. Following up the assembly with notes to parents that compliment students and explain how the students were recognized sends a clear message concerning what is important in that school. Recognition assemblies, in this way, not only serve as public relations tools but communicate cultural values to parents as well. Another effective strategy to report news to parents is through the student-led conference. These conferences, appropriate from kindergarten to the 12th grade, can be arranged as special events or as part of scheduled parent-teacher conference days. Student-led conferences give parents opportunities to observe and hear their children report and reflect on their progress. Whether teachers help students prepare working or showcase portfolios or specific samples of student work, students, by engaging in a dialogue with their parents and by showcasing their work, have an opportunity to demonstrate what they have learned. These conferences are a powerful tool, transcending, by far, the minimal effect provided by traditional report cards.

When considering how parents view schools, it is interesting to note that, as an institution, a school is one of the few professional organizations with which all feel some familiarity. We all attended school. The mysteries of medicine, for example, may cause parents to hesitate about questioning a particular diagnosis of their child. This is not the case when schools are concerned. Parents are likely to be much more assertive about questioning the school system. Their own experiences in school, good and bad, have left many parents with firm ideas on how to approach schools and how schools should operate. For some parents, school was a very unpleasant experience, and the school principal may remind them of memories better forgotten. Thus a smile, handshake, and warm welcome can be important icebreakers for those who feel less comfortable in schools.

The role that parents play in schools varies greatly and depends on factors such as whether the school is public, private, elementary, middle, or high; the nature of the parent community; the administrative approach with parents; current issues; teacher comfort with parental involvement; and the degree of parent input formally built into the system for educational and political reasons. Thus parents may play roles ranging from the more traditional role of attending school only on Back to School Night and during parent conferences, to volunteering several days a week as a class tutor, to serving on school boards and making general policy decisions, to becoming a member of a School Improvement Team involved in setting important yearly goals. Schools have the responsibility of informing parents about the various roles they can play.

Again, principals should be proactive with parents and not assume that they are an adversarial group. The overwhelming majority of parents will support the school as long as the school is communicating with them and has kept them aware of important issues. When there are interest groups that have a personal agenda that may interfere with the best interests of the students, it is very helpful to have a majority of parents familiar with the issues. When conflicts occur, a principal should look at the conflict or problem as a challenge and an opportunity to work out a solution. When working out solutions, principals must take the higher ground, not viewing the conflict as a personal battle. This, of course, is easier said than done.

When parents raise questions regarding general school issues or policies, the school philosophy or mission statement should play a major part in helping the principals and teachers remain focused regarding the direction of the school. This is why it is advisable to involve parents in mission building to create understanding and ownership. Certainly, change should be considered if the change will lead to progress, but school leaders constantly must consider the school mission when working with groups that are asking for change. One must consider the key question: Is the proposed change consistent with the school mission?

Additionally, it is important for the principal to actively listen to all ideas and factions. This does not mean that the principal is not aligned with a particular point of view—one should have strong feelings on significant issues—but the appearance of an inflexible position quickly tells parents that you are uninterested and not listening. It is important also for principals to meet routinely with the president or head of the parent association. Particular parents, however, should not be seen as the principal's favorite or the decision makers for other parents. Here is an interesting view from a principal on remaining neutral with parents:

> What I try to do is stay right on the fringes of all groups so that they're comfortable with me and me with them. But I don't want to drink beer with them, or whittle at the courthouse, or hunt and fish, or haul wood. I just want to be close enough to them so I can sit and be comfortable, and them with me. But that's it.

■ BUILDING BRIDGES WITH THE PARENT COMMUNITY

To build up parent interest in a school, an open house before school officially opens or early in the year can be held for parents (and students) to meet the administration and teachers. This kind of positive interaction can help build the bridges that will come in handy when communication on important issues is necessary.

Holding monthly parent coffees is an excellent proactive forum to discuss school issues. Although you cannot eliminate griping by some parents at these meetings, the forum can be used to present important school issues with the administration taking initiative. The following format has been used successfully to carry out monthly coffees: (a) general announcements updating parents on school events and student successes, (b) a presentation to parents on a topic in which they have expressed interest (e.g., the new school reading program, a sample of the hands-on science curriculum, trends in education, an update on new federal/state guidelines and expectations), (c) occasionally breaking up into small groups to talk about the presentation issues, and (d) open comments and announcements by parents. Holding these meetings in the morning or evening with a one-hour time limit lets the community know that the sessions will be both meaningful and doable given a parent's busy schedule. Furthermore, it emphasizes the value placed on two-way communication in a clear, concise way.

This format works because many parents attend coffees if they think a topic of substance is on the agenda. By setting a positive tone with planned presentations of interest to parents, the meetings proceed in a supportive climate. The climate of these morning or evening coffees can be an essential element in maintaining positive family-school relations throughout the year. It is important to stress that parents, guardians, and community members should be welcome at the coffees. The more the general public knows about what is actually taking place in the school, the less chance there will be for rumors or inaccurate information to be spread around.

Additionally, these coffees can serve as important opportunities—within a structured environment—to gain parent input on hot issues. For example, coffees can be used to exchange ideas on the adoption of a new science program, pilot testing of new standards, disappointing state testing results, rumors about new high school graduation requirements, or the institution of major changes in a disciplinary or homework policy. Principals can open these coffees to parent ideas, letting them know that the ideas will be brought back to the appropriate committees for consideration. Often, parents make excellent suggestions that can become part of the new policy or curriculum change.

Although it is more convenient for school personnel and many parents to hold the coffee on site, principals should consider parents' homes and community centers as other venues for coffees. For some constituencies, a community center may seem less threatening and an indication that the school is reaching out to the community. This may be particularly true in some low-income settings.

Parent reading groups sponsored by the school are another effective way to build bridges with the parent community. A school principal, assistant principal, counselor, librarian, or teacher can help sponsor the reading group. In one school system, the following books were used during a two-year period with various elementary and secondary school parent groups: *A Tribe Apart,* by Patricia Hersch (1998); *Emotional Intelligence,* by Daniel Goleman (1995); *Reviving Ophelia,* by Mary Pipher (1994); *Raising Cain,* by Dan Kindlon and Michael Thompson (2000); and *Letting Go: A Parents' Guide to Understanding the College Years,* by Karen Levin Coburn and Madge Lawrence Treeger (2003). *Letting Go* was the only book selected for a very specific group: parents of high school seniors, who were literally experiencing the anxiety of letting go.

Excerpts from the following letter to parents introducing the reading group for *A Tribe Apart* may help demonstrate the potential of this parent-school activity:

Dear Reading Group Parents,

We were quite pleased with the number of parents who expressed an interest in joining a high school reading group during our recent coffees. We've received the first order of 28 copies of *A Tribe Apart,* by Patricia Hersch. To pay for the book, please make a check out for _____ to (school name), or bring exact change to the high school office.

After reflecting on the book, and trying to pace our discussions, we'll divide the readings into three parts to follow the natural sections of the book as outlined by the author. Thus, for the November session, please read Part I, Stepping Inside, pages 3–120 (mostly about life in schools); for the December session, read Part II, Making Contact, pages 121–228 (about adolescent life outside of school); and for February read Part III, Making Sense, pages 229–375 (mostly about how adolescents try to make sense of who they are and where they are going). [Exact dates and times are provided for each meeting.]

A Tribe Apart follows eight teenagers through three years of their lives. The teenagers are Chris, Jessica, Jonathon, Joan, Ann, Charles, Courtney, and Brendon. You will know them well before you finish the book! A good theme and question for us to consider during the first session in November would be: Is teen culture really different for the present generation of adolescents, when compared to 20 years ago? Of course, many other questions will emerge from our discussion. Please bring questions to the reading group!

The fun and goals of the reading group should include intellectual stimulation, strengthening the relationships among the adults in the reading group, and engaging in a lively discussion. As with all reading groups, it will be important for us to be supportive of the comments made by others, stay relevant regarding the text, and develop questions and responses based primarily on our interpretations of the book. Additionally, the group will give all of us an opportunity to work on our listening skills as we gain insights from other group members. The PTA will be providing refreshments for each session.

Finally, we look forward to taking this journey with all of you these next few months. We suspect that we will all grow from the text and the ideas that we will share with one another.

Sincerely,

The traditional Back to School or Open House Night and parent conference days provide unique opportunities for schools to show what they are all about. Creative variations during these traditional activities can have very positive long-range results in the parent community. For example, teachers should be encouraged to show parents videos of students working and student-teacher interaction in their classes. Parents appreciate the effort made by teachers who prepare videos, and they love to see their children in action. As noted earlier, student-led conferences are very effective. The use of student portfolios displaying the work and progress of each student significantly affects parents. One parent, after viewing her child's portfolio, remarked, "I wasn't aware that my child was capable of that work." Furthermore, the walls of a school should be lined with student work every day, especially on these special days. Student work should be the heart of these events. Open School Night, if organized to start with presentations by the administration and the parent association, provides a special opportunity for principals to reassert the vision of the school, publicly thank teachers and parents, and recognize the important role that they play in the lives of children. One principal made suggestions to faculty members concerning the group meetings with parents on Back to School Night (usually held within two or three weeks after the opening of the school year) and concerning the individual meetings with parents later in the year. Both sets of guidelines follow.

Back to School Night Guidelines for Teachers

- Welcome parents at the classroom door.
- Clearly display, or verbally note, the room number, your name, and class (sometimes parents are lost and in the wrong room!).
- Review curriculum expectations of the class, sharing samples of books and instructional resources to clarify points.
- Review major class activity, assessment, and homework expectations, possibly showing samples of exemplary work.
- Let parents know that you are accessible to their children.
- Let parents know how you can be reached and that they are welcome to get in touch with you. Exchange appropriate phone numbers and e-mail addresses.
- Tell parents that if their child is experiencing difficulty, they will be notified (e.g., progress reports, e-mail), and that positive news will also be reported.
- If time permits, consider having parents write a short note to their child to be read privately by their child the following day.
- Try to have parent or student translators available if necessary.
- Finish with positive comments.

The following suggestions for teachers apply to individual parent-teacher conferences, usually held a couple of months after the school year begins.

Guidelines for Individual Conferences With Parents

- Pleasantly greet parents and thank the parents for taking the time to meet with you.
- Some parents know their children are doing poorly and are quite uneasy about the conference. It is especially important to comfort these parents and let them know that "we are in this together."
- Be specific about strengths and weaknesses, and include samples of student work to emphasize a point. Again, consider student-led conferences as an option for the evening.

- Ask parents for helpful information about their child that might be of assistance to you. For example, "Do you believe your child learns better by seeing, hearing, or through a hands-on approach?" Also, you might inquire as to whether a student has access to a computer or the Internet at home.
- Discuss specific strategies for their child to achieve success in your class.
- Ask parents for help, and review activities that they can do at home with their child to strengthen the home-school partnership.
- Avoid educational jargon when talking about the curriculum, instructional strategies, assessment, or concerns about a child.
- Before closing, ask parents if there is anything else that they would like to know, or share, about their child.
- Keep the meetings on time so waiting parents do not have to wait longer than expected.
- Try to finish on a positive note. Thank parents for coming, remind parents that you enjoy working with their child, and let them know that you are accessible and how you can be contacted. Exchange contact information.

(Principals should make sure that refreshments are available during conferences in central locations, or in each classroom.)

A school might consider a Saturday morning parent workshop or academy sponsored by the administration and teachers for parents to provide information on important topics. Topics might be faculty or parent generated and include helping children with homework, the role of technology in education, discussing learning styles, or suggestions to instill greater responsibility at home. In settings where parents' own experiences with school were so negative that they feared school, the school has extended an outreach program. In Hawaii, for instance, school personnel took blankets to the local park and set up learning stations for parents.

For years Joyce Epstein (2007) has been conducting research on how to develop and sustain effective partnership programs with families and the community. She recommends four essential components for success:

- *Action teams for partnerships:* Teachers, administrators, parents, community partners, and sometimes students serve as a committee or "action arm" of the school improvement team. The action team is responsible for improving a program of family and community involvement linked to school improvement goals.
- *The six types of involvement framework:* By selecting activities that focus on parenting, communicating, volunteering, learning at home, decision making, and collaborating with the community, schools can help all parents become involved in different ways.
- *Action plans that are linked to goals for student success:* Annual written plans for family and community involvement are linked to the school improvement plan and to specific goals for student learning and development.
- *Evaluation and ongoing improvement:* By documenting and assessing the quality of activities . . . the action team can continually improve outreach to more families and success for more students. (pp. 18–19)

ADDITIONAL WAYS TO BRING PARENTS ■ AND COMMUNITY MEMBERS INTO SCHOOL

Involving parents in school-related activities can build bridges with the parent community and help the school in areas in which resources may be scarce. To illustrate, parents can serve as volunteers to help with tutoring, with field trips, in the cafeteria, in the office, or in the media center. It is critical to conduct background checks prior to using parents in schools. Volunteer tutoring is especially helpful. Using retired community members for tutoring can be a wonderful experience for both students and retirees. It is important, though, that when tutoring takes place, volunteers are aware of the importance of confidentiality and working hand in hand with the classroom teacher. The school, at the appropriate time, should make sure that parents and other community volunteers receive necessary training in instructional and curricular strategies and are recognized for their work. For example, workshops could be held to review the primary objectives of the reading or math program, examples of confidentiality, and basic dos and don'ts about working with children to support their self-esteem. In one school, parents and community members joined together to create assistive technology devices, such as communication boards, to support special education students.

A parent or community resource file can be set up by each school to note parents and community members who have a particular expertise or hobby that they can share with the school. Having adults from the community visit classrooms to tell about their careers or hobbies brings the real world to the classroom and lets students know that there is a clear link between what they are doing and what is taking place in the world of work. Furthermore, it fosters great public relations, and the students, parents, community members, and school all benefit from the experience. One school invites students to shadow parents at work and then participate in a forum in which critical skills are discussed.

Also, booster clubs have been an important traditional way for parents to become involved in schools. Frequently, these clubs help with sports activities, but these organizations can also help purchase technology for a school, raise funds to improve playground equipment, and repaint the walls of a school. The variety of possibilities is limited only by one's imagination.

Many parents do not reach out to a school because they do not know how they might help. Some schools facilitate the outreach effort by sending home a list of suggestions. Suggestions range from supporting the school on campus to assisting students by sponsoring a homework group. Working parents may appreciate that even by saving labels from cans—something they can do with limited time—they can help. A school starting a new science program asked parents for jars, lids, and bottles to build up the science resource room supplies.

Each February, the national PTA supports a PTA Take Your Family to School Week to encourage parent and family involvement in schools (Hopkins, 2008). The event, commemorating the founding of the PTA, can include numerous fun activities to engage parents, the community, and students. For example, the PTA suggests holding an International Food Night, with families bringing dinners representing the various school cultures and the school providing information about countries represented. Another event, titled Community, Kids, and Parents, involves having community businesses working on various projects with students for one hour. A complete list of the creative activities can be found at www.pta.org/take_your_family_to_school.asp.

In summary, effective communication with parents is a primary responsibility of each school. Why? Because it is very difficult to succeed with children if relations with parents are unsatisfactory. We need to create a partnership. So often, a school looks to what parents can do for the school. We must also examine what the school can do for parents and the community. By taking a proactive stance, schools send the message that "we care, we want to work with children, and we welcome parent and community input." In the end, the school principal is in the most effective position to lead the way in taking the initiative with teachers, parents, and the larger community. Building this bridge can enhance learning opportunities for parents, community members, teachers, students, and the principal and thus enrich the overall school climate.

BROADENING SCHOOL ■
SUPPORT AND PARTNERSHIPS

Developing relationships with parents is essential. Schools, however, need to reach out and create partnerships with the broader community as well. This provides opportunities to counter the traditional skepticism about the effectiveness of schools in communities. Partnerships address the need to get public support for schools and enable schools to maximize existing and potential human and financial resources. In pursuit of building broader support, schools need to communicate with a wider circle of people. One principal suggested, "Schools need to meet folks on their turf." The outreach effort may extend to the beauty parlor, barber shop, senior citizens center, supermarket, plant nursery, local business association, chamber of commerce, churches, mosques, and synagogues.

Partnerships can bring both younger and older students to retirement communities for seniors or nursing homes to sing for the adults, provide companionship for walks, and play board games. In return, the senior citizens can serve as tutors, mentors, or surrogate grandparents. For these retired senior citizens, as noted earlier, the experience can be rewarding and meaningful. For students, these experiences build important values about reaching out and serving others. Also, senior citizens or disabled veterans served by community organizations can be invited to schools for special programs at the holiday season or even special programs just for them. When appropriate, professional development opportunities in a school can include participants from the business community who can benefit from the experience (e.g., learning styles workshop).

Today, approximately 70 percent of school districts are involved in some type of business partnership, a 35 percent increase since 1990 (Sloan, 2008). In Fairfax County, Virginia, Falls Church High School is partnering with Beanetics Coffee Roasters. David Star, co-owner of Beanetics, "has taught the students the ins and outs of the coffee business." According to the high school's assistant principal, Michael Brooks, "The students are learning everything from manufacturing to marketing through the partnership" (p. 3). Jay Engeln, an expert on school-business partnerships with the National Association of Secondary School Principals, states that, "In every partnership, the school and school district's mission must be first and foremost at all times" (p. 7). According to the *Guiding Principles for Business and School Partnerships* (Council for Corporate and School Partnerships n.d.), successful partnerships state clear missions for both parties, meet mutual needs, attain buy-in from key players, set goals, measure success, communicate successfully, and monitor the partnership.

COMMUNITY-BASED ORGANIZATIONS[1] ■

In urban and rural areas, community-based organizations (CBOs) may provide the greatest direct support to schools other than the help of parents. This is especially true in areas with large numbers of at-risk youngsters. Often, the organizations provide support that cannot be offered at home. CBOs provide direct or indirect assistance to schools, individual students, parents, and teachers. The organizations usually work in collaboration with a school to enhance educational opportunities and provide the kind of individual or family aid that can make the difference between dropping out of school and making it. CBOs provide support to help with such questions as these: Where do I go for a job? Where can I get adequate day care? Where can I find food or shelter? How can I get health care?

Both public and private agencies are involved in community-based support efforts. Community agencies are reaching into schools, and schools are learning how to reach out to the community. This is reflected in the growth of full-service schools and community-school partnerships. Jane Quinn (2002), assistant executive director of the Children's Aid Society of New York, emphasizes that as a result of these partnerships, "The principals in these schools no longer have to double as educational leaders and social workers because our agency provides social services (as well as medical, dental, and mental-health services; before and after-school enrichment; summer programs; and parental involvement opportunities)" (p. 40). Quinn emphasizes that joint planning will be a key to successful partnerships in the future.

Harkavy and Blank (2002), of the Coalition of Community Schools, state their views on the effectiveness of full-service community schools based on a vision of partnership representing the ideas of 170 organizations:

> Community schools are public schools that are open to students, families, and community members before, during, and after school, and throughout the year. . . . These schools, as family support centers, help with parent involvement, child rearing, employment, housing, and other services. . . . Community schools use the community as a resource to engage students in learning and service, and help them become problem solvers in their communities. Volunteers come to community schools to support young people's academic, interpersonal, and career success. (pp. 38, 52)

Beyond the focus of high-stakes testing, Harkavy and Blank (2002) maintain that successful community schools will foster "after-school enrichment opportunities, programs in such areas as violence prevention, service learning, family literacy, mentoring, mental health, and others, and services that go beyond a narrow focus on core academics" (p. 52). Community-based support efforts may include the following:

- health clinics, including dental facilities
- hospitals
- neighborhood associations
- religious organizations
- women's centers
- community colleges and universities
- youth centers
- art organizations
- museums
- YMCAs and YWCAs
- merchant associations
- drug and alcohol rehabilitation centers
- sports associations
- Girl Scouts and Boy Scouts
- zoos
- teachers' unions
- parks and recreation departments
- U.S. Forest Service and National Park Service
- U.S. Postal Service
- U.S. Armed Forces
- police, fire, and emergency service personnel
- newspapers, television networks, and radio stations

Often, major city school districts or local, state, and federal agencies will list the CBOs in a particular area that provide resources to schools. For example, the New York City Department of Education maintains an Office of Public and Community Affairs that partners with numerous organizations, which are listed on its Web site: http://schools.nyc.gov/Offices/OPCA/. These organizations often receive financial support primarily from the United Way or the city's Department of Education.

The services in the New York area are broad and attempt to meet educational, family, and community needs. Services available for students and adults include assistance for students at risk of dropping out of school; academic support for first-time youthful offenders; support for academically talented youths in need of college scholarships; training for substance abuse prevention; education for adults and their prekindergarten children; service to combat alcohol and drug abuse for elementary school children; nutrition awareness for school staff; homework assistance for at-risk youth; employment preparation; special employment preparation for disabled students; child care so parents can attend school conferences; programs on effective parenting skills, coping with domestic violence, stress reduction, and crisis intervention; and education in conflict resolution for children, parents, and staff.

SEEKING SCHOOL SUPPORT ■
THROUGH EDUCATIONAL GRANTS

In addition to CBOs, another source of assistance for individual schools can be public or private grants. Millions of dollars in grants are available to schools from public and private sources for worthy and innovative school programs. These grants may be from federal, state, or community agencies; from private industries or foundations; or from different educational associations. Often, a grant is targeted for a specific community or general region in which an industry operates. The hope is that the grant will eventually "pay off" for the community or possibly the corporation. One source of information about grants is the weekly report *Education Grants Alert.* A typical issue will list grants from federal agencies (e.g., Department of Labor, Department of Commerce, Department of Health and Human Services) and many industrial or private industries and foundations (e.g., Scott Paper, Bill and Melinda Gates Foundation, Danforth Foundation, Annenberg Foundation). Grants can range from a few hundred dollars to millions of dollars and may be available for early childhood learning; academic achievement; innovative educational reforms; environmental issues; consensus building; substance abuse education; teen pregnancy prevention and assistance; afterschool and summer activities for inner-city youths; professional teacher reform; Native American education; and math, science, and technology projects. Interestingly, with the move toward site-based management, grant proposals often need to be approved by district personnel, principals, teachers, and union and parent representatives.

REACHING OUT AND ■
WORKING WITH THE MEDIA

Newspapers, television, and the radio are always competing for an audience. They compete with other newspapers or stations and with one another for stories that attract the largest audience. Unfortunately, conventional wisdom and marketing strategies indicate that the news vacuum is often filled with stories that are negative: "If it bleeds, it leads." The public sometimes complains that the media are only interested in selling bad news. Yet we know that news organizations do extensive surveying for marketing purposes. If good news sold, then good news is what would be presented most often.

How can schools overcome this conventional logic concerning news stories? Well, they cannot overcome it completely, but interestingly, some schools have succeeded incredibly well in getting their story across. For example, one school district in Washington State conducted a news audit and found out that during a 180-day school year, 105 articles were printed about the district in local papers—only 3 articles were negative! How did this occur? What can a school district do to minimize the negative news and get the true message out about school success? Larger districts do this by hiring a public information specialist (that "PR" person!) responsible for collating and distributing news about the schools for dissemination to various media. Smaller school systems must rely on superintendents, principals, and classroom teachers to work with the media. Regardless of whether you are a principal in a big city system or in a small town, the following guidelines can help you reach out to spread the message of success:

1. *Focus on the school vision and mission.* Every television appearance, radio interview, and newspaper article that you are involved in should focus on teaching and learning and the health and welfare of the students. Always consider the school mission and your responsibility to students, teachers, and the community. Of course, there will be many situations that do not directly relate to these issues, but school leaders need to bring the subject of the media event back to these issues. A trick of the trade is to quietly ask oneself before an interview: How can I focus on teaching and learning during this media opportunity? Remember, each time an administrator speaks with the media, it is an opportunity to step forward, be an advocate, and state what is best about the school. Even when a violent incident occurs, drawing media to the school, the direction of the interview from the school's standpoint should be toward the health and welfare of the students and getting back to teaching and learning.

2. *Build a reputation based on honesty and trust.* Successful public information officers will tell you that it is vital to build an honest and trusting relationship with the media. This is especially true when there is bad news to report—and the bad news should be reported just as we report the good. The community is entitled to know what takes place in the tax-supported public schools. Sadly, there are times when an administrator, teacher, or classified worker engages in inappropriate or criminal behavior. Trying to hide a major incident will backfire on the school district. After receiving legal advice, schools must be up front about incidents that may hurt the image of the school. However, if a trusting relationship between a reporter and a school district has been nurtured, even the most difficult situations can be ameliorated at times. For example, in one school district an embarrassing incident concerning a staff member was going to be reported in the local newspaper. Because of the trusting relationship between a reporter and a school administrator, the school was told when an article about the incident would be in the paper and whether the incident was going to be in the widely circulated main section of the newspaper or in the "zone" (local) section. This forewarning helped the school prepare for the fallout. Trust is also maintained with a little common sense. For example, never ask to see a story in advance, and send a brief "thank you" note when a positive story is published.

If a school leader is unhappy with a story because of inaccurate or biased reporting, he or she should avoid contacting the news service when angry. When calm, one should send a letter presenting one's point of view. And, if possible, contact the reporter who actually reported the story. If you initially contact the editor, the message of "going to the boss" may embarrass the reporter. The consequences can hurt the school district. Of course, contacting the editor should be an option if inaccuracy or bias continues.

3. *Recognize that each story needs an angle.* Consider that the average 30-minute television news show may select from hundreds of stories for the evening broadcast. Maybe 10 stories will be selected as "news," with only about 20 minutes of actual broadcasting time. Why should the station

show a story about a school? What makes your story news? Whether we like it or not, it is only news if the media says so! So the story needs to be unique or have an angle that will get the viewer to stick with the story instead of switching to another station. A story about school service might pique a station's interest. For example, the ecology club in one school created a trail with Braille signs for visually impaired hikers. A newspaper and a local television station picked up the story. The story was inspirational and sent a strong signal to the community about the school's devotion to service and its ecological mission.

Interestingly, because of No Child Left Behind (NCLB), standards, high-stakes testing, and accountability issues, school test results are big news. Public interest on national, state, and local levels means that test scores often are listed in newspapers as columns of statistics with a school's score, compared to others in the district or state. When school leaders are asked to comment on these data, it is important to keep a perspective. Thus, if interviewed about a school's test results, one might consider avoiding the appearance of being overly thrilled or overly disappointed depending on a school's scores. (Don't set yourself up for the surprises that next year's scores may hold!) Further, one might let reporters know that high-stakes testing is only one of many ways to assess students and that some students simply do not test well.

4. *Seize opportunities to showcase the students.* In small and midsize cities, newspapers and television networks will often showcase stories about students receiving awards or special recognition. This is especially true when a major state or national honor is achieved. In small towns, local newspapers will publish honor roll information, and zone editions of some major papers will publish local school information about awards, the work of clubs, special class activities, and big school events. A key to all of these opportunities is that they are about local kids, with local names that stakeholders will know. If a newspaper lists the names of 300 high school students who made the honor roll or a photo of the citywide chorus made up of four middle school groups, there is a good chance that all of the parents or guardians of the children mentioned would buy papers.

5. *Serve as an educational resource.* Although reporters are college educated, it is unlikely that they are familiar with all of the issues facing schools. A commandment of working with non-school personnel is avoid jargon, yet it is sometimes difficult to do so completely. A familiar and simple comparison can help a reporter or the public understand an important educational issue. To illustrate, Meek (1999) offers the following advice: "If you try to explain 'alternative assessments,' you are likely to use education jargon that is not clear to the public. If you must explain, use examples people are familiar with. To explain portfolios and exhibitions, you should use examples such as an artist's portfolio as a collection of work over time or a basketball game as an exhibition in which performance is judged, the same as a science fair" (p. 129).

Additionally, you may be asked about issues related to testing, data-driven assessment, students with special needs, NCLB, and so on. Reporters may not have a comprehensive understanding of an issue and will want to check with a trusted educator they know. Help out! Tell the reporters what they need to know. If the information is not at your fingertips, let the reporters know that you will check it out and call back. Likely, the favor will pay off in the future.

6. *Be accessible and visible.* As with other principalship roles, accessibility is critical. When the media calls, try to get back to them as soon as possible. Obviously, if there is a serious issue, it may be necessary to check with the superintendent, and in larger districts with the public information specialist, before returning a call or accepting an interview. When positive or negative issues arise, the community expects the principal to be there. Events like Principal for the Day are excellent opportunities for the principal to be visible. In one high school, this event was featured on the front page of the school newspaper, giving the principal an opportunity to be seen in a very positive manner.

7. *Approach news proactively—good or bad.* Districts should keep a steady stream of school news flowing to the media. As noted previously, there will be negative stories that need to be shared. Keep the media informed consistently about district and school events; the number of positive stories will greatly outnumber the negative. Moreover, schools must advocate for students at every opportunity and get the message out. The best way to do this is by raising the consciousness of all staff about the importance of sharing school successes beyond the classroom walls and by developing a system in which interesting stories are routinely sent to the principal and the district's public information specialist. These administrators can select the stories that will likely receive recognition and make decisions concerning which media source would best suit the school's needs.

8. *Respect deadlines.* Because newspapers, television, and radio are different media, they handle deadlines differently. Check with newspaper reporters and editors and radio and television producers to find out about local deadlines. For example, ask: What kind of advance notice is necessary for a human interest story? If you request a photographer, will that change the deadline? For a crisis or emergency situation, schools need to know print and broadcast deadlines. For example, television producers often meet about 10 A.M. with the anchors and reporters to decide on the evening stories. Anyone who has been in a television studio before an evening news show or in a newspaper's newsroom knows that the deadline pressure is extraordinary; schools do not need to complicate the situation.

9. *Write effective news releases.* Newspapers thrive on good, crisp writing. They expect those who wish to have stories published to do the same. A news release should be written in the active voice with a strong first paragraph, arousing the interest of editors and reporters. Furthermore, the news release should be no longer than one page, with a notation of "more" at the bottom of the page if additional information is included. The traditional who, what, where, when, how, and why questions need to be answered in the news release. In addition, the news release must include a date line (noting the date the story is released by the school), contact line (noting the contact person at the school), and release line (noting when the story should be released to the public). Calling the newspaper to find out if the release was received is perfectly acceptable. Normally, newspapers prefer about a five-day notice for news releases. Warner (2000) makes the following wonderful suggestions concerning news releases: "One way to get the reporter's attention is to print a special news release envelope that identifies it as such. To further catch the reporter's eye, you might consider using a neon-colored envelope that stands out in a stack of mail" (p. 91). Using district and school stationery to identify your releases and sending out a routine release form (e.g., Activity TIPS for the Week) for regular school athletic, social, and parent events keeps the media current about school activities.

10. *Get to know the key media players.* Part of building a professional relationship with the media is simply getting to know the key players. For example, find out if there are particular newspaper, television, and radio reporters who cover the education beat. Identify the influential editors and producers. Keep this information easily accessible in a Rolodex or personal digital assistant for future use. Meet these important contacts for lunch, invite them on a tour of your school, and prepare a press kit for them with essential and lively information about your school (include sample news release forms in the kit). Also, it is essential that all media are treated equally, especially because reporters are with competing newspapers and radio and television stations. Equal treatment includes returning calls promptly and recognizing deadlines. If the relationships are trusting and strong, ask for advice regarding the best way to handle a story.

11. *Develop partnerships with the media.* Members of the media should be actively courted for school-community partnerships. Career Days, journalism classes, media technology production

classes, and social studies and English classes all present opportunities to actively involve the media. Classes can visit newspaper offices and radio and television studios for worthwhile field trips. School-to-work courses and media internships are excellent credit-earning possibilities for high school students. Also, the media should be routinely invited to unique class events, showcase assemblies, science and math exhibitions, fund-raisers, and other major academic and nonacademic programs and sporting events.

12. *Prepare for interviews.* A public information officer once advised one of the authors to remember the following admonition when giving an interview: "Don't say dumb things, and don't do dumb stuff!" Of course, this basic admonition is ignored too often. Nonetheless, there are a few general points that can help a principal prepare for an interview. First, decide on the critical points of your message, and state the message by sticking to the facts during the interview. Second, remember that short 10- to 20-second sound bites are what the public remembers. Thus, brevity! Third, because the brain remembers beginnings and endings best, state your point firmly at the beginning and repeat it at the end of the interview. Fourth, when television interviews are recorded, the dead time will likely be edited, so patiently collect your thoughts before answering. Fifth, school leaders represent what is best in society. If a reporter gets argumentative, stay calm and ethically above the fray. Sixth, at the end of the interview, express your thanks for the opportunity to talk about the school.

13. *Recognize that there are no "off-the-record" comments.* Reporters are trained to supply the public with news. When school leaders try to confidentially share a little news with reporter, sometimes hoping to avoid an unfortunate consequence, the school leaders force the reporter into an ethical dilemma. It is unfair to do this to a reporter. Thus, principals should only make comments that are on the record. In fact, even during a newspaper interview, it is a good idea to record the interview so both sides can recognize that the whole story is on the record.

14. *Contact non-English-language newspapers and television and radio stations.* A very powerful message is sent to all of the school communities when an effort is made to contact non-English-language newspapers and television and radio stations about school events. Through the non-English-language media, the school can notify the non-English-speaking community that translators are needed or will be available especially for events like Back to School Night. This action sincerely tells the non-English-speaking community that the school is reaching out. It may also be possible to initiate a liaison relationship to share information between the English media and non-English-language media.

15. *Respect the legal and moral privacy of your students.* Recently, one of the authors noticed a front-page newspaper photo of a student in a school lunchroom being admonished by a police officer for poor attendance. The story's purpose was to highlight budget cuts that would curtail the services that city police could offer to schools. However, the photo was disturbing because anyone who read the paper would know about the child's attendance issues—and yes, the child's name was written below the photo. The budgetary cuts, purportedly the purpose of the article, could easily have been stressed with a positive photo of students and the police officer. The child's rights (e.g., privacy of attendance records) under the 1974 Family Educational Rights and Privacy Act (Public Law 93–380) may very well have been violated.

16. *Keep the superintendent informed.* Skip Bonuccelli, the former public information specialist with the Central Valley School District in Spokane, Washington, has the following advice for all school principals: "Remember, little kids love surprises; superintendents do not!" As with all important school issues, the superintendent or an appropriate assistant superintendent must be kept informed. There are very few administrative gaffes that annoy a superintendent more than finding out for the first time about a major school district story via the evening news or the morning paper.

Actually, this type of communication oversight is really more than just about keeping a superintendent informed. One would hope that with years of educational experience, the superintendent would be consulted as a rich source of information on how to handle a problem before it becomes news.

■ A REFLECTION ON PARTNERING WITH PARENTS AND THE COMMUNITY

Today, the needs of many students extend far beyond the resources schools have traditionally offered. Thus, teachers and administrators cannot accomplish their mission alone. School leaders must creatively reach out to the community to bring in resources that can positively impact students. Resources can range from programs that enrich academic and extracurricular activities to essential survival services for students in need. Collectively, through relationships with parents and partnerships with the broader community and public and private agencies, schools can provide the services to enhance student life in and out of school.

NOTE

1. We would like to thank Richard Shustrin from the New York City school system for his assistance with the Community-Based Organizations section of the chapter.

REFLECTIONS

This space provides for you a place to write in ideas that have been generated by this chapter, things you want to try, or adaptations of ideas presented herein.

1. Thinking about the school in which you work, in what ways are parents involved?

2. What strategies would you introduce to increase parent involvement?

3. What are some possible risks when parents play an active role in schools? What are the possible benefits?

4. What kinds of school-community partnerships are established in your school and district?

5. Based on ideas from this chapter, how can the partnership arrangement be enriched?

6. What community-based organizations play an important role in your school? What organizations would you like to see play a larger role in your school? How can this be achieved?

7. What insights or new questions do you have as a result of reflecting on ideas presented in this chapter?

18

Making a Difference for Students

The Heart of the School

Our school goes home at night.

—A principal's voice

It is not the building or instructional resources that make a school; it is the students, teachers, and parents. A school is made up of people. When the doors close, we only have a building, an empty shell without a soul. The soul of the school is the students.

In this chapter, we will try something a bit unusual. It is often through anecdotes about students that we get our greatest insights regarding their needs and how they think. Humorous anecdotes are especially interesting and often poignant. We find relief in the comical stories of children as they remind us of our special connection to students and the joys of innocence. Thus a portion of the chapter will be spent on anecdotes about students from elementary school through high school. However, we will begin the chapter by examining social justice and the challenge of excellence and equality. Following the humorous anecdotes we will review important components of the Individuals with Disabilities Education Act and how principals should respond to remain in compliance. We will then discuss ways to structure student success by encouraging greater student responsibility. Next, this chapter offers key considerations for developing an effective school discipline plan, including addressing the issue of bullying. The alarming high school dropout rate will then be examined, with suggestions to address the crisis. The chapter will close with reflective thoughts about the horrific events of September 11, 2001, and how school and student resiliency emerged as an important aftermath of the tragedy.

■ SOCIAL JUSTICE AND THE CHALLENGE OF EXCELLENCE AND EQUALITY

Success in North American schools and those of other progressive nations presents a much greater challenge because the intent is to enable each student to reach for both excellence and equality. As we move further away from ability grouping and traditional high school tracking, provide the least restrictive environment for children with disabilities, and successfully meet the needs of students from diverse backgrounds, our democratic ideals can become a classroom reality. Many nations track students early for high schools, colleges, and careers; in this context, the "late bloomer" would not have a chance to reach his or her potential. Reaching for both excellence and equality is a tall order, but it is a noble goal and one that very few nations seek to attain.

Today, this quest for excellence and equality has become an important moral issue for school principals, and educators in general, under the phrase *social justice.* In fact, Standard 5 of the *Educational Leadership Policy Standards: ISLLC* (2008), related to integrity, fairness, and ethical leadership, includes social justice as a critical principalship function: "Promote social justice and ensure that individual student needs inform all aspects of schooling." McKenzie et al. (2008) define three social justice goals to help school leaders make decisions for students with moral purpose. The goals include the following:

- rais[ing] the academic achievement of all students in their school, that is, test scores do matter. . . . Thus, although we advocate for a variety of measures of student learning and are well aware of the problems associated with standardized achievement tests, we contend that they still have a place in the social justice discourse.
- requir[ing] that educational leaders for social justice prepare their students to live as critical citizens in society. . . . Thus, it is not enough for leaders to focus on student achievement only to produce students who can read, write, and compute at high academic levels but who do not use their academic skills to challenge injustices in society and thus become no more than uncritical operators in the production economy.
- require[ing] leaders to structure their schools to ensure that students learn in heterogeneous, inclusive classrooms. Thus, the third prong of our definition of social justice links social justice to inclusive schooling. (p. 116)

The current interest in social justice comes at an important time for schools and school leaders. Leaders often feel torn between meeting mandates and addressing individual needs. For example, leaders worry that high-stakes testing may be forcing some students to drop out of school. We often see issues as either/or propositions. Yet as the above social justice goals demonstrate, excellence and equality are both worthy objectives. In Chapter 5 we reviewed the notion of the bifocal principal who recognized the need to both lead and manage creatively, to resolve what appeared to be conflicting objectives. Social justice objectives remind us that leaders need to do whatever it takes to make a difference for students.

■ "THOSE KIDS" AND THEIR STORIES

Let us talk about kids for a few minutes. First of all, to consider kids, it is important to get into their shoes. A good way is to try to recall your own school experience. What do you remember about school? Do you recall a specific class? An incident in the hallway? What special events do you remember? Which teacher had the greatest effect on you? Why? As a school principal, are you promoting the kinds of experiences for students in school that reflect your own positive memories of school?

As ideas flash through your mind, consider what you remember about your school principals. We all remember our interactions as students with principals. How many of us, when growing up, never saw the principal except on the stage during school assemblies or in his or her office because of a disciplinary infraction? One of the authors recalls playing with drumsticks on the school stairs as an eighth grader. All of a sudden, two legs appeared on the stairs. They belonged to the principal. Fortunately, the principal's reprimand was in a soft tone—he had obviously decided that this was not a major infraction. More than 30 years later, the feeling of that incident remains!

A principal recalls many memories of students. At high school graduation, pride flows when the student speeches surpass those of celebrities and politicians who are asked to address the senior class. The humor of simulated U.S. presidential debates by students in middle or high school always brings a smile to the principal's face. In one example, the principal recalled the vehicles with their tops down bringing the "candidates" to the debate accompanied by "secret service" personnel with secure earphones (from their iPods). The goal of both excellence and equality emerges when a teacher, assessing students for entrance to calculus class, mentions to the principal that a student new to the school who did not have the grades and did poorly on the assessment test asked some great questions during the test. The teacher indicates the student should be given a shot at taking calculus. The student eventually received a B in the course. High expectations pay off! Another memory is crystallized when recalling the high school student whose captivating violin solo led to a standing ovation during a school assembly. The student's reputation among the faculty as indolent and unmotivated needed to be revisited after the memorable performance.

The elementary school stories often tend to be comical, yet valuable. During the morning of the first day of school, one principal walked into every classroom to greet students. He mentioned to the second-grade students how lucky they were to have Ms. Smith as their teacher and that this would be a special year for them with this special teacher. A little girl smiled and raised her hand. The principal confidently called on her. She said, "You said the same thing last year."

In the beginning of the year, one child new to the school saw the principal a few days after school began as he was walking downtown. The child looked at the principal with an odd expression on his face and then smiled and said, "Do you know who you are? You're the principal!" A first grader walked up to his teacher a few days before the school year ended and said, "You know, in the beginning of the year I didn't like you. But now I like you better than I like my dog!"

In kindergarten class, a teacher told students that 10 bears were going on a picnic. They had only eight cups. Would that be enough cups? All the students, except one child, said no. When the single child was called on to explain his answer, he said that eight would be enough because "they could share." In another kindergarten class, a teacher asked the students to draw a picture of a birthday party. One child approached the teacher with a picture of a house, flowers, trees, and a picket fence. After looking at the picture, the teacher immediately thought to herself, "This child is a product of poverty and has never experienced a birthday party. I was foolish to assign this project." Still the teacher asked the child, "Where is the birthday party?" The student, after hearing the teacher's question, fashioned a facial expression that could only mean one thing: The teacher must be an idiot! The student proudly pointed to his picture and announced, "The birthday party is out back!"

While saying good-bye to students by the school buses one day, another principal asked Nicholas, a second grader, "Did you learn a lot in school today?" He said, "No." (The principal was immediately disappointed.) Then Nicholas added, "You don't learn a lot in one day. You learn a lot in a whole year."

A library teacher shared a story in which she was explaining to the children that previously it was legal to separate Blacks and Whites in some parts of the United States. She asked the children to state the word that indicates a separation between races. The children could not come up with the word. So she gave them a clue and said that the word starts with the letter *s*. A student raised her hand and said that the *s* word for separating the races is the word *stupid!*

■ THE RIGHT TO BE A CHILD AND TO MAKE MISTAKES

Janucz Korczak is one of the best-known European educators from the first half of the 20th century. He was a Polish doctor, teacher, and great advocate of children's rights. Tragically, he was killed with his students in Nazi concentration camps. Korczak was so famous the Nazis offered to let him escape the camps, but he chose to remain with his students, knowing that they would be arrested and later murdered. This story is told of him:

> In 1919 Korczak was giving a series of lectures at the Institute of Special Pedagogy in Warsaw. His first lecture was titled "The Heart of the Child." He asked the assembled group to accompany him with a child he was holding by the hand to the X-ray room of the children's hospital. The child was placed behind a fluoroscope and the lights in the room were dimmed. Everyone assembled could see only one light. It was the light of the child's heartbeat. Korczak then stated: "Look, and remember in the future, sometime, when you are tired or angry, when children become unbearable and distract you from your thoughts . . . remember what a child's heart looks like" (quoted in Brendtro & Hinders, 1990, p. 239).

Korczak also wrote a Bill of Rights for Children, which included the admonition that "children have a right to make mistakes." This is a key point to keep in mind when encouraging students to take risks as they answer questions or respond in class. In the end, if school does not provide an environment where it is safe to make mistakes and learn from them, where might this occur?

For students to grow intellectually, they must be encouraged to become risk takers and make mistakes. Therefore, we must help children overcome their concern about failing in front of classmates or their teachers. If failure can be viewed as a source of learning, rather than a defeat, it takes on a positive air. This cannot be accomplished without caring. We have to nurture students so they are not afraid of trying to experiment, even though they may not succeed. Trial and error are part of learning. The risk for society is that a fear of failure may inhibit a child's desire to take on new challenges or creative enterprises. Many important intellectual leaps for our society have come about as the result of risk-taking, intuitive, and creative behaviors.

■ MAXIMIZING OPPORTUNITIES FOR STUDENTS WITH DISABILITIES

Introduction

Special education programs have mushroomed since the original Individuals with Disabilities Education Act (IDEA; Public Law 94–142) legislation in 1975, which mandated Individualized Education Programs (IEPs), free and appropriate education for students with disabilities in the Least Restrictive Environment (LRE), and due process rights. Today, 6.9 million students receive special education services (Miller, 2007). Approximately 95 percent of special education students spend at least part of their day in a general education classroom (Morrison, 2009), while 25 percent of special education students are in self-contained classes and 3 percent are in special schools or facilities (Ornstein & Levine, 2003). In a study of parents of special education students, the parents reported that teachers cared about their children and were able to properly work with their children. Yet parents maintained that school districts do not really provide the maximum assistance possible. Ann Duffett, reporting on the study sponsored by the advocacy group Public Agenda, found that more than 80 percent of the 510 parents surveyed thought teachers cared about their children with disabilities, and almost 70 percent of the parents indicated that they were satisfied with a teacher's knowledge of their child's disability. However, 55 percent of the parents said they "must work to find out what help is available and 16%—about one in six—said they have considered suing or threatening to sue a school district over an issue related to a child's education" (Associated Press, 2002, p. 2A).

The 2004 IDEA Legislation: Continuing the Academic Emphasis of the 1997 Law

Federal law mandates that all students, regardless of their degree of disability, must receive a free and appropriate public education. The 1997 IDEA legislation, stipulating that special education is a service, sent a clear message that special education students should not be isolated. A key feature of the 1997 law, reinforced in the 2004 law, was the mandate that IEPs must relate more clearly to the general curriculum. The 2004 legislation took this notion a step further, aligning IDEA legislation with No Child Left Behind (NCLB) accountability requirements. Umphrey (2006) notes, "When the requirements of IDEA 2004 and NCLB are combined, students whose academic performance could at one time blend into the background and go unnoticed are now readily visible on a school's accountability landscape. IDEA 2004 raises the bar for a good reason—to support all students as they pursue an education and prepare for life" (p. 6).

Although many in the education community have complained about the 2004 requirement that students with disabilities be included in the district and state assessments, some teachers welcome the change. One veteran California special education teacher stated, "Finally my kids get the same books as the general education students because now our test scores count, just like every one else. Previously, we received old or outdated resources."

The 2004 law also provides for more flexibility on the part of the school related to disciplinary issues. The legislation "does not require that schools hold an IEP meeting or a manifestation determination review (MDR) before suspending a student for 10 days" (Arnberger & Shoop, 2006). The new legislation also permits schools to place students in an alternative educational setting for up to 45 school days (increased from 45 calendar days in the 1997 legislation) for weapons or drug charges.

Individualized Education Plans and Programs (IEPs)

The IEP is at the heart of the movement to serve students with disabilities. IEPs must be developed before permanent placement is decided upon. The goal is to place a student in the least restrictive environment with appropriate accommodations and resources. It is critical that principals recognize that the IEP is a contract and any decisions made to provide a particular service or meet an expectation becomes part of the contract. To reinforce this point, a lawyer representing a school district on special education issues counsels principals with this simple advice: "If it is on the IEP, the school must comply. If the IEP states that a paraprofessional will serve a child in a general education classroom, then that paraprofessional must be in place. Compliance is nonnegotiable, otherwise lawsuits will occur." Also, legislation requires that the IEP team consist of parent(s), school social workers, regular and special education teachers, school psychologists, an administrator, the student (if appropriate), "and other individuals who have knowledge or special expertise about the child who can help plan for the student's unique needs" (Miller, 2007). Armenta and Beckers (2006) note that although the legislation does not specifically require that the school principal attend the IEP meeting, "some state statutes may require it. Other state laws simply mandate that a principal's designee attend. If that is the case in your state, care should be exercised in selecting that designee" (p. 23).

Some Important Components of an IEP

- A statement of the child's current educational performance level
- A statement of measurable annual goals, with short-term objectives
- A statement of related services, instructional aids, and modifications to be provided
- An explanation of program modifications or supports from school personnel
- Administration of state- and districtwide assessments
- The projected date when services will begin, with information on frequency, location, and duration of services
- An indication of how annual goals will be measured
- An explanation of transition goals from school to postschool activities beginning soon after one's 15th birthday
- A statement of how parents will be informed about their child's progress concerning annual goals (Morrison, 2009; National Association of Elementary School Principals & Council for Exceptional Children, 2001)

The Principal's Role

Principals can set an ethical tone for a school by embracing the spirit and law of the IDEA legislation. For example, although a principal's designee can attend an IEP meeting, attendance by the principal sends a strong message of support for special needs students. Principals can also address the needs of special education faculty, and the parents, by providing time for staff to meet and plan lessons for special education students. Arranging teacher schedules to accommodate parent meetings can be very helpful. In addition, principals can facilitate relevant professional development for special education, regular, and paraprofessional staff. Using faculty meetings for professional development is a worthwhile option.

Recognizing the accomplishments of special education students, displaying their work, and paying attention to the students in one-on-one situations will send a strong and positive signal to students, staff, parents, and the community. Principals can help "cut through the red tape" to ensure that proper assistive technology devices are available and that regular instructional resources are modified. Spending time with parents of special needs students, and giving them an opportunity to share their hopes, can help build trust and confidence in the school's program.

Social Justice, Equity, and Students With Disabilities

Ornstein and Levine (2003) note that "Data on special-education placement show that students from some racial minority groups are much more likely to be designated for mental retardation programs than are non-Hispanic white students" (p. 390). This news is disturbing. Fair testing, with extensive documentation and a variety of culturally sensitive assessment tools, is necessary. States, therefore, are required to gather data to ensure that school districts are not identifying and placing minority students and limited-English-proficiency students disproportionately in special education classes. School principals must examine disaggregated data to ensure that race and ethnicity are not student placement factors.

Further, principals must ensure that students with special needs do not feel isolated from the general population. It is an issue of social justice. When portable classrooms, resource rooms, or study skills classrooms with special needs students are located away from general education classes, the "spirit of educating these students in the least restrictive environment" is compromised (Armenta & Beckers, 2006). At the end of the day, principals must ask: Have I done everything possible to address the needs of students with special needs?

Section 504 of the Rehabilitation Act of 1973

"Section 504 prevents discrimination against students with any disabilities in all programs and activities receiving federal financial assistance. Examples of Section 504 handicapped conditions not covered by the 13 categories specified in the IDEA legislation include disabilities such as HIV, asthma, allergies, attention deficit disorders, behavioral difficulties, and temporary medical problems" (Alvy & Robbins, 1998). Other common disabilities covered by Section 504 include alcohol or drug abuse (but not illegal drugs), hepatitis, and environmental disabilities. Student accidents that require home schooling for a temporary period are also covered under Section 504.

Although Section 504 assistance does not provide the extra funding or extra services that the IDEA legislation requires, it does offer a broad range of services to level the playing field for students who are experiencing difficulty in school. Although an IEP is not mandated for a Section 504 child, a specific plan to help the child is required. Furthermore, parents must be notified regarding identification of needs, evaluation, placement, and significant changes made in the child's program. Again, if our mission is to meet the needs of all students in the school, Section 504 special needs students also must receive the attention of school principals to ensure that proper services are provided.

STRUCTURING STUDENT SUCCESS   ■

When thinking about student success, schools should encourage behaviors that include responsibility within a nurturing environment. The environment, as much as possible, must address student behavior positively and proactively so students feel a commitment to the order and structure necessary in schools.

Involving students in worthwhile community or school projects that contribute to improving the quality of one's life or the school environment can teach responsibility and be a valuable aspect of a student's school experience. Activities that focus on making a difference—helping the elderly, tutoring other students, cleaning up the environment—help students feel like they are making a difference. Moreover, these students take pride in their school because the outreach activities tell the community "we care." At some middle and high schools, students, along with teachers, serve poor neighborhood children each week. They distribute snacks to the children, teach them health habits, tell stories, watch DVDs, and enjoy one another's company.

Peer counseling in high schools and tutoring by high school students is a wonderful way to teach responsibility and give students an opportunity to feel good about themselves. Tutoring can give students who may not be popular in other arenas (e.g., sports, music) a chance to feel good about themselves and recognize their talents. The tutoring can be one on one or with a class. When high schools can coordinate tutoring programs with middle or elementary schools, it is very satisfying to see high school students assisting a teacher by working with a few students or serving as a "buddy" to an elementary school student. High school seniors in a French IV class in Elizabethton, Tennessee, visited first-grade classrooms once a week to practice their French and teach first graders a second language. An additional benefit of this service project was the positive relationships students developed, the opportunity to model a love of learning, and a sense of empathy.

Elementary school principals should strongly consider instituting formal student government activities or informal representative assemblies, just as they occur in middle and high schools. Of course, the level of activity or structure will not be as sophisticated as the model for older students, but similar principles and activities can occur. These include such events as charity drives, cleaning up the school, fund-raisers to increase school resources, and presentations in which students make suggestions to improve the school. The student organization can study some of the principles of American government or American history to apply to their activities. The school principal and teacher advisors can meet with the students periodically during lunch to support the students and teachers organizing the activity. The National Association of Elementary School Principals (NAESP) and the National Association of Secondary School Principals (NASSP) distribute literature to support elementary, middle, and high school student government activities.

■ DISCIPLINE GUIDELINES

Another aspect of structuring student success rests in a sound discipline program, often one that reflects the input of students. Such programs enable students to be clear about expectations and provide the information students need to be successful in school. Specific school rules must, of course, align with federal, state, district, and local school board policies. School law and the legal system often are in flux, yet general guidelines concerning the extent of the school's responsibility with regard to discipline and student rights must be followed by school principals. Taking a school law class and following legal updates in principalship journals is a must. For example, school principals must be familiar with laws related to due process, random drug testing, search and seizure, truancy, disruptive students in special education, zero tolerance, censorship, and bullying prevention related to violence, intimidation, sexual harassment, and cyberbullying. Access to a lawyer with school law training is an imperative for today's school leaders.

When developing disciplinary guidelines for a school, consider the following:

1. State the guidelines positively and with clarity. A list of don'ts sets a negative tone.

2. Except when absolutely necessary (see Guideline 3), avoid guidelines that are too specific; consider general principles that include specific offenses.

3. Guidelines that should be absolutely specific include the right to undisturbed teaching and learning and total intolerance for weapons, physical violence, and drugs; hurtful, sexual, sexist, or racist language; bullying behavior; academic dishonesty; and vandalism.

4. If you are not sure that a particular guideline (e.g., students are not permitted to smoke within three blocks of the school) is the responsibility of the school, consider leaving the guideline out.

5. Safety must be the prime consideration when developing guidelines; a school must first be safe.

6. If students can be involved in developing guidelines, their commitment will increase—however, remember that student responsibilities go along with student rights.

7. All guidelines should have a rational basis. "It has always been a rule" is not good enough.

8. School rules should align with the school mission.

9. School rules must reflect district, state, and federal legal statutes.

The following is an example of one elementary school's rules:

Students care and come to school prepared to learn and to do their best. In order to do this, we

- Are polite and helpful
- Take care of our school
- Respect others—teachers, aides, students, secretaries, and support staff
- Care about ourselves and take responsibility for our behavior
- Practice good health habits
- Enjoy games in the proper areas
- Are responsible for our belongings

Students are "Safe, Smart, Clean, and Friendly."

The following section of the *American Embassy School Board Policy Manual* was written by administrators, teachers, board members, and members of the high school student association. The document is based on the premise that although students have many rights, these rights are meaningless unless each individual accepts the responsibilities that accompany rights.

Students' Rights and Responsibilities

The American Embassy School [AES] endorses the belief that education should be directed to the strengthening of respect for human rights and the fulfillment of students' responsibilities. All students shall be informed of their rights and responsibilities.

AES is a community of learners, and in any effective community, rights and responsibilities balance one another. Consequently, at AES, student rights and responsibilities are interdependent. The rights are dependent upon each member of the student body exercising the responsibilities of respect for the educational process, consideration for others, honesty, and accepting the consequences of one's actions.

In order for students to be able to conform to the community's standards of conduct, rights, responsibilities, and expectations must be articulated. At the same time, it is impossible to describe and specify all situations, hence common sense and trust must be used. Indeed, an atmosphere of mutual trust, synonymous with the sense of community for which we strive, is best achieved by establishing a few clearly described universal expectations rather than a host of rules which anticipate misconduct.

Students' Rights

1. Students are entitled to all the rights set forth in this policy, without distinction of any kind, such as race, color, sex, language, religion, political or other opinion, national or social origin, property, birth, or other status.

2. Students have the right to pursue education in a climate of mutual trust, respect, and interpersonal concern where openness and integrity prevail.

3. Students have the right to a meaningful education which will prepare them to be confident and independent learners in the lifelong search for understanding.

4. Students have the right to a curriculum which is relevant to the world in which they live and a right to provide input into determining that curriculum.

---

5. Students have a right to safety of both person and property, including the right to safe and clean school facilities.

6. Students have the right to freedom of thought, conscience, and religion.

7. Students have the right to protection from arbitrary interference with privacy, family, home, and correspondence.

8. Students have the right to freedom of opinion and expression. This right includes the freedom to hold opinions without interference and to seek, receive, and impart information and ideas, unless this would violate the rights of others.

9. Students have the right to express an opinion and have that opinion considered in any matter affecting a student or students.

10. Every student has the right not to be a witness against himself or herself.

11. In any action against a student that could result in expulsion, the student has the right to obtain assistance for his or her defense and should be informed of that right.

12. Students have the right to freedom of peaceful assembly and association, unless this would violate the rights of others.

13. Students have the right to choose freely whether to belong to an association.

14. Students have the right to confidentiality of individual student academic records.

15. Students have the right to confidentiality of counseling sessions and records.

16. Students have the right to inspect and review all academic records directly related to the student.

17. Students may seek a correction or deletion where a record is felt to be inaccurate, misleading, or otherwise in violation of the privacy or other rights of the student.

18. Students have the right to seek representation on the Board of Governors and may attend any committee meeting when dealing with matters directly related to students.

19. Students have the right to have their views solicited and considered by teachers, administrators, and the Board of Governors when dealing with matters directly related to students.

Students' Responsibilities

Students safeguard their rights by taking full responsibility for their actions. Students are responsible for their own behavior. They must care for the individual rights of others and help to provide a safe and positive school environment within which to learn. Specifically, students have the responsibility to:

1. Conduct themselves with honesty and integrity

2. Exercise self-discipline

3. Be courteous, communicate respectfully to other members of the school community, and treat with respect the views of others

4. Respect the educational process and learning environment by refraining from any classroom behavior which diminishes the rights and opportunities of others to receive an education

5. Act in a manner which safeguards the health and well-being of others

6. Respect the property of fellow students and the property of the school

7. Dress in a neat attire which takes into account cultural sensitivities

EFFECTIVE CLASSROOM MANAGEMENT: ■ HANDLING DISCIPLINARY PROBLEMS

The very best disciplinary guidelines may reduce, but will not prevent, disruptive behavior. Handling disruptive behavior is certainly one of the most difficult and potentially controversial aspects of a principal's job. Helping students behave properly is one of the most important aspects of our job. Setting limits and showing a caring attitude when disciplinary problems occur can be a very important lesson for all students. Major responsibilities for principals, then, include helping teachers develop effective classroom management plans and consistent schoolwide plans as well as working directly with the more difficult disciplinary problems. Often, middle and high schools assign an assistant principal to be responsible for discipline. However, principals need to let these administrative colleagues know that the principal should be kept informed and consulted when difficult situations occur. Ultimately, the principal is responsible for disciplinary decisions taken by the assistant principal.

Before discussing discipline management plans, it is important to define *effective classroom management:* Effective classroom management is the conscious use of proactive strategies and procedures to help students behave in a way that provides maximum learning opportunities for each student in the class. Through such a management system, students are encouraged to develop skills for self-discipline. Based on this definition, attention should be devoted to behavior management at both an individual and a schoolwide level. Thus there should be an overall school procedure for handling disruptive behavior and specific recommendations to teachers on how to resolve problems with individual students. Both situations, however, must always be viewed as "embedded in a social system; it [a disciplinary problem] is never an isolated event" (Ross, 1981, p. 211). This is a critical point because principals and teachers must act on the assumption that every student is a witness to the decision. In this setting, fairness and a justifiable rationale are essential.

The social context is especially important when examining Curwin and Mendler's (1988) "80-15-5 Principle" describing the typical classroom. Curwin and Mendler maintain that 80 percent of the students infrequently break school rules and come to school prepared to learn, 15 percent break rules somewhat frequently and show inconsistent motivational tendencies, whereas 5 percent are frequent rule breakers and come to school with almost no motivation or direction in their lives. The social context is critical here as the teacher has the seemingly insurmountable task of keeping the 80 percent motivated while using appropriate disciplinary strategies to control the 15 percent and firmly deter the 5 percent. Curwin and Mendler believe that the key is helping the 15 percent improve their behavior without antagonizing the other students.

When developing a disciplinary plan, it is, of course, a good idea to examine what research has told us about what effective teachers do to maintain discipline in a caring environment. Curwin and Mendler (1988) reviewed the research of Emmer, Evertson, and Anderson to stress "that effective teachers teach classroom rules and procedures, monitor compliance with the rules, follow through with consequences quickly and consistently, establish a system of student responsibility and accountability for work, communicate information clearly, and organize instructional activities" (p. 13). Ross (1981) also stresses the importance of clear rules but adds that showing praise—catching the child being good—and ignoring undesirable behavior when possible have proven to be effective management techniques.

The strategy of catching the child being good raises, also, the important issue of intrinsic versus extrinsic motivation. If, while catching the child being good, the teacher uses too many extrinsic rewards, students may become dependent on external reinforcement and teacher behaviors that diminish the value of being good simply because it is the right thing to do. Too often in school we resort to instant extrinsic rewards and reinforcement (e.g., stickers, exaggerated praise) to promote desired behaviors. As Kohn (1996) reminds us, "The promise of a reward is sometimes not just ineffective but counterproductive, that is, worse than doing nothing at all" (p. 33). We need to adopt long-term strategies to foster intrinsic behaviors that encourage the joy of learning or the personal satisfaction of reading a book or helping a classmate who is having difficulty with a math problem.

Based on the previous suggestions of Curwin and Mendler (1988) and shared experiences of many educators, the following steps are recommended for principals and teachers when consequences need to be administered to an individual student:

1. In a balanced tone, let the student know what he or she did wrong.

2. Ask the student to explain why the behavior is unacceptable. If his or her answer is inadequate, explain why the behavior is unacceptable.

3. Discuss the consequence and how it will be administered. Begin with the least threatening intervention and, when possible, give the student a choice of consequences.

4. If necessary, describe and model the desired behavior.

5. Ask the student if he or she has anything else to share with you.

6. Finish the meeting by emphasizing that although you are displeased with the unacceptable behavior, you separate that behavior from your positive feelings about the student.

7. If the inappropriate behavior continues, reflect on the environment in which the behavior occurred. Should changes take place?

8. Communicating with parents or guardians should be considered depending on the frequency or degree of the misbehavior.

When viewing the big picture, principals should remind teachers, especially new teachers, that everyone experiences disciplinary problems—and one should not take the problems personally. Also, teachers should keep administrators informed when problems occur frequently. Such happenings usually indicate that the student feels troubled. This warrants further study. Teachers need to know that they can speak with administrators about disciplinary issues without worrying that the administrators will think they are ineffective teachers. A principal must be there for teachers.

■ REDUCING BULLYING BEHAVIOR

"Bullying is frequently mentioned as a possible contributor to school violence . . . [and] bullying is one of the most common forms of victimization at school" (Harris, Petrie, & Willoughby, 2002, p. 3). Although it would be an overstatement to assert that all incidents of extreme school violence, including school shootings, are a result of bullying behavior, clearly bullying has contributed to some of the most tragic events. Bullying should be stopped, and not just because it may lead to the worst-case scenario of a school shooting. Bullying is unacceptable because it is wrong to verbally or physically intimidate or harass others. And obviously, students cannot learn successfully when fear is a part of their lives. Also, those who exhibit bullying behavior at school often "experience a greater degree of depression than is found among adults who did not bully others at school." Moreover, bullies are more likely to receive future criminal convictions (Harris et al., 2002, p. 6).

School principals must communicate to the school community that bullying is unacceptable. Sadly, the victims of bullies do not feel that school officials care, and bullied students are unlikely to tell about their victimization for fear of reprisals. To support these students and schools, states and school districts are establishing antibullying policies. For example, Washington State's law describes bullying as "Harassment, intimidation or bullying . . . when the intentional written, verbal or physical act (a) physically harms a student or damages a student's property; (b) has the effect of substantially interfering with a student's education; (c) is so severe, persistent, or pervasive that it creates an intimidating or threatening educational environment; (d) has the effect of substantially disrupting the orderly operation of the school" (Substitute House Bill 1444, State of Washington, 2002). Washington State has mandated as part of the bill a section that provides immunity to school employees, students, or volunteers who willingly report incidents of harassment, intimidation, and bullying. Furthermore, staff workshops and other professional development programs that stress positive character traits and values as part of an antibullying policy are mandated by state legislation.

Goleman (1995) notes that bullies often lack empathy, are unable to interpret social cues, and misread neutral expressions as hostile actions against them. Elias (2002) indicates that if bullies are going to change their behavior, they must learn to internalize and practice appropriate skills. One program described by Elias that is used to minimize inappropriate behavior is called the "Keep Calm Force." Elementary school students who display appropriate behavior are selected for the Keep Calm Force and help maintain good behavior on the playground wearing their Keep Calm Force T-shirts. When they observe dissension or fighting, the students walk over to the conflict and point to their T-shirts. Among the Keep Calm Force students are former "troublemakers." Also, students who no longer qualify for the Keep Calm Force (possibly because of bullying behavior) are reminded that they are Keep Calm Force alumni—good behavior is part of their history!

Based on the recommendations of Harris et al. (2002), our own experiences, and the suggestions of other educators, the following recommendations are suggested to reduce bullying behavior in schools:

- If possible, organize large schools into smaller "units, families, or houses" to reduce the feeling of alienation some students may experience in larger settings.
- Initiate programs that connect an adult with every student in the school, and that connect students with peers. Mentoring programs and peer intervention programs should both be instituted so that every student has someone to talk with and receive effective intervention strategies from when difficulties occur.
- Use community resources to help students prone to bullying, especially those students from families unable to provide positive support.
- Survey students concerning their perceptions about bullying, and share results with staff, parents, and community members.
- Ensure that students who are victims of violence recognize that the administration, counselors, classroom teachers, and community resources are firmly in their corner and are there to support them.
- Use student leadership organizations or other appropriate avenues to get the message out that a dialogue concerning antibullying prevention and intervention strategies is a major school priority.
- Recognize that bullying behavior is everyone's responsibility and that overt acts of bullying (e.g., violence) are not the only concern; verbal harassment and intimidation must also be addressed.
- Supervise areas where bullying behavior may occur. These areas include hallways, lockers, cafeterias, restrooms, playgrounds, buses, areas immediately surrounding the school, and even classrooms. Provide extra supervision in areas that are especially problematic.

- Initiate professional development programs that emphasize character and values, and work with the faculty to model and support a positive school climate and a culture that promotes antibullying behaviors.
- Keep students informed concerning the school's antibullying policy and consequences relating to suspension and expulsion for students who defy the policy.
- Initiate programs to assist students who bully others by providing social, emotional, personal, and academic skill support to cope appropriately in a school environment.

■ CYBERBULLYING AND SOCIAL RESPONSIBILITY

The Center for Safe and Responsible Internet Use has defined cyberbullying as "being cruel to others by sending or posting harmful material using the Internet or a cell phone" (Willard, 2005). Cyberbullying includes online verbal attacks with hostile or vulgar language; sending or posting hurtful messages, rumors, or photos; intimidating through cyberstalking; disclosing private information; and blocking someone from online access (Parker-Roerden, Rudewick, & Gorton, 2007). Cyberbullying is particularly pernicious because the bully (who perpetrates the Internet, text messaging, or other electronic bullying act) can easily remain anonymous while engaging in harmful behavior toward an innocent target. Often the bully sends a copy of the hurtful message to bystanders, similar to the act of the schoolyard bully who punishes another in front of a crowd. Bystanders, who may initially be innocent recipients of the "message," have three basic choices: (1) they can forward the hurtful message to others and become bullies themselves, (2) they can remain as bystanders, or (3) they can intervene to end the bullying behavior.

How a bystander responds to cyberbullying can determine whether the hateful behavior continues, and "experts agree that addressing the bystander is the best way to curb cyberbullying. By encouraging the bystander to have the courage to intervene rather than take part, most incidents of cyberbullying would fizzle before catching fire online" (Long, 2008). However, behaving with courage is not easy, especially for teenagers surrounded by peers who are participating in cyberbullying or other forms of harassment. Teaching students how to be socially responsible can be a first step in minimizing bullying behaviors.

According to Brunner and Lewis (2008), social responsibility can be taught and proactive preventive behaviors can become community values. Adults and teens need to take a stand against racial harassment, gay bashing, and physical and relational aggression. Brunner and Lewis recommend four principles of social responsibility:

- I will not intimidate or embarrass others.
- I will be a friend to those being harassed, teased, or embarrassed.
- I will invite students who are left out of activities to join me.
- When I see students being harassed, teased, or embarrassed, I will tell responsible adults. (p. 40)

Additionally, school leaders must make sure that student disciplinary policies define cyberbullying and the consequences for inappropriate behaviors. Because cyberbullying can begin off school grounds, students may rationalize that it is not a school issue. Administrators need to let students know that cyberbullying is a form of harassment, bullying, and intimidating behavior. Parents must also be informed about the anticyberbullying policy and provided with guidelines to help them understand the issue and what they might be facing at home. Finally, staff professional development should be included as part of a school's anticyberbullying strategy, just as professional development has been offered in response to other forms of inappropriate behaviors.

THE HIGH SCHOOL DROPOUT CRISIS ■

Graduating from high school is a first step to opportunity. For students and society, failure to graduate has far reaching implications. For example, California "loses $46.4 billion for each cohort of . . . residents that reach age 20 without a diploma, after the lifetime costs of their lower earnings, higher medical costs, and increased likelihood of needing public assistance or committing crimes are taken into account. Each year, that number is about 120,000 young people" (Jacobson, 2008, p. 8). Although states use various formulas to calculate their high school dropout rates, the overall statistics are sobering. While about 70 percent of U.S. high school students graduate, 1.2 million students fail to do so each year. Former Secretary of Education Margaret Spellings referred to the crisis as the "silent epidemic." Colin Powell called the 1.2 million figure a "catastrophe" ("Feds Take on Dropout Crisis," 2008). When the high school dropout data is disaggregated, the statistics are even more sobering. Seventeen of the nation's 50 largest cities report graduation rates of less than 50 percent. After four years of high school, only 58 percent of Hispanics, 55 percent of African Americans, and 51 percent of Native Americans graduate ("Diplomas Count 2008," 2008).

At a conference on the crisis sponsored by the UCLA Civil Rights Project, four common reasons for dropping out of school were identified in a report compiled by Johns Hopkins University:

- Life events such as pregnancies, arrests, or a pressing need for a full-time income.
- Frustration or boredom with curriculum that leads [dropouts] to lose sight of the "reason for coming to school."
- Subtle discouragement from teachers or school administrators who label a student "difficult, dangerous, or detrimental to the success of the school."
- Repeated failure to succeed can wear students down. ("Educators Told Schools Face a Dropout Crisis," 2008)

Academic Press and Social Support

Although the challenge of reducing the number of students dropping out of school appears overwhelming, it must be addressed. Fortunately, promising practices are being implemented throughout North America. An approach reporting the results of the Chicago Annenberg Research Project and supported by the Chicago Annenberg Challenge (Lee, Smith, Perry, & Smylie, 1999) recommends a two-pronged strategy employing both *Academic Press* and *Social Support* to make a difference in the lives of students. Although the study concentrated on sixth and eighth graders, fieldwork involved observing high schools that were using both social support and academic press strategies. Social support is defined as "the personal relationship that students have with people who may help them do well in school" (p. 9), while "academic press . . . focuses on the extent to which school members, including teachers and students experience a normative emphasis on academic success and conformity to specific standards" (p. 10). The power of this approach rests on rejecting the notion that schools must choose between providing emotional and social support *or* press for academic achievement. The results of this study indicated that when both academic press and social support were instituted, achievement scores were highest. Thus, school systems should aim for both social relationships *and* accountability and rigor. Interestingly, the approach to supporting students in historically Black colleges and universities is provided as an example of the success of this dual approach. These institutions of higher education succeed due to "strong academic programs and strong systems of social support to help students succeed academically" (p. 6).

Based on the research study, strategies to enhance social support include supplemental one-on-one tutoring, creating smaller learning communities, personalized learning, schools within schools, parent education programs, and building relationships with mentors and older community members. Academic press strategies include higher expectations for students, professional development related to higher order thinking and challenging student work, and formative assessments to impact instruction (Lee et al., 1999, pp. 21–22). Finally, the researchers report, "For students who may receive little support from home, peers, and community, it becomes even more important that principals, and teachers create school and classroom environments that provide personal support for learning" (p. 25).

Breaking Ranks II

The recommendations of the Chicago Annenberg Research Project parallel the objectives of the NASSP (2004) in its publication *Breaking Ranks II*. In that document, the NASSP calls for (1) personalization through smaller learning communities, advisory programs, and personal connections among students, teachers, and administrators related to social and academic issues; (2) aligning curriculum with state standards and at the same time ensuring the material is relevant to students; (3) teacher professional development related to engaging instructional and assessment strategies and creating flexible scheduling to address student needs; and (4) developing Professional Learning Communities in which leadership is distributed and teachers, students, families, and the community communicate successfully and exchange ideas to foster student success (pp. 6–18).

The Chicago Annenberg Research Project and NASSP clearly articulate the notion that to reduce the number of high school dropouts, school leaders and teachers need to make personal connections with students that intentionally focus on academic rigor and success. Additionally, creating community is a major element stressed by both groups. Personalization cannot rely only on the one-on-one connection; administrators, teachers, students, families, and community members must all see the calling and engage in the moral challenge that will lead to increasing the number of high school graduates to a figure of which we can all be proud.

One school principal from a high school with a large population of at-risk youth took an unusual but powerful approach to address the dropout problem. As you read this principal's story, consider how a vision can be realized when school leaders, faculty, and students are committed to the idea.

Leaders as Builders of Dreams

"Sometimes, leaders are 'keepers of the dream' when it comes to students' aspirations. But sometimes, the leader encounters students who are dreamless. They are beaten down and have a sense of hopelessness. In this case, the leader must help construct dreams for, and with, students. Last year, I took on the role of 'builder of the dream.' I shared this idea with teachers and asked them to collaborate as 'builders of the dream.' During the first week of school, we called in every senior. We shared our collaborative vision of graduation day. We asked the seniors to put themselves in the picture, specifically the lineup to receive a diploma. Then we said, 'To make this vision closer to reality, put on a cap and graduation robe. And we'll take your picture.' Students seemed surprised, but pleased. We photographed every one of them in a cap and gown, approaching a podium where they would be handed a diploma. That picture served as a magnet for many of the kids—it pulled them through the year, despite tough times. As a staff, we are convinced many more graduated because of this approach. We'll plan to do this again every year."

STUDENT AND TEACHER RESILIENCY ◼

As the tragic events of September 11, 2001, were unfolding, we learned a great deal about heroes. "On September 11th, more than 8,000 children—from day care to high school seniors, from fully mobile to multiple-handicapped—were safely evacuated from the vicinity of Ground Zero in lower Manhattan. Not a single child was harmed or lost in all of the chaos. The principals, teachers, staff, and parents were heroes in every sense of the word" (Lehmuller & Switzer, 2002, p. 54). Paul Houston (2002), executive director of the American Association of School Administrators, reflected,

> Perhaps the most powerful lesson for me was to find that all I had learned about heroes was wrong. Most of us were raised to think of heroes as those extraordinary people in history books who do extraordinary things. What we learned on September 11th was that we are genetically programmed to act heroically. Heroes are ordinary people who do extraordinary things and they are all around us. It is in each of us to act heroically when called upon. What a wonderful lesson for our children. (p. 46)

School principals all around the country were tested concerning their leadership skills on September 11, 2001, and the following days. On September 11 teachers, students, and parents wondered if their schools would be closed or if lockdown procedures would be implemented. Following September 11, teachers looked to principals to determine whether they should stick to their routine or teach about death, grief and anxiety, tolerance, current events, the tenets of American democracy, or the geography of Afghanistan.

Let's recall that a consistent theme in all of the nation's schools was a desire to express appreciation to New York and Washington firefighters, police officers, and emergency service workers and to the heroic civilian and military men and women who were attacked at the World Trade Center and the Pentagon. Students created banners, drew pictures, collected money, and wrote thousands of letters to express their feelings. Like thousands of other classrooms across the nation, Shannon Collinge's class of second graders in Spokane, Washington, received the following thank you from the Uniformed Firefighters Association of New York:

> Thank you for the drawings and letters from the children in your class. Please convey to them our gratitude for the concern and compassion they have shown us in this difficult time.
>
> We have received an outpouring of kindness from the children of America in such letters as those you sent and we have taken the letters and drawings to fire stations all over the city so that they can be displayed where firefighters can see them. We also placed as many pictures as would fit in the front window of our building so that other New Yorkers could see them as they pass by.
>
> Again, please let the children know how much their kindness means to us.
>
> Sincerely,
> Uniformed Firefighters Association
> Widows' and Children's Fund

Richard L. Curwin (2002), in the inspiring article "Finding Jewels in the Rubble," noted that "Character is not determined by what happens to us, but rather by how we deal with what happens to us" (p. 80). Curwin gathered information from schools all across the nation to find out how they were coping with, and responding to, the events of September 11 as part of their school programs. Altruism, building community, accepting others, and finding a common ground were some of the themes emphasized by schools. Positive action was taken, such as visiting nursing homes, collecting food for the homeless, considering the negative effects of cliques and bullying, and refining the art of compromise. As noted earlier, we have redefined heroes and heroism as a result of September 11th. Curwin suggests the following:

> Schools can take the opportunity to explore the notion of heroism, pointing to new role models for students to emulate as alternatives to sports figures and movie stars. More important, students can begin to explore their own heroic qualities and choices and discover how they can be heroes in their own school communities by, for example,
>
> - Stopping fights
> - Reporting dangerous behavior
> - Standing up to bullies and defending their victims
> - Watching the school neighborhood for suspicious outsiders
>
> Even low-achieving students and those with behavior problems can find heroic qualities within themselves. They may not be top students or great athletes, but they can defend the defenseless. Gang members can help eliminate drug sales around the school perimeter and patrol for dangerous strangers. Why not reward those who demonstrate these qualities with New York Fire Department hats? Everyone has the potential to be a hero in small, meaningful ways. (p. 81)

■ FINAL THOUGHTS ON "THOSE KIDS"

When considering our quest for excellence and equality, it might help to consider the ideas of Howard Gardner (2006), who reminds us to recognize that students may display intelligence in different areas. Gardner asks us to consider nine separate areas of possible intelligence, including the verbal-linguistic, logical-mathematical, musical, bodily-kinesthetic, visual-spatial, naturalist, interpersonal, intrapersonal, and existential areas. When we recognize that students' talents may vary and when we show our respect for various talents, whether they be linguistic or musical, we are telling students that we admire them for their strengths and are not simply looking to find their weaknesses. The popular disciplinary refrain to "catch the kids being good" should go beyond discipline and into the multidimensional intelligence areas—"catch their strengths" and help students build from areas of strength.

Students remember not only the rules but how they are treated and what others think of them. School leaders cannot afford to miss opportunities to support students and celebrate their strengths. Terry Deal reflects that industries can recycle poor products, but a "lost child is a lost treasure." Caine and Caine (1991) remind us that creating a positive climate in school can directly affect how students think and function. They stress that under threat, the brain actually "downshifts" and does not perform at its maximum capacity. Thus communicating often with students, setting a supportive tone in class, and sending positive nonverbal signals are as critical as the rules. Finally, learning what responsibility is all about is a lifelong challenge. If schools can foster responsibility through positive guidelines and valuable activities, then the possibility of developing the tools for lifelong learning can become a reality.

REFLECTIONS

This space provides a place for you to write down ideas that have been generated by this chapter, things you want to try, or adaptations of ideas presented here.

1. What do you remember about your school principals?

2. What aspects of social justice resonate with you?

3. What humorous anecdotes can you recall about students in your school that tell a larger story?

4. What are some of the effective strategies used in your school to assist students with disabilities? Which strategies need to be improved?

5. What are some guidelines that should be included in a student disciplinary code?

6. Review the recommendations in this chapter described to reduce bullying behavior. What else would you suggest to solve this problem?

7. Why has the high school dropout rate become a major issue today? Do you believe it has always been a challenge for educators? What solutions do you think could be offered to reduce the crisis?

8. What insights or new questions do you have as a result of reflecting on the ideas presented in this chapter?

PART VII

The Principal's Professional and Personal Worlds

19

The Newcomer to the Principalship

There were some days, you know, I can't describe this feeling. It's like when you're a kid and you're about to go up [to bat], and there are three guys on base, and it was the bottom of the ninth, and there were two out, and you were up, and there were two strikes on you. Your stomach has this feeling like, boy, I've got to do it! There were some days I had that feeling all day long in my stomach. And that is a bad feeling.

—Comment from a first-year principal

First-time principals experience five interrelated threads of influence (Alvy & Robbins, 2008) that help explain why the job is so complex. The unique experiences of all newcomers affirm their individual signatures. Review each factor below, and consider your personal situation.

Newcomer experiences—negotiating the many "firsts" one encounters during any fresh experience such as moving to a new community, meeting new people, driving a new car, or operating a different computer.

Challenges all principals face—experiencing the daily work of any principal, new or seasoned.

Personal and professional baggage—considering all the experiences one brings to the job, including family background, education, values, teaching experiences, previous supervisory relationships, one's unique career ladder, social and communication skills, attitude, and talents.

Local and immediate context of the school culture—reflecting on the special nature of each school, district, and community that newcomers encounter during their initial principalship.

The chemical mix—reflecting on the unique "mark" that emerges for each individual when the above four factors are synthesized.

By reflecting on these factors, new principals gain important insights about the challenges of the job, previous experiences that influence present behaviors, and one's performance. Most important, these factors should provide newcomers with a sense of relief, reminding them that they are not alone. But the relief does not diminish the daily challenges that new principals face; on-the-job training is not an option. From day one, you have full principalship responsibilities. Schools obviously cannot afford to suspend operations while new principals are learning the ropes. Thus it is crucial to identify the problems that are especially challenging for new principals and offer practical suggestions to assist new and prospective principals. Experienced principals, who find themselves "new again" in a different setting, will find the ideas discussed in this chapter useful, as will superintendents and veteran principals serving as mentors for new principals.

PROBLEMS THAT ■
CHALLENGE NEW PRINCIPALS

The literature on the principalship indicates there are several areas of difficulty that seem to frequently surface with new principals (Alvy, 1983; Alvy & Robbins, 1998). In the following paragraphs these difficulties are described, not to scare off prospective principals or newcomers but to reduce their anxiety about what they might face. This chapter will then move forward with suggestions to acquaint prospective as well as new principals with important socialization concepts and offer some practical suggestions to get started on the job.

The limitations of preservice training. When moving into the principal's role, newcomers usually find that the preservice training could not possibly duplicate all of the challenges that one immediately faces. For example, there are many unique situations in each school, regarding staff relations, student needs, and the physical plant, so that on-the-job trial and error is simply a necessity. For some, it has been helpful to experience the realistic and practical training provided through a vice principalship, administrative internship, or administrative assistantship. Preservice courses generally do not address how to use the latest administrative software, design a temporary schedule to implement the statewide testing of all middle school students, or operate a fire drill system. Yet these frequently are the responsibilities of a principal. Universities and principals' centers are working to improve their ability to provide more realistic experiences (e.g., case study analysis, simulations, internships with support networks) so prospective principals are more familiar with some of the challenges they will face. Increasingly, school districts and universities are pursuing mentoring programs to link up prospective or new principals with seasoned veterans or retired principals to help newcomers face the job challenges. An effective mentoring program benefits the protégé and the mentor. The protégé gains an ally and sounding board, while the mentor may find the relationship renewing, enabling the veteran principal to gain new meaning from his or her leadership career.

It's lonely at the top. New principals are not only on unfamiliar ground but will find that, by virtue of their positions at the top of the management hierarchy in their schools, they do not have professional peers with similar responsibilities in their immediate environments. Quite simply, there may be no one else around who can relate to the problems being faced. Elementary principals may find themselves even lonelier because many elementary schools have only one administrator in the building. Role models and on-site assistance may be desired but not possible. "I felt like I was alone. I couldn't go across roles and confide with somebody" (a principal's voice). Because the superintendency and high school principalship in many areas are still dominated by males, the loneliness of the principalship may be heightened for women in some contexts where the male-dominated old boys' network still exists.

Ironically, although the principal may be lonely with regard to having a professional peer on the same organizational level, a principal is anything but alone during the school day. The principal is constantly interacting with teachers, students, secretaries, parents, salespeople, student teachers, and community partners. Thus, for someone who enjoys human interaction, the principalship can be very rewarding and an opportunity to meet interesting people from various walks of life. Yet opportunities to sit down at the lunch table with other principals may occur only at districtwide meetings or at annual regional, state, or national association meetings.

Time management—finding time to visit classes and juggling the various roles. It is an understatement to say new principals quickly learn that there are frequent and various demands on their time. For many newcomers, time management becomes their most significant problem. Unfortunately, the first casualty of a new principalship may be the instructional responsibility of taking the time to visit classes (Alvy, 1983). If one's early actions are a predictor of future actions, it may be difficult for newcomers to reverse patterns that develop early in their principalship. Managing one's time, then, becomes a challenge to be addressed from the first day on the job.

New principals may also feel resentment about the amount of time required of them. Why do I have to return to school in the evening? Should I turn off my cell phone during dinner? Should I check my e-mail before going to bed? What happened to my summer holiday? "I've been surprised at the amount of time, and weekends, that this particular superintendent has asked me to give. . . . It surprises me, and that's the one thing about the job that bothers me" (a principal's voice).

A related time and responsibility management issue is juggling the various roles one has to play. Principals can pretty much forget their job description. In addition to serving as instructional leaders, principals must be child advocates, budget managers, personnel directors and mediators, cheerleaders during "down" days, community healers, public relations experts, basketball timers, culture shapers, actors in school plays . . . and what else?

Staff relations and introducing change. There is always some nervousness when a principal is new to a school—especially when a first-timer takes over responsibilities. The nervousness, of course, is mutual. Newcomers usually find that staff resistance to change is one of the major obstacles they face. The resistance may be even more pronounced with the more experienced teacher veterans, who may comment, "We tried this two principals ago." Implementing change may be especially hard for the principal who is hired in-house. Relationships with longtime friends may have to change. In this context, the teacher evaluation process can be a particularly difficult hurdle to overcome.

Satisfying the various constituencies. Teachers, students, superintendents, unions, school boards, parent associations, specific parent interest groups, businesses, and other community groups often have conflicting interests. Just trying to find out what these individuals and groups desire is a considerable task for the new principal. Principals may be tempted to state simply, "My responsibility is to follow the directives of the superintendent, who is acting on the authority of the board in the best interest of the students." But reality tells us that interest groups will not be satisfied with this bureaucratic response. Various constituencies will disagree on the purpose of schooling. Group conflict and the consequences are a given. Staff and parents will be very interested to see how the newcomer reacts when conflicts emerge. Principal must manage the fallout but should also seek opportunities when conflict occurs.

Unrealistic expectations—making immediate instructional changes. When hired for the principalship, one usually can take pride in knowing that he or she was selected for the job over some pretty stiff competition. Also, with all of the literature on the principal as instructional leader, often the newcomer hopes to make a quick and significant curriculum change or implement an instructional innovation. However, these ideas usually will need time to be nurtured as staff members adjust to the newcomer and the newcomer learns about the culture of the school. Thus implementing immediate curricular, instructional, or assessment changes will probably have to wait until the principal has the opportunity to assess the context and build trust with staff members. For a change to be institutionalized, one should know the organization well—the mission, teachers, parents, students, and resources—so the change can become a part of the way business is conducted at the school. This is, however, usually a disappointment for the first-timer who is ready to jump in and immediately have an impact on the organization. One veteran principal advises newcomers to be patient with the staff: "Trust took almost five years to build. But we created a world together."

Meeting individual student needs. Principals and teachers want to address the needs of each student. However, many new principals see the school population as a whole—instead of considering individual students. After all, principals see all the students at an assembly, in the hallways, by the buses, in the cafeteria, or during a fire drill. This is quite a change, especially if the principal recently served as a teacher. It is a challenge and a dilemma. One must take responsibility for the whole institution but still consider the personal needs of each individual. The same dilemma can be applied to faculty, classified staff, and the parent community.

It's difficult to become an instant sage. A new principal in his mid-30s had a veteran teacher, who was close to retirement, enter the office one afternoon after school to ask the principal for advice about what to do in retirement. The newcomer was struck by this image of the older, white-haired teacher coming to this newcomer for advice. If anything, it was the new principal who should be going to the veteran teacher for advice. However, as the weeks progressed, many others asked critical questions that required the principal to respond. The newcomer slowly realized that because of his position many people just expect the principal to know. If only they knew the truth!

A PROFILE OF THE NEW PRINCIPAL   ■

The following brief characterization summarizes the previous remarks concerning the school life of a new principal.

After a few days on the job, the newcomer realizes that the preservice training program insufficiently prepared her for the job. The new principal is having trouble with experienced staff who are resisting necessary changes and two former teaching colleagues from a previous school who refuse to take the beginner seriously. The principal is not sure how to respond to a few teachers who seem very frustrated concerning students who are experiencing academic difficulties. The principal is struck by the notion that too many students are not succeeding. She too is frustrated and thinks, "This job has more responsibilities than I had anticipated. However, I am eager to accept the challenges."

As the year progresses, the new principal is somewhat disheartened because numerous daily interruptions, job details, and personal ambivalence concerning the evaluation process stand in the way of spending more time as an instructional leader. She wants to visit classrooms, observe student work, and assist teachers. Yet the beginner is still unsure—and a little fearful—about delegating responsibilities to free herself to engage in more instructional leadership. The new principal also is learning about the norms and customs of significant others in the school, district, and community and is embracing some of the customs. Finally, toward the end of the year the newcomer is becoming more confident in her work and open to asking veteran district administrators about important end-of-year responsibilities. She reflects while shaking her head, "Why didn't I ask for assistance in August and September? I certainly will seek assistance next year!"

■ HELPING PROSPECTIVE AND NEW PRINCIPALS MAKE THE GRADE

Identifying the problems of new principals is, of course, a first step in helping newcomers make the grade. From there, we need to consider socialization strategies necessary for the principalship and close by offering practical suggestions to succeed during those critical first years.

Socialization for the Principalship

Developing a positive mind-set is critical to success in a new position. As you reflect on the ideas that follow, consider how these suggestions can enhance your performance.

The leader as learner—a habit of mind. The leader-as-learner mind-set is essential to a new principal's success. Why? Because the concept is based on the premise that the leader who is willing to learn has an excellent chance to succeed. Thus, when new principals ask questions and solicit ideas about how the school works, they are not revealing a weakness or ignorance but a strength, the desire to learn. Let others know that their ideas are important and that without their information you could not succeed. This is a refreshing attitude to see in a leader; most professional colleagues will appreciate the newcomer who wants to know how things really work. The key, though, is to keep this characteristic throughout your career.

Reflecting on your professional background. Sarason (1982) reminds us that as teachers we often remember the supervision and evaluation process with some disdain. With regard to teaching experiences, prospective principals need to consider their feelings about classroom isolation; how they felt when supervisors entered their classrooms; relationships with teachers and supervisors, students and parents; and the professional climate in their schools. For example, what kind of supervisory role models has one worked with? In addition to teaching experiences, new principals need to evaluate the type of university training received and how previous administrative positions may affect their performance. For instance, if one has served for several years as an athletic director, will he or she be able to make budgetary decisions fairly when the athletic budget may need slicing to provide more funds for a major group of non-English speakers entering the school district?

Developing a broad view. When teaching or taking responsibility for a particular program, one does not have to consider the broad scope of responsibilities and decisions that a principal experiences. To illustrate, imagine a cone-shaped funnel. The teacher can look toward the narrowing end of the funnel while the principal must look at the funnel becoming wider with increased responsibilities.

> There is a tendency, and I went through it myself, for teachers to feel that administrators forget that they were teachers once, too. I don't think that's the case. I think that once you start operating from a different frame in the system, your outlook changes from single program to total program, and that causes some real problems. (A principal's voice)

Thus, for the principal, it is critical to look at the big picture. What is the mission of the school? What are the important goals of the school? Are we meeting the needs of all students with disabilities? Is our school providing a caring environment for students, teachers, parents, and the community? When one sees the big picture, then it becomes easier to discern which battles are worth fighting. For example, is it really important that a particular bulletin board was not changed on the due date? Shouldn't the real question be: How effective is that teacher with students? A principal must "Step back, look at the whole program, and then step in again" (a principal's voice).

Exercising patience and flexibility—yet holding on to your convictions. Leaders often have to deal with impatient individuals who want to see things change—immediately. A principal must remain patient when that irate parent shows up or a teacher is upset because the server is down or the school air conditioning system is broken. Listening patiently is very important. However, when false information is presented, it is important to politely correct the errors. For example, an angry parent might say, "That teacher just doesn't care for my child." The principal's response: "I'm sorry you feel that way, Mr. Smith, but if the teacher did not care about your child, or any other child in this school, he would not be working here. We just don't operate that way."

Remaining flexible and actively listening is critical during discussions if one is going to remain open to various points of view. Yet when all is said and done, it is very important to state your convictions. People need to know where the principal stands on issues.

> But the one thing about change is that you're supposed to do it over a long period of time, and I've got to learn that. You are supposed to go in and be very low-key the first year, and then the second year you're supposed to do that, and then the third year you're supposed to hit. Well, that's just not my personality. And people have to learn that that's not going to happen. If I know something has to be done to change academic achievement of kids or their mental health, I'm not willing to wait one, two, or three years. I simply will not settle for that. (A principal's voice)

Coping with the loneliness and time factors. As stated previously, two problems that many newcomers face are loneliness and the difficulty of managing time effectively. Interestingly, these two factors are connected since there are extensive periods after school, in the evenings, or on the weekends when principals are alone at the office or working at home. However, because the principal's job can be so fragmented, it may be that productive work only occurs during these "lonely" times when true reflection take place.

PRACTICAL SUGGESTIONS ■
FOR NEWCOMERS

The buck stops here . . . for everything. Harry Truman was right. Thus it is important that the new principal accepts responsibility for whatever takes place in the school. Regarding the school operation, it is especially important to take responsibility for items that may appear to be petty but are very significant for teachers in the beginning of the year. For example, the principal needs to make sure that there are enough desks in each room, drinking fountains are working, and toilets are flushing. Another critical consideration is lighting. It is very difficult to educate children if classroom lighting is inadequate.

Although whatever takes place in the school may, in the end, land on the principal's doorstep, it is important that one does not misinterpret "the buck stops here" to mean the principal cannot delegate and trust others with responsibilities. Competent people welcome and need responsibilities.

Seek out people—especially the experienced staff and the secretary. If the three rules of real estate investing are location, location, location, then the three rules of the principalship are communication, communication, communication. In the principalship, you are investing in people. New principals should track down experienced staff (especially the school secretary) and gain their opinions about what works and what does not. They know the history of the school. Also, send a letter to faculty during the summer, letting them know that you look forward to meeting with them. At the first faculty meeting, let the faculty know that you are eager to learn and you would appreciate having them visit with you.

One principal spent time before school began in August with a longtime veteran and asked, "What, in your opinion, separates this school from others?" The veteran stated, "Our teachers are always accessible to students." The new principal used that information as a positive theme with students, teachers, and parents whenever he wanted to describe the school culture.

As the year progresses, continue to take the initiative regarding relationships with faculty, students, and parents. As you develop relationships, try as much as possible to meet on their turf. The principal's office is daunting for many, and until others see you as approachable, it may not be the best place to meet. Teachers appreciate the principal who says, "Let's meet in your room."

Be visible and support the school vision and mission. Visibility is crucial. The teachers and secretary need to know that you believe the most important events in the school take place in classrooms, not the principal's office. Thus, principals need to Lead and Learn by Wandering Around (LLBWA). Research indicates that finding time to visit classrooms is especially difficult for new principals. By visiting the classrooms, library, cafeteria, labs, gymnasium, art studios, and music rooms, the principal is sending a strong message to the staff and students that what they are doing is important. Also, consider the school mission, vision, and School Improvement Plan during your school walks. When opportunities emerge, compliment individuals for behaving in ways that support these school goals. For instance, one principal regularly celebrates teachers who consistently share good news and seek feedback from parents and the larger community. These efforts address the school improvement goal of enhancing two-way communication between the school and the community.

Keep in mind that LLBWA may very well be a new approach for faculty. Make sure you let them know during the beginning-of-the-year faculty meetings that you believe the important events of a school take place in classrooms, so you intend to be visible, use walk-throughs, support the school mission and vision, and celebrate teaching and learning. Some of the staff may be skeptical about your motives at first, but most will soon appreciate the effort. As a consequence, classroom visits later in the year for teacher observations will be less stressful.

Control your schedule. This book provides several suggestions regarding time management strategies. However, a few points should be emphasized for newcomers. Although it is very difficult, try to take control of a significant part of your schedule. Block out time for events that demonstrate your commitment to the educational goals of the school. If the effort is not made, "events" will quickly fill up your schedule. During the year, constantly think about the school priorities and consider whether your schedule reflects them. There will certainly be days and even weeks when you will not be able to meet your objectives, but keep coming back to them. The teachers and your secretary should know your basic strategy concerning time use. The secretary needs to know that teachers should never feel shut out when they want to see the principal. If the principal is unavailable at a particular time, then the secretary should take the initiative and set up an appointment for the next available time. LLBWA also allows for numerous miniconferences during the day.

Additionally, it is crucial to learn to say no and to take a backseat on some committees and community requests for your time. For example, if the Cub Scouts ask you to speak at their annual awards ceremony, you should probably say yes, but that does not mean you should also say yes to the request that you join them on the overnight campout in April.

Make sure that you leave time for your own lunch and for leisure activities. Otherwise, your productivity and spirit will suffer, and resentment may surface if the job becomes all-consuming.

There have been some things that just wear on me personally. Part of that is the time factor that you're expected to spend, and expected by others, and you inflict on yourself. You just have to spend that amount of time. But I don't think it surprises me. It kind of eats away on me because I'm not real comfortable with it. (A principal's voice)

Model the desire to grow professionally. In the long run, this may be the area in which you make your most significant contribution in serving students and teachers. Begin modeling a desire to grow professionally as a principal. Share professional articles and recommend journals and Web sites to the staff. Let staff know about professional growth opportunities. Share with them your professional growth objectives during your first year. For example, as a new principal, one should try to get involved with a mentor, either in the district, through a local university, or possibly through a state principals' association. Subscribe to professional journals, and try to attend state and national association meetings. Share your learning experiences with the staff. When you have time, continue to read about the principalship. It can be very therapeutic—and you will find out that you are not alone!

FINAL THOUGHTS ON THE NEWCOMER EXPERIENCE

Coping with the daily events and constituencies in a school can be very overwhelming for a new principal. Yet there is no greater feeling than to be part of a school community and to know that you made a difference. New principals during their first year can make a contribution to their school communities every bit as significant as that of the 10-year veteran.

Often, new principals are told they will experience a honeymoon period and be forgiven for early mistakes. However, it may be foolish to hope for such a present. It is more important for the newcomer to assume that many mistakes will be made, not only during the first year. If the principal is a learner, he or she will grow professionally through each mistake. If the teachers, students, and parents perceive that the newcomer is growing, trust will build. Everyone wants to be proud of the principal. Together, as a community of learners, the principal, teachers, and students can grow together.

REFLECTIONS

This space provides a place for you to write down ideas that have been generated by this chapter, things you want to try, or adaptations of ideas presented here.

1. What were some of the major challenges you faced (or are facing) during your first year as a principal?

2. What characteristics would be suitable for a principal mentor? On what areas of study would you like to focus, given the opportunity to work with a mentor?

3. Do you agree with the characterization of the principalship as a lonely position?

4. To add to the advice offered in this chapter, what suggestions do you have for aspiring or new principals?

5. What insights or new questions do you have as a result of reflecting on the ideas presented in this chapter?

20

Taking Care
of Yourself

Educators would do well to ponder Elizabeth Cady Stanton's injunction that self-development is a higher duty than self-sacrifice.

—Barth (1990, p. 47)

Principals must take care of themselves in order to care for others. Setting an example as a leader does not end with the leadership, instructional, and management roles of a principal. How a workplace "feels" plays a profound role in influencing creativity, commitment, and productivity. The leader is observed by organizational members and serves as an emotional barometer and guide. Does your job performance impact your home life and vice versa? In all professions, if the leader comes to work unhappy or stressed out, it takes a tremendous amount of energy and psychological manipulation to reverse one's disposition in order to function effectively for others and oneself. If a leader wants the staff to perform optimally, the leader must model both a zest for professional learning and enthusiasm for leadership that influences learning. Just as important, however, is modeling taking time to relax, reflect, and renew. If the school leader and staff are not refreshed when the year begins, then the school year is off to an ominous start.

■ THE SELFISH NATURE OF MARTYRDOM

School leaders, because of pressure and long hours, can easily begin to see themselves as martyrs and burn out in their quest for martyrdom. Much has been written about the effect of burnout on principals and about good people leaving the profession because of too much stress. Principals have to learn to take care of themselves. It seems that everyone wants a piece of the principal's time. But if the slices are too small, no one can derive the benefits. One principal shared the following personal experience:

> I was very proud of myself because I did not take time for lunch during my first six years in the principalship. How foolish! I thought I was setting an example for the staff of how

to effectively use time by meeting with teachers during my lunch hour. Often, I would eat my sandwich during a meeting, demonstrating how hard I was working. My favorite line was "Do you mind if I eat during our meeting?" Undoubtedly, I enjoyed the martyrdom. Two years ago, I started taking 30–40 minutes a day for lunch to have real time away from my office. And do you know, the school did not burn down! In fact, I doubt if anyone noticed that I was out. I think the staff probably felt more at ease with my decision. Moreover, skipping lunch was not a healthy example for the teachers. Following lunch I was relaxed and refreshed. I was ready to work in the afternoon. (A principal's voice)

What Is Burnout?

According to Miller and Smith (1993), "If in the beginning your job seems perfect, the solution to all your problems, you have high hopes and expectations, and would rather work than do anything else, be wary. You're a candidate for the most insidious and tragic kind of job stress—burnout, a state of physical, emotional, and mental exhaustion caused by unrealistically high aspirations and illusory or impossible goals" (p. 107). Other possible causes of burnout may include a loss of meaning for the work and frustration resulting from top-down mandates that lack alignment with what is best for students. A toxic school culture, and the daunting task of transforming the culture, can also be a contributing cause of burnout. Finally, many principals cite the long hours and time away from family and friends as another burnout factor.

TAKING CONTROL OF YOUR ■
SCHEDULE TO CARE FOR YOURSELF

Unless we proactively organize our schedules with a lunch hour, leisure time, exercise, and other activities that refresh us, they will not happen. Thus, as you plan your schedule, build in leisure time. Place it on your schedule just as you place a school meeting on the calendar. The idea, obviously, is not to place these activities during the school day at prime times but, rather, to allocate time for daily personal activities at the beginning or end of the day to recharge your batteries. For example, if you need to leave at 5:00 p.m., it should be noted on your appointment calendar so you do not miss that jog, basketball game, or tennis match.

Interestingly, the professional development time that you might take to read a journal to stay current in the field is the first thing to go when unimportant but pressing items arise in the schedule. Yet if we are to grow and our staff are to grow, we need to recognize that reading a professional journal in our office is as important as any other aspect of the job. Professional reading time should be identified on the calendar and used accordingly. This can also be a time to inform our practice. One principal routinely writes quotations down on index cards from articles she reads. She uses these to open faculty meetings with an approach called "Quote of the Day." Individuals read a quotation they are handed and can swap quotations with others. Also, we need to allocate time to reflect, write, and read about the principalship and follow other professional interests. These interests need to become part of our professional and personal schedules. Taking time out for yourself gives you an opportunity to reflect upon your own experiences and your interaction with the staff. You can gain a greater understanding of the faculty by taking the time to ponder why a teacher acted in a particular way or made a comment that seemed inappropriate. This can help a principal respond appropriately when addressing the needs of colleagues. Reflection often affords a principal a valuable new perspective, providing valuable insights not available when one is rushing from one task to the next.

■ A PERSONAL MISSION STATEMENT

An interesting and productive activity is to develop a personal mission statement based on your professional and personal goals to transcend the day-to-day responsibilities and keep your long-term vision in mind (Covey, 1989). As you develop the mission statement, consider the following questions:

- When you retire from education, how do you want to be remembered?
- What do you want teachers, parents, and, most of all, students to say about you?
- What will you, and those with whom you work, say are the highlights of your life story?
- What will be your legacy as a principal?
- What kind of a friend are you?
- How productive are you outside of your professional work?
- What would you want written on your tombstone?

Such questions cause one to connect daily activities with a meaningful, long-range vision. After your mission statement is developed, post it in a place where you can glance at it during the week. Reflect upon your actions and decisions. Do your actions and decisions align with the mission statement?

■ GAINING PERSPECTIVE BY SPENDING TIME WITH STUDENTS

When a principal feels stressed, the "batteries can be recharged" by taking time to visit with a class or spending a few minutes with students on the playground, in the halls, or in a courtyard. Students appreciate spending time with the principal, and this helps spread the message that the principal is more than the office figure or school disciplinarian. Having students see you as a real person helps in the process of building relationships with all students. One principal rides the bus with students once a month. Another greets students at the door when they arrive every morning. Still another participates regularly in book club discussions with different classes. These acts not only build relationships but also inform the principal about the pulse of the school.

■ BODY AND MIND: HEALTHY AND ILL TOGETHER[1]

If you do not feel well, it is hard to help others while on the job. From a practical viewpoint, the better you feel, the better you will perform. Your personal level of health and well-being must be maintained if you are to perform effectively on or off the job. This concept of well-being is dependent on attention to four areas: physical, physiological, emotional, and psychological. Although these are four separate areas, their functions are interrelated. For example, when you are stressed, often you do not sleep well or eat properly. You may indulge in too many sweets, which can adversely affect your blood sugar level and put your system out of balance. A quick examination of these four interrelated categories can help you assess your personal well-being and identify areas you wish to monitor or change.

Physical Awareness

We all value having energy. An essential way to gain greater energy is to exercise. We all recognize how increased energy and endurance can sustain us with a greater degree of alertness throughout the day. Yet we often fail to take the necessary steps, before or after work, to fine-tune our bodies to perform at a higher physical level while on the job.

The physical aspect of well-being can be maintained through systematic exercise to improve our cardiovascular fitness. Also, systematic exercise releases endorphins in the body that can have a soothing, pleasurable effect on the mind and relieve stress. And, of course, from a physical standpoint, exercise, energy, and longevity are inextricably linked for most people.

Unfortunately, when time gets tight on the job, exercise is often the first thing to go. Planning your own prescheduled exercise program or joining an exercise group or club that meets at a specific time may be a good start. Needless to say, the exercise program should be written on your schedule, and you should not be shy about saying that you need to leave work at a certain time to make your appointment. Because of the facilities often available in schools, you may be able to get your exercise on site if you do not feel that you need a different environment in which to relax. Another possible solution is to try to commit to an exercise program or sports activity with a friend. This serves two purposes. First, the friend will expect you to show up! Second, having a friend to talk with can provide a sounding board for dilemmas and someone with whom to share private victories. Many principals in Clark County, Las Vegas, Nevada, wear pedometers to measure how much exercise they derive from daily activity. They set targets for the number of daily steps they will take. This action makes the principal more visible.

Physiological Awareness

The old adage "You are what you eat" holds some truth. Although nutritionists and physicians may disagree on some specifics as to what is good to eat and what is not, there are certain principles that apply to most people. For example, moderation of consumption is better than excess. Overindulgence in food or inappropriate foods can lead to adverse consequences for your body and mind. Excessive food intake at meals can lead to marked swings in blood sugar levels. This physiological occurrence can lead to unwanted alterations of brain function, adversely affect attention and creativity, and contribute to lethargy. Unfortunately, overindulgence or erratic eating habits are most common when we are under stress.

Even when one strives to maintain a balanced diet, often the rapid pace of the day makes a principal skip meals or choose inappropriate foods. Principals should prepare for this eventuality by planning ahead and having some healthy food that is quickly accessible and provides for both energy and brain power. Also, complex carbohydrates such as fruits and vegetables are a good source of nutrients. Low-fat foods are helpful. For example, there are many low-fat breakfast foods and snacks on the market (e.g., bagels, granola bars, low-fat crackers). Keep these items readily available in your desk or refrigerator. Too often, it is a temptation to have a candy bar and indulge in the wrong snack when under stress or when a busy schedule may lead to omitting a meal.

Emotional Awareness

As discussed in Chapter 4, the leader's emotions influence the emotions of constituents. In fact, it has been said that the heart gives out an electromagnetic signal that is perceivable within three feet! Keep in mind that emotionally intelligent leaders exceed their goals by at least 20 percent (Goleman, 1995).

Psychological Awareness

Psychological rest or peace of mind takes place when your behaviors match your values and beliefs. There is more to life than the job. If you have peace of mind, that feeling can positively affect the level of energy that you give to your job or personal life. Unfortunately, principals may often experience psychological discomfort by doing things that they do not enjoy (e.g., completing reams of paperwork, responding very politely or patiently when one would like to take a more aggressive stance). You need to anticipate that this will happen and have a plan for it. In a proactive way, anticipate that stress will enter your life and plan how you will cope. Different people handle stress in different ways. Some take comfort in spending time with family or friends; others go for a walk, exercise, read a book, travel, or pursue a hobby such as art or music. Having an outlet is very important because it gives us an alternative to reduce stress and brings a richness to our lives, enabling us to be more well rounded and aware of other ways of doing things.

Finally, it cannot be emphasized too often that it is very difficult to make an effective contribution to an organization if one is functioning below par because of physical, physiological, emotional, or psychological reasons. Principals owe it to themselves, their families, their colleagues, and their profession to do what they can to maintain a high level of physical, physiological, emotional, and psychological well-being.

■ MAINTAINING INSTITUTIONAL AND INDIVIDUAL BALANCE

Principals also need to be careful about letting the institutional and bureaucratic values smother them; one's individuality can be lost with the pressures to conform. It is hard to feel good about yourself if you know that your individual convictions are always being sacrificed to preserve the status quo. But it is very difficult to overcome the socialized pressures within the system. Interestingly, principals to a great extent have been socialized as "school folks," sometimes for their whole lives—responding to bells; following a certain calendar; and always relating to students, teachers, and administrators.

The classical business and sociological theorists Barnard (1938, pp. 8–21) and Merton (1957, pp. 195–201) agreed that over time, bureaucracies depersonalize or stifle individuals to satisfy bureaucratic needs. Merton maintained that bureaucratic controls such as career promotions and salary increments force individuals to adapt their behavior to official regulations. Furthermore, individuals can become so engrossed in bureaucratic roles that they may disregard their responsibility to assist clientele to preserve the common interests of colleagues. For schools, this can mean neglecting the needs of children or blocking necessary change to satisfy the professional or support staff.

These valuable insights clearly indicate that a strong possibility exists for principals to become the organization. Often, principals are required to implement top-down federal, state, or district mandates. Principals become increasingly socialized as the years of service increase. Moreover, one is less likely to promote change in the organization if maintaining the bureaucratic status quo becomes one's mission and personality. Reflective activities can help principals maintain their individuality and keep the organizational or institutional bureaucracy in perspective. Activities such as reading, writing, and exercising while away from the job can help reduce the bureaucratic ties to the organization and help the practitioner hold on to his or her individuality.

Taking Care of Yourself

Marcy Holland, a graduate student at Eastern Washington University focusing her research on teacher burnout, found the following useful advice from the Georgia Association of Educators (1998–2001): "Understand that the only people without stress are in the cemetery! It is not so much the stress in our lives that hurts us, but how we respond to it." The Georgia Association of Educators offered many techniques to avoid burnout, among them:

- Exercise.
- Don't schedule all of your leisure time.
- Get plenty of sleep.

- Pursue a project or hobby.
- Find a friend.
- Don't procrastinate.
- Don't feel that you must do everything.
- Keep a "things to do" list.
- Recognize and accept your limitations.
- Learn to tolerate and forgive.
- Learn to plan.
- Be a positive person.
- Learn to play.

Consider how you will integrate these techniques into your calendar. Both you and the organization will benefit!

Highly effective leaders work to find an inner balance or harmony within themselves. Doing this builds the capacity to portray oneself as a caring leader. Zach Kelehear (2004) suggests some useful strategies for doing this:

- Reflect on what matters most in your life; strive to align your decisions and actions accordingly.
- Remember, "Attitude is everything."
- Make time to take care of your health.
- Ask yourself, at the end of the day, "Has the practice of my life today reflected what matters most to me? In what way have I made the life of at least one child better?"

In the fast-paced life of the principal, it is tempting, and sometimes necessary, to dash from task to task. Only when we pause to reflect do we find the inner resources we need to serve others.

NOTE

1. We would like to thank Dr. David Jay Caro, from San Mateo General Hospital, for his assistance with this section of the chapter.

REFLECTIONS

This space provides a place for you to write down ideas that have been generated by this chapter, things you want to try, or adaptations of ideas presented here.

1. Have you learned how to say no in order to provide yourself with quality time away from the job? Think of three school situations. and practice how you would say no in each situation.

2. How do you feel about reading a professional journal while in your office? How do you think the staff would react to seeing you read a journal during the day?

3. How much have you become "the organization"?

4. What are you doing or might you do to take care of yourself?

5. Google "The Last Lecture by Professor Pausch." Read or listen to it. Reflect on how the messages embedded in the lecture might influence your life. Share your insights with a trusted colleague.

6. What insights or new questions do you have as a result of reflecting on the ideas presented in this chapter?

21

Keeping the
Professional Candle Lit

Through learning we re-create ourselves.

—Senge (1990, p. 14)

How does a practitioner remain on the cutting edge of the profession? Before accepting the principalship, he or she is often taking courses and learning as much as possible about the job. Unfortunately, once in the position, the practitioner is so busy that it is difficult to keep the professional candle lit. It's easy for those professional journals to stack up. And it's difficult to commit time away from the school site for professional growth experiences. Taking a proactive approach is the only way to stay current in the field regarding leadership and educational literature. This chapter will provide suggestions for taking a proactive approach to keeping the professional candle lit.

■ INSTITUTIONALIZING PROFESSIONAL GROWTH ACTIVITIES

The key to remaining proactive is to institutionalize specific activities through memberships, conferences, writing, relationships, and the creative use of time. As has been emphasized throughout this book, the personal example set by the principal can be a strong motivator and influence staff. Teachers will notice if you are current in your field and if you can be counted on to keep them current. By staying abreast of the field through professional activities and professional relationships, routines are broken, which helps keep the practitioner stimulated, thus reducing the possibility of burnout. Infusing new learnings into faculty, team, or department meetings helps build staff members' capacities to help students succeed.

There are many activities that can be institutionalized and will require your professional dedication and attention. It is just a matter of choosing what is best for you. Probably the most important action the practitioner can take is to become actively involved in one or two professional organizations. Active involvement means attending the state and, if possible, national conferences of the organization and reading the journals sponsored by the organization. The logical organizations for principals are the National Association of Secondary School Principals and the National Association of Elementary School Principals (both organizations address the needs of middle school principals, as does the National Middle School Association). The Association for Supervision and Curriculum Development (ASCD) and the National Staff Development Council are also key national organizations for principals. All five organizations and state affiliates hold annual conferences that keep practitioners on the cutting edge in the field. Each one publishes excellent journals and newsletters.

The national associations also sponsor leadership academies in the form of 1- or 2-day workshops throughout the school year and longer workshops during the summer. Many states have principals' centers, often affiliated with universities. The opportunity to network with colleagues through the associations, workshops, webinars, principals' centers, and universities should not be missed. In fact, the loneliness of the principalship as a day-to-day feature of the job almost makes the networking through the various organizations imperative.

The opportunity to meet with other principals is especially important for the newcomer who needs affirmation that he or she is on the right track. Developing a mentor relationship through an organization can be an asset for newcomers and veteran principals. Becoming a member of specific associations will ensure that time will be set aside to meet with colleagues and keep up on issues in the field.

The principal should acquire subscriptions to several journals for him- or herself and the school. The national principal associations all publish journals for elementary, middle, and high school principals. *Educational Leadership* (ASCD), *Phi Delta Kappan,* and the *Journal of Staff Development* would be excellent additional choices. *Teacher* and *Instructor* would be good hands-on choices for elementary school principals. *Education Week* is a good source of information about current events in education, especially as related to national and state political agendas.

To keep the professional candle lit for teachers, each school should be getting journals in the various disciplines. Publications for elementary, middle, and high schools are produced by all the major organizations such as the National Council for Social Studies, the National Council of Teachers of English, and the National Council of Teachers of Mathematics. Each department should keep up to date. In elementary schools, *Arithmetic Teacher* or *Reading Teacher,* for example, should be subscribed to and distributed to the staff or kept in a professional library. All organizations such as these maintain active Web sites that carry important information about available resources.

As principals are in key leadership positions, they have much in common with those leading noneducational organizations. Thus it can be very helpful to subscribe to a professional journal outside of the educational field. For example, *Harvard Business Review* has excellent articles on leadership that not only give ideas that principals can use but also let principals know what is taking place "out there." This can be very helpful information when making curriculum decisions to prepare students for the world of work.

Beyond journals, the practitioner should maintain a professional library with modern classics in the educational field (to revisit) and current books of interest on leadership and educational issues. A good selection would include books on educational philosophy, curriculum, the life of principals and teachers, and leadership books from the business and education world. (It goes without saying that books other than those that are education related are certainly welcome.) Important educators of the last century are always interesting to study; this enables one to compare contemporary writers with classical ones (e.g., Dewey, Tyler, Hutchins, Cremin).

Listening to books on CDs or podcasts when driving to and from work or jogging can also be professionally productive. These can be ordered from professional conferences, association catalogs, or bookstores. Watching professional DVDs or videos has become a very popular activity with colleagues in school or in the comfort of one's home. Principals and teacher leaders can play a key role in ensuring that schools provide these resources for all school professionals.

Visiting other schools also can be informative. Drucker (1992) refers to this as managing by wandering around—outside. Spending a day in another school with another principal can offer insights on how others do the job. The opportunity to visit a school outside of your district or in another state may be advantageous because one is likely to see activities and curriculum projects a bit differently from those in the home district. These experiences may even lead to strong professional friendships and resource sharing across district lines.

■ REFLECTION AS A TOOL

The importance of reflection has been stressed throughout this book. Keeping a personal journal certainly can help one reflect about the principalship and any other aspect of one's life. Often, the experience of seeing one's ideas in writing helps affirm convictions and brings greater insight to a particular problem. As the journal grows, one can reflect on past experiences—so that is how I handled this problem last time! Reflection is a great asset and can help one avoid making the same mistake. To illustrate, in July of 1993, golf great Jack Nicklaus played the Senior Open Golf Tournament. As he led the tournament until the 12th hole, he recalled playing on the same course and approaching the 12th hole more than 30 years ago. He reflected back to that earlier tournament. He vowed not to make the same mistake that he had made in 1960. He won the Senior Open by one stroke!

Writing can extend beyond the journal to professional articles authored alone or with colleagues. Writing with another principal, teacher, consultant, or university professor may be the best route for the practitioner because it becomes very easy to drop a project when you are working alone and busy with the day-to-day responsibilities of the principalship. It is very helpful to have someone driving you on. (The computer will hold your ideas until you are ready to return to them!) Involvement in Action Research projects with teachers in your school also can be very rewarding. Presenting the results of a research project as a workshop during a state or national conference can be an important extension of the effort.

Holding a miniconference in a school or on a university campus could be a great way to intellectually stimulate a staff. The faculty could get together to recommend speakers to the administration. Administrators and faculty members could present at the conference, possibly during a staff development or inservice day or afternoon. This highlights the importance of keeping learning as a valued centerpiece of the school.

■ A PRINCIPAL'S PORTFOLIO

Whether a principal is remaining in a school for several years or preparing to move on, developing and updating a principal's portfolio is a valuable resource to keep a record of and reflect on one's growth during a particular school year and over one's career. The portfolio could open with a personal mission statement, professional goals, and schoolwide goals and objectives. The orientation of the portfolio should be to demonstrate growth within a particular area or areas. At times, principals may elect to identify themes for their portfolios: enhancing student work, building positive parent-community-school relationships, professional development, teacher supervision and evaluation, professional presentations, or reflections. The portfolio can serve as a valuable resource when applying for new positions.

Artifacts may include photographs of the faculty, students, and classroom activities; important professional development ideas; journal entries; speeches; staff evaluations; newspaper articles about the school; successful grant applications; important memos; faculty meeting agendas; letters or notes from students, parents, community members, and faculty; a DVD or video of school activities and the activity calendar of the school year; notes for possible journal articles; student work; information on awards given to students or faculty; data on student performance; information on workshops or conferences attended; presentations made to the school community or at professional meetings; organizations that one belongs to; and family photos.

OTHER GROWTH OPPORTUNITIES ■

A strategy for ensuring one is current is to examine the *Educational Leadership Policy Standards* (2008). These are highlighted on the inside cover of this book. One can reflect upon these and assess personal strengths and areas for professional growth. Another opportunity to assess personal strengths is to examine the work of Marzano, Waters, and McNulty (2005), who identified 21 leadership responsibilities associated with student achievement. These highlight leadership behaviors that impact student performance.

Involvement in a support group on a topic of interest can also be rewarding. The support group may sponsor topics such as global education, the at-risk student, closing the achievement gap, differentiated instruction, working with special needs students, brain research, or effective instructional practices. The group may meet at lunch or even during dinner at various homes during the year. In one school district, K–12 administrators and department heads got together for dinner and conversation prior to board meetings. They read and discussed *Classroom Instruction That Works* (Marzano, Pickering, & Pollock, 2001) chapter by chapter. This was so rewarding that they elected to read a second book, *True North* (George, 2007).

Working to develop an inviting professional resource area in the school can be a significant professional boost for administrators and teachers. This should be an area to exchange professional articles, books, and ideas. Principals should encourage teachers to pass on professional articles to colleagues and the principal to help him or her stay on top of particular issues and, probably more important, remain informed regarding what teachers think is important. Having an area in the school for professional reading just might make it easier for administrators and teachers to spend time there during a school day—actually building the time into their weekly schedules. The actual physical structure for professional reflection can symbolize the importance of remaining on the cutting edge.

Finally, remaining intellectually stimulated throughout one's career is a tall order. Yet doing so benefits the principal, staff, students, and the organization. For instance, underlining important quotations while reading a journal and sharing these at faculty meetings, followed with a discussion, can show that the leader is academically up to date and can provide valuable resources to staff members in a time-efficient way. We need to create our own opportunities for professional growth through institutionalizing interaction, reflections, and readings. It is through these encounters that we remain alert and ready to approach the next challenge. Focusing on our own professional development builds an incredible resource bank from which to draw. By nurturing our own growth, we are able to enhance our ability to serve and to help others grow.

REFLECTIONS

This space provides a place for you to write down ideas that have been generated by this chapter, things you want to try, or adaptations of ideas presented here.

1. Are you keeping your professional candle lit? Discuss this with a colleague.

2. Which two or three professional development activities discussed in this chapter can you use?

3. What inspirational article or book have you read recently? What about an inspirational story? How might you share it?

4. What insights or new questions do you have as a result of reflecting on the ideas presented in this chapter?

22

Reflections
on the Principalship

The power of personal example is the essence of true leadership.

—Covey (1989)

A school is much more than a physical structure; it is a community made up of adults and children engaged in a journey that will lead to greater understanding, learning, and a force in society. To help students, a principal serves teachers by empowering them to be the best they can be. As servant leaders, school principals find that their professional vocation is, in many ways, a calling. When principals answer that calling and serve teachers, students, and parents effectively, students have a greater opportunity to enhance their skills in a climate that promotes growth, understanding, and a love of learning. Principals, through their words and deeds, grow the citizens of tomorrow.

SERVING THE SCHOOL COMMUNITY ■

As a school leader, a principal's foremost asset may be his or her ability to lead by example. How principals conduct themselves on the job—what they pay attention to—says more about ethical practice and their leadership ability than any specific decision, regardless of how important. Nair (1997), commenting on the life of Gandhi, notes that "leadership is not a technique, but a way of life." Leading by example must be sincere; if a principal is uncomfortable with small children or teenagers, the nonverbal cues will quickly be picked up by the students. Moreover, if the personal example lacks consistency, others will soon comment about the lack of sincerity on the part of the principal. Thus, when reflecting on the principalship and considering experience and sound theory, the authors believe that the following behaviors and characteristics, if modeled consistently, can go a long way in helping a principal best serve a school.

Principals thrive on the ethical responsibility to help teachers grow so they can make a difference for children. As suggested above, principals serve teachers by empowering them to be the best they can be. James MacGregor Burns (1978), in his classic study on transformational leadership, noted that "Transforming leadership ultimately becomes *moral* in that it raises the level of human conduct and ethical aspirations of both leader and led, and thus it has a transforming effect on both" (p. 20). George (2007) adds, "authentic leadership is empowering others on their journey. This shift is the transformation from 'I' to 'We.' It is the most important process leaders go through in becoming authentic" (p. 44). Principals who enthusiastically accept the responsibility of helping others grow foster the aspirations of teachers by distributing leadership throughout the system. Promoting teacher growth also includes helping colleagues become autonomous decision makers who engage students successfully when the classroom door is closed. These teachers are confident in their decisions, partially because they are part of a school culture that thrives on collaboration, peer coaching, mentoring of new teachers, and teacher-generated professional development opportunities so that, at the end of the day, they can impact student learning.

Principals respect and dignify others. The importance of positive human interaction has been a main feature of this book; therefore, it should not surprise the reader that leading by example must include respecting and dignifying each individual connected with the school. Students must see the principal as someone who believes in them and respects them for what they are and what they can become. Teachers must see in the principal someone who has great respect for the teachers' professional role and what they can bring to students. Dignifying the classroom teacher is of paramount importance and should be modeled often by the principal during public and private occasions. Parents should see the principal as someone who listens to them and displays concern and interest when they are with students.

Principals lead through learning. There is no setting in which this concept of the leader as learner is more applicable. This leadership role can be achieved by promoting several ideas. For example, when working with teachers in a supervisory role, principals must create an atmosphere that fosters mutual trust and growth. Trust is a requisite characteristic if one is to take chances in a professional relationship. Teachers must feel that they can trust the principal if risk taking is to occur during a class lesson. Furthermore, principals and teachers need to believe that they will grow from the relationship if they are to talk honestly during conferences about their profession and discuss what they think they are doing right and ways they can improve.

Additionally, as a leader of learners, the principal needs to provide the structure and forum to ensure that a dialogue concerning curriculum, teaching, assessment, and student learning takes place throughout the school. The principal needs to participate in this dialogue as an equal member, sharing articles and Web sites, structuring faculty meetings to facilitate conversation, promoting professional development in and out of the school, analyzing and discussing data, creating areas in the school for professional discussion, promoting classroom visitations by colleagues, and recognizing those teachers who are growing professionally. The dialogue that develops can create lasting relationships and a synergy that demonstrates the strength, potential, and desire of the group to never be completely satisfied with the current state. As Collins (2005) reminds us in *Good to Great and the Social Sectors,* "Greatness is an inherently dynamic process, not an end point. The moment you think of yourself as great, your slide toward mediocrity will have already begun" (p. 9).

Principals promote and embrace the success of others. As ideas are generated, the school principal must give credit to teachers and others whose ideas and dedication improve the school and contribute to student success. Stephen Covey (1989) calls this strategy *the abundance principle* in which credit for successful actions is spread around as much as possible. Furthermore, principals need to hire the best personnel available and show a willingness to give them the freedom to use their talents to maximize student learning and address the never-ending challenges that face schools.

Giving credit to others, inspiring colleagues to take on difficult tasks, and taking satisfaction when the accomplishments of associates bring them into the limelight may be difficult for some, but it is a necessary requirement for successful leadership. Thus Drucker (1992) emphasizes,

> Precisely because an effective leader knows that he, and no one else, is ultimately responsible, he is not afraid of strength in associates and subordinates. . . . [A]n effective leader wants strong associates; he encourages them, pushes them, indeed glories in them. Because he holds himself ultimately responsible for the mistakes of his associates and subordinates, he also sees the triumphs of his associates and subordinates as his triumphs, rather than as threats. . . . An effective leader knows, of course, that there is a risk; able people tend to be ambitious. But he realizes that it is a much smaller risk than to be served by mediocrity. (pp. 121–122)

Encouraging others to be strong associates and distributing leadership can be frustrating for principals who have been raised on the formula of the principal as the sole instructional leader or the one who must say "The buck stops here." Yet these are the days of distributed leadership and shared decision making. Are distributed leadership and shared decision making consistent with "the buck stops here"? Some make a distinction between shared decision making, in which the principal takes input but ultimately decides and takes responsibility, versus shared governance, in which decision makers exchange ideas and share accountability. We have learned that the factory worker may know more about how the company works than the executive on the top floor. Barth's insight regarding this dilemma may be helpful: "It's far more powerful to join with others to do what needs to be done" (quoted in Sparks, 1993, p. 20). School principals are joining with others to try to make schools work better. But principals know and accept that, for the most part, teachers, students, parents, and the community continue to expect the principal to take ultimate responsibility.

Effective principals recognize active listening as an essential communication skill. The image of the leader who dominates a group discussion is inappropriate in a setting that thrives on teamwork and developing ideas through mutual understanding. Many school leaders who achieved their success because of their decisiveness and public speaking ability may have a difficult time becoming good listeners and reflective thinkers. Yet creative ideas and solutions often occur after listening, reflecting, and working in groups.

Real listening with patience and attention is critical if one is truly trying to support and foster growth in others. Showing concern for students, teachers, and parents means hearing them out. Listening shows support and may go a long way in meeting the needs of colleagues or others in the school community. Often, individuals do not come right out and say what is bothering them. In fact, Soder (2001) warns leaders "that many people will be likely to tell you what they think you want to hear, and the likelihood poses dangers for the leader" (p. 33). Active listening, then, means trying to find out the subtle messages—what is really being said? At that point, it is possible to begin meeting the needs of others. To illustrate, when conferencing with teachers, principals will find that as the trust relationship begins to grow, teaching colleagues will take small leaps of faith to explore how sincere the principal is about trust and working with them. Unless a principal is listening carefully to the teacher, the principal may very well and quite inadvertently miss the leap on the part of the teacher.

Principals address their own needs. The school principal should also remember that it is important to recognize one's own basic needs. That is, one's private life, responsibility to family, and need for leisure and recreation should not be sacrificed. A workaholic is not a better principal than someone who knows how to manage his or her time and who takes the time for family and friends. A principal's life outside of school must receive the time and energy necessary for success so a positive attitude on the job results. Principals have to understand themselves, their strengths, and weaknesses. George (2007) insightfully reminds leaders, "First, you have to understand yourself *because the hardest person you will ever have to lead is yourself. . . .* Second, to be an effective leader, *you must take responsibility for your own development*" (p. xxxiii).

Principals accept success and frustrations. As part of our basic humanity, it is important also to take in stride both the successes and frustrations of the job. One should not be too enthralled with the positive press—when it happens. On the other hand, do not get too upset with the negative reviews. Reflection is a characteristic needed in both situations. What happened? What can I learn from this experience? Find the humorous side when possible. Bringing in humor often helps relieve tension, reduce one's feelings of self-importance, and place an issue in a more realistic perspective.

Effective principals take the high road. When the negative reviews appear or when individuals complain, one should behave in an ethical manner. Regardless of tactics used by others, the school leader should always represent the best in society. Character is very important when crises occur. In fact, character is the key in a crisis, and character is often judged not by what one says but by how one acts. Persons who whisper but act righteously are heard loud and clear. Stay above the fray and avoid the shouting match. As one principal said, "What you do speaks so loudly I can't hear what you say!"

■ WHERE DO WE GO FROM HERE?

Of course, there are no formulas for successful leadership that can be universally applied. An individual who exhibits or models some of the above characteristics may still fail if he or she is unable to analyze situations appropriately. The challenge is to find out what works in a particular setting. In his seminal work, Newell (1978) stressed that "effective leadership is possible only through an analysis of the situational elements in a particular system" (p. 242). Each school is different; therefore, each leadership situation is different. In the end, the effective leader, collaborating and building relationships with teachers, parents, and students, must discover how to meet the needs of students in a specific setting. And the discovery will show that no secret formula exists; the setting will dictate the approach.

Because there are no secret formulas, frustration can be a constant companion in the principalship. Yet the frustration can lead to success if one always searches for solutions and has faith in one's ability to face challenges with the help of others. In facing the challenges, a vision of the good school is essential. So what is our vision of the good school? What will one see on entering the doors of the school?

■ THE GOOD SCHOOL

When entering the school, a visitor quickly perceives that students and teachers are enjoying their time there. Here is where they want to teach and learn. The visitor notices that most students are actively interested and engaged in learning. Teachers are enthusiastic about their work. Student interest is shown through obvious excitement while working at a hands-on activity or through a look of serenity when quietly reading a book.

Some classroom teachers may, at first, be difficult to spot—they are sitting with students or with groups of students and examining student work. In another room, a teacher is talking to the class, his gestures indicating excitement about a student comment. In fact, the visitor notices that most teachers are enjoying their work and are patiently listening to and helping students. In various classes, students display looks of concentration and puzzlement, mixed with expressions of satisfaction and frequent smiles. The school visitor observes that some students seem less interested than others, yet the teachers are giving them equal time and showing patience when necessary. No students appear to be overlooked.

The visitor observes that the library and computer labs are busy throughout the day. In both areas, there are students working individually, in groups, or with teachers. Several students are gathered around computers. One group is sending an e-mail to a scientific team in Antarctica while another group is analyzing a recent presidential speech. In other areas such as the music, art, physics, or foreign language rooms, students are all actively engaged, talking about their work, singing, writing, reading, drawing, experimenting, and showing interest in what they are doing. In the cafeteria the visitor notices that various racial and ethnic groups, and younger and older students, are sitting together and interacting during lunch. Also, several students are helping new Russian immigrant students with their English. Two elderly individuals, likely retired, are engaged in serious conversations with two older students.

Dropping into various classrooms with the principal, the visitor and principal notice a variety of teaching techniques. Some teachers are using document cameras or overhead projectors while speaking with students, others are using PowerPoint presentations and SmartBoards to communicate the content of the lesson, some teachers are sitting with students, and a couple of teachers are walking around their rooms observing groups or watching students work individually. One teacher is lecturing, another is reading silently with his class, and another is writing in her journal with the class. Interestingly, the principal and visitor observe a lot of lively, engaged, and smiling faces in the various classrooms. The principal notices that students are unafraid to give "incorrect" answers and, at times, respectfully challenge a teacher's answer.

Our visitor notices that the teachers' lounge is frequented by colleagues who enjoy one another's company and share in the joys and frustrations of their classroom experiences. While in the lounge, teachers share a light experience, the humor of a classroom event. One teacher asks a colleague to read a poem written by a student the previous class period. It is clear that this group of teachers works and plays together. They share professional articles, problem solve, and encourage one another to pursue professional development opportunities. They team teach, coplan, and peer coach.

On the playground, students are obviously enjoying themselves playing games or sitting and talking. In the middle and high schools, peer counselors are spending time with students who are new to the school or are having some difficulties. In the elementary school, a couple of kindergarten students run up to the principal, proudly announcing that they picked up some litter from the sidewalk to keep the school clean.

The school buildings and grounds are inviting. The entrance doors to the school are murals, painted in bright colors by students. The halls of the school are lined with student work. The high school includes a fine arts display that rotates the art, poetry, photographs, and ceramic work of various students. The restrooms and cafeteria are clean and graffiti free.

In general, the visitor perceives pride and a caring attitude regarding how adults feel about students and the school. The visitor's perception is based on the positive interaction observed between teachers and students, secretaries and teachers, maintenance personnel and the principal, and students and the cafeteria workers.

At the end of the day, the visitor notices that neither teachers nor administrators rush to leave the school. Many staff members remain in their classrooms either working quietly, helping individual students, or conferencing with parents. The principal is seen standing by the school buses saying good-bye to students and asking them how the school day went.

■ TAKE TIME TO SMELL THE ROSES

A vision of the good school can help principals hold on to their convictions concerning what schooling should be all about. The vision and one's convictions can steer the school through rough seas and keep the school on course—a course guided by the needs of the students, needs that can be satisfied when exposed to a challenging school experience in a climate nurtured by caring adults.

As you reflect on your role in accomplishing this, take time to celebrate your deeds, learn from mistakes, smell the roses daily, make connections with others, and maintain a positive outlook for the future.

REFLECTIONS

This space provides a place for you to write down ideas that have been generated by this chapter, things you want to try, or adaptations of ideas presented here.

1. In *True North*, George (2007) states, "True North is the internal compass that guides you successfully through life. It represents who you are as a human being at your deepest level. It is your orienting point—your fixed point in a spinning world—that helps you stay on track as a leader" (p. xxiii). Describe your True North. What guides you successfully through life?

2. Create two or three questions representing your own reflections on the principalship. Share these with a colleague.

3. What actions will you take as a result of these readings?

4. What topics do you want to explore in greater depth?

References and Additional Readings

■ REFERENCES

Alvy, H. (1983). *The problems of new principals.* Unpublished doctoral dissertation, University of Montana, Missoula.

Alvy, H., & Robbins, P. (1998). *If I only knew: Success strategies for navigating the principalship.* Thousand Oaks, CA: Corwin.

Alvy, H., & Robbins, P. (2008, March). *Helping new principals succeed: Strategies to support courageous leadership.* Presentation at the Association for Supervision and Curriculum Development Annual Conference, New Orleans, LA.

Amrein-Beardsley, A. (2008). Methodological concerns about the education value-added assessment system. *Educational Researcher, 37*(2), 65–75.

Armenta, T., & Beckers, G. (2006). The IEP: How to meet its demands and avoid its pitfalls. *Principal Leadership, 6*(9), 22–26.

Armstrong, D. G., Henson, K. T., & Savage, T. V. (2009). *Teaching today: An introduction to education* (8th ed.). Upper Saddle River, NJ: Merrill/Prentice Hall.

Armstrong, T. (1994). *Multiple intelligences in the classroom.* Alexandria, VA: Association for Supervision and Curriculum Development.

Arnberger, K., & Shoop, R. (2006). A principal's guide to manifestation determination. *Principal Leadership, 6*(9), 16–21.

Associated Press. (2002, June 17). Comments by Ann Duffett of Public Agenda. *Great Falls Tribune Nation,* p. 2A.

Bagin, D., & Gallagher, D. (2001). *The school and community relations* (7th ed.). Boston: Allyn & Bacon.

Barnard, C. (1938). *The functions of the executive.* Cambridge, MA: Harvard University Press.

Barth, R. (1990). *Improving schools from within: Teachers, parents, and principals can make the difference.* San Francisco: Jossey-Bass.

Barth, R. (2001a). Teacher leader. *Phi Delta Kappan, 82,* 443–449.

Barth, R. (2001b, February 28). Teachers at the helm. *Education Week,* pp. 32–33, 48.

Bennis, W. (1991). *Why leaders can't lead.* San Francisco: Jossey-Bass.

Bennis, W., & Nanus, B. (1985). *Leaders: The strategies for taking charge.* New York: Harper & Row.

Berman, P., & McLaughlin, M. W. (1978). *Federal programs supporting educational change, Vol. VIII: Implementing and sustaining innovations.* Santa Monica, CA: RAND.

Bird, T., & Little, J. W. (1984, April). *Supervision and evaluation in the school context.* Paper presented at the annual meeting of the American Educational Research Association, New Orleans, LA.

Blanchard, K., & Johnson, S. (1983). *The one minute manager.* New York: Berkley.

Bransford, J., Brown, A., & Cocking, R. (Eds.). (2000). *How people learn: Brain, mind, experience, and school.* Washington, DC: National Academy Press.

Brendtro, L., & Hinders, D. (1990). A saga of Janusz Korczak, the king of children. *Harvard Educational Review, 60,* 237–246.

Brunner, J., & Lewis, D. (2008). Tattling ends but bullying continues. *Principal Leadership, 8*(6), 38–42.

Burns, J. M. (1978). *Leadership.* New York: Harper & Row.

Caine, R., & Caine, G. (1991). *Making connections: Teaching and the human brain.* Alexandria, VA: Association for Supervision and Curriculum Development.

Caro, D. J., & Robbins, P. (1991). Talkwalking: Thinking on your feet. *The Developer,* pp. 3–4.

Chaltain, S. (2006, October 25). To make schools safe, make all children visible. *Education Week,* p. 48.

Champion, R. (2002). *Good principals use informal and formal approaches to staff development: White paper for principals.* Alexandria, VA: Association for Supervision and Curriculum Development.

Coburn, K. L., & Treeger, M. L. (2003). *Letting go: A parents' guide to understanding the college years* (4th ed.). New York: HarperCollins.

Collins, J. (2005). *Good to great and the social sectors.* Boulder, CO: Author.

Costa, A., & Garmston, R. (1991, April). *Cognitive coaching action lab.* Workshop presented at the Association for Supervision and Curriculum Development Annual Conference, San Francisco.

Costa, A., & Garmston, R. (1994). *Cognitive coaching: A foundation for renaissance schools.* Norwood, MA: Christopher-Gordon.

Cotton, K. (2003). *Principals and student achievement: What the research says.* Alexandria, VA: Association for Supervision and Curriculum Development.

Council for Corporate and School Partnerships. (n.d.). *Guiding principles for business and school partnerships.* Retrieved October 2, 2008, from http://www.corpschoolpartners.org/principles.shtml

Covey, S. (1989). *The seven habits of highly effective people.* New York: Simon & Schuster.

Crow, T. (2008, Summer). Declaration of interdependence: Educators need deep conversations about teaching and learning to spark real changes in practice (Q & A with Judith Warren Little). *Journal of Staff Development, 29*(3), 53–56.

Cunningham, W., & Gresso, D. (1993). *Cultural leadership: The culture of excellence in education.* Boston: Allyn & Bacon.

Curwin, R. (2002). Finding jewels in the rubble. *Educational Leadership, 59*(6), 80–83.

Curwin, R., & Mendler, A. (1988). *Discipline with dignity.* Alexandria, VA: Association for Supervision and Curriculum Development.

Danielson, C. (1996). *Enhancing professional practice: A framework for teaching.* Alexandria, VA: Association for Supervision and Curriculum Development.

Deal, T. (1985). Cultural change: Opportunity, silent killer, or metamorphosis. In R. H. Kilmann, M. J. Saxton, & R. Serpa (Eds.), *Gaining control of the corporate culture* (pp. 292–331). San Francisco: Jossey-Bass.

Deal, T., & Kennedy, A. (1982). *Corporate culture.* Reading, MA: Addison-Wesley.

Deal, T. E., & Peterson, K. D. (1990). *The principal's role in shaping school culture.* Washington, DC: U.S. Department of Education.

Deal, T., & Peterson, K. (1993). Strategies for building school cultures: Principals as symbolic leaders. In M. Sashkin & H. J. Walberg (Eds.), *Educational leadership and school culture* (pp. 89–99). Berkeley, CA: McCutchan.

Deal, T., & Peterson, K. (1994). *The leadership paradox.* San Francisco: Jossey-Bass.

Diplomas count 2008: School to college. Executive summary. (2008, June 5). *Education Week,* pp. 3–4.

Drucker, P. (1992). *Managing for the future: The 1990s and beyond.* New York: Dutton.

DuFour, R. (2001). In the right context. *Journal of Staff Development, 22*(1), 14–17.

DuFour, R. (2004). What is a "professional learning community"? *Educational Leadership, 61*(8), 6–11.

DuFour, R., & Eaker, R. (1998). *Professional learning communities at work: Best practices for enhancing student achievement.* Bloomington, IN: National Educational Services.

Dwyer, K., Osher, D., & Warger, C. (1998). *Early warning, timely response: A guide to safe schools.* Washington, DC: U.S. Department of Education. Retrieved October 6, 2008, from http://cecp.air.org/guide/guide.pdf

Dyer, K. (2001). The power of 360-degree feedback. *Educational Leadership, 58*(5), 35–38.

Eaker, R., & Keating, J. (2008). A shift in school culture. *Journal of Staff Development, 29*(3), 14–17.

Education Week. (2000). *Lessons of a century: A nation's schools come of age.* Bethesda, MD: Editorial Projects in Education.

Educational Leadership Policy Standards: ISLLC 2008. (2008). Washington, DC: Council of Chief State School Officers.

Educators told schools face a dropout crisis. (2008, June 1). *Anchorage Daily News.* Retrieved October 23, 2008, from http://www.adn.com/news/alaska/story/422977.html

Elias, M. (2002, March). *Building character education and social-emotional programs: A school leadership manual.* Presentation at the Annual Conference of the Association for Supervision and Curriculum Development, San Antonio, TX.

English, F., & Hill, J. (1994). *Total quality education.* Thousand Oaks, CA: Corwin.

Epstein, J. (2007). Connections count. *Principal Leadership, 8*(2), 16–21.

Feds take on dropout crisis. (2008, April 2). *eSchool News.* Retrieved October 23, 2008, from http://www.eschoolnews.com/news/top-news/?i=53380

Friedman, T. (2005). *The world is flat.* New York: Farrar, Straus, and Giroux.

Fullan, M. (2007). *The new meaning of educational change* (4th ed.). New York: Teachers College Press.

Fullan, M., & Miles, M. (1992). Getting reform right: What works and what doesn't. *Phi Delta Kappan, 73,* 745–752.

Fullan, M., & Stiegelbauer, S. (1991). *The new meaning of educational change.* New York: Teachers College Press.

Gardner, H. (2006). *Multiple intelligences: New horizons.* New York: Basic Books.

George, B. (2007). *True north: Discover your authentic leadership.* San Francisco: Jossey-Bass.

Georgia Association of Educators. (1998–2001). *Teacher tips: Avoiding burnout and staying healthy.* Retrieved October 8, 2001, from http://www.gae.org/teacher/te_burnout.html

Glickman, C. D., Gordon, S. P., & Ross-Gordon, J. M. (2007). *Supervision and instructional leadership* (7th ed.). Boston: Allyn & Bacon.

Goldring, E., & Rallis, S. (1993). *Principals of dynamic schools.* Newbury Park, CA: Corwin.

Goleman, D. (1995). *Emotional intelligence.* New York: Bantam.

Goleman, D., Boyatzis, R., & McKee, A. (2002). *Primal leadership: Learning to lead with emotional intelligence.* Boston: Harvard Business School Press.

Goodwin, D. (2005). *Team of rivals.* New York: Simon & Schuster.

Granada, J., & Vriesenga, M. (2008). Web-based walk throughs. *Principal Leadership, 8*(7), 24–27.

Gregorc, A. (1985). *Inside styles: Beyond the basics.* Maynard, MA: Gabriel Systems.

Grimmett, P., Rostad, O., & Ford, B. (1992). The transition of supervision. In C. Glickman (Ed.), *Supervision in transition: 1992 ASCD Yearbook* (pp. 185–202). Alexandria, VA: Association for Supervision and Curriculum Development.

Grove, K. (2002). The invisible role of the central office. *Educational Leadership, 59*(8), 45–47.

Hall, G. E., George, A. A., & Rutherford, W. L. (1979). *Measuring stages of concern about the innovation: A manual for the use of the SoC questionnaire.* Austin: University of Texas, Research and Development Center for Teacher Education.

Hall, G., & Hord, S. (1987). *Change in schools: Facilitating the process.* Albany: State University of New York Press.

Hall, G., & Loucks, S. (1978, April). *Innovation configurations analyzing the adaptation of innovations.* Paper presented at the annual meeting of the American Educational Research Association, Toronto, Ontario, Canada.

Hargreaves, A., & Dawe, R. (1989). *Coaching as unreflective practice.* Paper presented at the annual meeting of the American Educational Research Association, San Francisco.

Harkavy, I., & Blank, M. (2002, April 17). Community schools: A vision of learning that goes beyond testing. *Education Week,* pp. 38, 52.

Harris, S., Petrie, G., & Willoughby, W. (2002). Bullying among ninth graders: An exploratory study. *NASSP Bulletin, 86*(630), 3–14.

Harrison, C., & Killion, J. (2007). Ten roles for teacher leaders. *Educational Leadership, 65*(1), 74–77.

Healy, J. M. (1990). *Endangered minds: Why children don't think and what we can do about it.* New York: Touchstone.

Hersch, P. (1998). *A tribe apart: A journey into the heart of American adolescence.* New York: Ballantine.

Herzberg, F., Mausner, B., & Snyderman, B. (1959). *The motivation to work.* New York: John Wiley.

Hirsh, S. (1995/1996, December/January). Approaches to improving schools start with developing a shared vision. *School Team Innovator.*

Hopkins, G. (2008). Ten ideas for a successful take your family to school week. *Education World.* Retrieved October 2, 2008, from http://www.educationworld.com/a_admin/admin/admin509.shtml

Hord, S., Rutherford, W., Huling-Austin, L., & Hall, G. (1987). *Taking charge of change.* Alexandria, VA: Association for Supervision and Curriculum Development.

Houston, P. (2002). From tragedy emerge positive lessons for leaders. *School Administrator, 3*(59), 46.

Hyman, R. T. (1974). *Ways of teaching.* Englewood Cliffs, NJ: Prentice Hall.

Jacobson, L. (2008, April 30). Project aims to tackle dropout problem, California style. *Education Week,* p. 8.

Johnston, R. C. (2001, March 7). Central office is critical bridge to help schools. *Education Week,* pp. 18–20.

Joyce, B., & Showers, B. (1981). Improving inservice training: The message of research. *Educational Leadership, 37,* 379–385.

Joyce, B., & Weil, M. (1972). *Models of teaching.* Englewood Cliffs, NJ: Prentice Hall.

Jukes, I., & McCain, T. (2007a). *Beyond technology to the new literacy/shifting gears.* Retrieved October 1, 2008, from http://heartandsoulmadison.org/Info%20Lit%20pdfs/BeyondTech.pdf

Jukes, I., & McCain, T. (2007b). *Developing an instructional model for effective technology usage.* Retrieved October 1, 2008, from http://web.mac.com/iajukes/thecommittedsardine/Handouts_files/daim.pdf

Kanter, R. M. (1997). *On the frontiers of management.* Boston: Harvard Business School Press.

Kelehear, Z. (2004). Reflection helps good leaders find inner balance. *Journal of Staff Development, 25*(2), 72.

Kirn, W. (2007). The autumn of the multitaskers. *Atlantic Monthly, 300*(4), 72–76.

Kindlon, D., & Thompson, M. (2000). *Raising Cain: Protecting the emotional life of boys.* New York: Ballantine.

Koch, J. (2009). *So you want to be a teacher?* Boston: Houghton Mifflin.

Kohn, A. (1996). *Beyond discipline: From compliance to community.* Alexandria, VA: Association for Supervision and Curriculum Development.

Kouzes, J. M., & Posner, B. (2002). *The leadership challenge.* San Francisco: Jossey-Bass.

Kouzes, J. M., & Posner, B. A. (2006). *The encouraging the heart workbook.* San Francisco: Jossey-Bass.

Kriegel, R. (1991). *If it ain't broke . . . break it!* New York: Warner.

Lachat, M., Williams, M., & Smith, S. (2006). Making sense of all your data. *Principal Leadership, 7*(2), 16–21.

Lawton, W. (2002, April 2). Expert gives lesson in crisis communication. *The Oregonian,* p. C5.

Lee, V. E., Smith, J. B., Perry, T. E., & Smylie, M. A. (1999). *Social support, academic press, and student achievement: A view from the middle grades in Chicago.* Chicago: Consortium on Chicago School Reform.

Lehmuller, P., & Switzer, A. (2002). September 11: An elementary school at ground zero. *Principal, 81*(4), 52–54.

Lerner, M., Volpe, J., & Lindell, B. (2003). *A practical guide for crisis response in our schools.* New York: American Academy of Experts in Traumatic Stress.

Lewin, K. (1951). In D. Cartwright (Ed.), *Field theory in social science: Selected theoretical papers.* New York: Harper.

Lewis, C. (2002). Everywhere I looked: Levers and pendulums. *Journal of Staff Development, 23*(3), 59–65.

Lewis, T., Amini, F., & Lannon, R. (2000). *A general theory of love.* New York: Random House.

Little, J. W. (1982, May). Keynote address to Napa mentor teachers, Napa, CA.

Long, C. (2008, May). Silencing cyberbullies. *NEA Today,* 28–29.

Maeroff, G. (1993). *Team building for school change.* New York: Teachers College Press.

Manobianco, M. (2002). Guiding practices for using data to improve student learning. *The Principal News: A Journal of the Association of Washington School Principals, 31*(1), 16–17.

Marzano, R., Pickering, D., & Pollock, J. (2001). *Classroom instruction that works.* Alexandria, VA: Association for Supervision and Curriculum Development.

Marzano, R., & Waters, T. (2007, March). *Balanced leadership framework: School leadership that works.* Presentation at the annual conference of the Association for Supervision and Curriculum Development, Chicago.

Marzano, R. J., Waters, T., & McNulty, B. A. (2005). *School leadership that works: From research to results.* Alexandria, VA: Association for Supervision and Curriculum Development.

Maslow, A. (1954). *Motivation and personality.* New York: Harper & Row.

Maxwell, L. (2006, October 11). School shootings in policy spotlight. *Education Week,* pp. 1, 16–17.

McKenzie, K., Christman, D., Hernandez, F., Fierro, E., Capper, C., Dantley, M., et al. (2008). From the field: A proposal for educating leaders for social justice. *Educational Administration Quarterly, 44,* 111–138.

Meek, A. (1999). *Communicating with the public: A guide for school leaders.* Alexandria, VA: Association for Supervision and Curriculum Development.

Meier, D. (1995). How our schools could be. *Phi Delta Kappan, 76,* 369–373.

Merton, R. (1957). *Social theory and social structure* (rev. ed.). Glencoe, IL: Free Press.

Miller, G. (2007). Individuals with disabilities education act (IDEA) overview. Washington, DC: Committee on Education and Labor, U.S. House of Representatives.

Miller, L. H., & Smith, A. D. (1993). *The stress solution: An action plan to manage stress in your life.* New York: Simon & Schuster.

Mintzberg, H. (1973). *The nature of managerial work.* New York: HarperCollins.

Morrison, G. (2009). *Teaching in America* (5th ed.). Boston: Allyn & Bacon.

Nair, K. (1997). *A higher standard of leadership: Lessons from the life of Gandhi.* San Francisco: Berrett-Koehler.

National Association of Elementary School Principals. (2001). *Leading learning communities: Standards for what principals should know and be able to do.* Alexandria, VA: Author.

National Association of Elementary School Principals & Council for Exceptional Children. (2001). *Implementing IDEA: A guide for principals.* Arlington, VA: Authors.

National Association of Secondary School Principals. (2004). *Breaking ranks II: Strategies for leading high school reform.* Reston, VA: Author.

National Association of Secondary School Principals. (2008). *NASSP leadership skills assessment.* Retrieved September 16, 2008, from http://www.principals.org/s_nassp/sec_inside.asp?CID=39&DID=39

National Mental Health Association. (2006). *Coping with the war and terrorism: Tips for college students.* Retrieved October 6, 2008, from http://www.nmha.org/reassurance/collegetips.cfm

National School Public Relations Association. (1996). *NSPRA's complete crisis communication management manual for schools.* Rockville, MD: Author.

National Staff Development Council. (2001). *NSDC standards for staff development.* Oxford, OH: Author. Retrieved September 23, 2008, from http://www.nsdc.org/standards/index.cfm

Newell, C. (1978). *Human behavior in educational administration.* Englewood Cliffs, NJ: Prentice Hall.

Newmann, F., & Wehlage, G. (1995). *Successful school restructuring.* Madison: University of Wisconsin.

O'Neill, J., & Conzemius, A. (2002). Four keys to a smooth flight. *Journal of Staff Development, 23*(2), 14–18.

Oates, S. (1994). *With malice toward none.* New York: Harper & Row.

Olson, L. (2008, January 16). Assessment to rate principal leadership to be field-tested. *Education Week,* pp. 1, 11.

Ornstein, A., & Levine, D. (2003). *Foundations of education* (8th ed.). Boston: Houghton Mifflin.

Parker-Roerden, L., Rudewick, D., & Gorton, D. (2007). *Direct from the field: A guide to bullying prevention.* Retrieved February 9, 2009, from the Commonwealth of Massachusetts Web site: http://www.mass.gov/Eeohhs2/docs/dph/com_health/violence/bullying_prevent_guide.pdf

Parsley, D., Dean, C., & Miller, K. (2006). Selecting the right data. *Principal Leadership, 7*(2), 38–42.

Peters, T., & Austin, N. (1985). *A passion for excellence.* New York: Warner.

Peterson, K. (1982). Making sense of principals' work. *Australian Administrator, 3*(3), 1–4.

Pipher, M. (1994). *Reviving Ophelia: Saving the selves of adolescent girls.* New York: Ballantine.

Quinn, J. (2002). Must principals "go it alone." *Education Week, 21*(36), 40.

Reeves, D. B. (2008). *Reframing teacher leadership to improve your school.* Alexandria, VA: Association for Supervision and Curriculum Development.

Robbins, P. (1991a). *The development of a collaborative workplace: A case study of Wells Junior High.* Unpublished doctoral dissertation, University of California, Berkeley.

Robbins, P. (1991b). *How to plan and implement a peer coaching program.* Alexandria, VA: Association for Supervision and Curriculum Development.

Robbins, P., & Alvy, H. (2004). *The new principal's fieldbook.* Alexandria, VA: Association for Supervision and Curriculum Development.

Rosenholtz, S. (1989). *Teachers' workplace.* New York: Longman.

Ross, A. (1981). *Child behavior therapy.* New York: John Wiley.

Sack, J. (2002, May 1). EPA pushing improved air quality for schools. *Education Week,* pp. 1, 12.

Samuels, C. (2008, April 30). Principals at the center. *Education Week,* pp. 26–28.

Sarason, S. (1982). *The culture of the school and the problem of change* (2nd ed.). Boston: Allyn & Bacon.

Schein, E. (1985). *Organizational culture and leadership.* San Francisco: Jossey-Bass.

Scherer, M. (2001). How and why standards can improve student achievement: A conversation with Robert J. Marzano. *Educational Leadership, 59*(1), 14–18.

Schlechty, P. (2001). *Shaking up the schoolhouse: How to support and sustain educational innovation.* San Francisco: Jossey-Bass.

Schmoker, M. (2004). Tipping point: From feckless reform to substantive instructional improvement. *Phi Delta Kappan, 85,* 424–432.

Senge, P. (1990). *The fifth discipline.* London: Century Business.

Skretta, J. (2007). Using walkthroughs to gather data for school improvement. *Principal Leadership, 7*(9), 16–23.

Sloan, W. (2008). Collaborating over coffee: Creating a successful school-business partnership. *Education Update, 50*(5), 1–7.

Smith, R. (May 2, 2005). *World news tonight* [Television broadcast]. New York: American Broadcasting Company.

Soder, R. (2001). *The language of leadership.* San Francisco: Jossey-Bass.

Solomon, G., & Schrum, L. (2007). *Web 2.0: New tools, new schools.* Eugene, OR: International Society for Technology Education.

Sparks, D. (1993). The professional development of principals: A conversation with Roland Barth. *Journal of Staff Development, 14*(1), 18–21.

Sparks, D. (1999). Try on strategies to get a good fit: An interview with Susan Loucks-Horsley. *Journal of Staff Development, 20*(3), 56–60.

Starratt, R. J. (2004). *Ethical leadership.* San Francisco: Jossey-Bass.

Stewart, M. (2006, June). The management myth [Electronic version]. *The Atlantic Monthly.* Retrieved September 16, 2008, from http://www.theatlantic.com/doc/200606/stewart-business

Stiggins, R. (2005). Assessment for learning: Building a culture of confident learners. In R. DuFour, R. Eaker, & R. DuFour (Eds.), *On common ground: The power of professional learning communities* (pp. 65–83). Bloomington, IN: National Educational Services.

Sylwester, R. (1995). *A celebration of neurons: An educator's guide to the brain.* Alexandria, VA: Association for Supervision and Curriculum Development.

Teeter, A. (1995). Learning about teaching. *Phi Delta Kappan, 76,* 360–364.

Tierney, R., Carter, M., & Desai, L. (1991). *Portfolio assessment in the reading-writing classroom.* Norwood, MA: Christopher-Gordon.

Tucker, P. (2001). Helping struggling teachers. *Educational Leadership, 58*(5), 52–55.

Umphrey, J. (2006). IDEA: A tool for students. *Principal Leadership, 6*(9), 6.

U.S. Department of Education. (2007). *Practical information on crisis planning brochure.* Washington, DC: Author.

Walton, M. (1986). *The Deming management method.* New York: Perigee.

Warner, C. (2000). *Promoting your school: Going beyond PR* (2nd ed.). Thousand Oaks, CA: Corwin.

Wayne, L., & Kaufman, L. (2001, September 16). Leadership, put to a new test. *New York Times* (Money & Business Section 3), pp. 1, 4.

Wheatley, M. (1992). *Leadership and the new science.* San Francisco: Berrett-Koehler.

Wiggins, G., & McTighe, J. (1998). *Understanding by design.* Alexandria, VA: Association for Supervision and Curriculum Development.

Willard, N. (2005). *Educator's guide to cyberbullying and cyberthreats.* Retrieved October 23, 2008, from http://csriu.org/cyberbully/docs/cbcteducator.pdf

Wolfe, P. (2001). *Brain matters: Translating research into classroom practice.* Alexandria, VA: Association for Supervision and Curriculum Development.

Wood, F., Thompson, S., & Russell, F. (1981). Designing effective staff development programs. In B. Dillon-Peterson (Ed.), *Staff development/organizational development* (pp. 59–91). Alexandria, VA: Association for Supervision and Curriculum Development.

Zemelman, S., Daniels, H., & Hyde, A. (2005). *Best practice: Today's standards for teaching and learning in America's schools* (3rd ed.). Portsmouth, NH: Heinemann.

■ ADDITIONAL READINGS

Alvy, H. (2005). Preventing the loss of wisdom in our schools: Respecting and retaining successful veteran teachers. *Phi Delta Kappan, 86,* 764–766, 771.

Deal, T., & Peterson, K. (1999). *Shaping school culture: The heart of leadership.* San Francisco: Jossey-Bass.

Fullan, M. (1997). *What's worth fighting for in the principalship.* New York: Teachers College Press.

Gardner, J. W. (1990). *On leadership.* New York: Free Press.

Marzano, R. (2003). *What works in schools.* Alexandria, VA: Association for Supervision and Curriculum Development.

Murphy, J. (2005). Unpacking the foundations of ISLLC standards and addressing concerns in the academic community. *Educational Administration Quarterly, 41,* 154–191.

Robbins, P., Gregory, G., & Herndon, L. (2000). *Thinking inside the block: Strategies for teaching in extended periods of time.* Thousand Oaks, CA: Corwin.

Sparks, D., & Loucks-Horsley, S. (1990). Models of staff development. In R. Houston (Ed.), *Handbook of research on teacher education* (pp. 234–250). New York: Macmillan.

Index

CORWIN

A SAGE Company

The Corwin logo—a raven striding across an open book—represents the union of courage and learning. Corwin is committed to improving education for all learners by publishing books and other professional development resources for those serving the field of PreK–12 education. By providing practical, hands-on materials, Corwin continues to carry out the promise of its motto: **"Helping Educators Do Their Work Better."**